Microsoft® EXCEL/VISUAL BASIC®

Step by Step

Other titles in the *Step by Step* series:

Microsoft®

EXCEL/VISUAL BASIC®

Step by Step

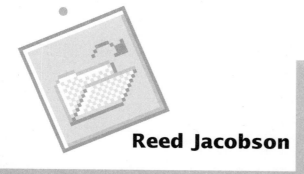

Reed Jacobson

Microsoft *Press*

PUBLISHED BY
Microsoft Press
A Division of Microsoft Corporation
One Microsoft Way
Redmond, Washington 98052-6399

Library of Congress Cataloging-in-Publication Data
Jacobson, Reed.
    Microsoft Excel/Visual Basic step by step / Reed Jacobson.
        p.   cm.
    Includes index.
    ISBN 1-55615-830-0
        1. Microsoft Visual BASIC   2. Microsoft Excel (Computer file)
    I. Title.
    QA76.73.B3J352   1995
    005.369--dc20   95-38367
                                                               CIP

Printed and bound in the United States of America.

1 2 3 4 5 6 7 8 9   QMQM   9 8 7 6 5

Distributed to the book trade in Canada by Macmillan of Canada, a division of Canada
Publishing Corporation.

A CIP catalogue record for this book is available from the British Library.

Microsoft Press books are available through booksellers and distributors worldwide. For further
information about international editions, contact your local Microsoft Corporation office. Or
contact Microsoft Press International directly at fax (206) 936-7329.

Paradox is a registered trademark of Ansa Software, a Borland Company. Macintosh is a
registered trademark of Apple Computer, Inc. dBASE is a registered trademark of Borland
International, Inc. FoxPro, Microsoft, Microsoft Press, MS, PivotTable, TipWizard, Visual Basic,
and Windows are registered trademarks of Microsoft Corporation. ORACLE is a registered
trademark of Oracle Corporation.

Companies, names, and/or data used in screens and sample output are fictitious unless
otherwise noted.

Acquisitions Editor: Casey D. Doyle
Project Editor: Laura Sackerman
Editing and Production: WASSER, Inc.

About the author

Reed Jacobson owns Jacobson GeniusWorks, a company that specializes in creative training, consulting, and custom development services for Microsoft Excel and other Microsoft Office products. Jacobson GeniusWorks is one of the original partner companies in the Microsoft Excel Consulting Relations Program.

Reed received a BA in Japanese and Linguistics and an MBA from Brigham Young University, and a graduate fellowship in Linguistics from Cornell University. He worked as a Software Application Specialist for Hewlett-Packard for ten years.

Reed is the author of *Excel Trade Secrets for Windows* and has given presentations on Excel at Tech-Ed and other Microsoft conferences and seminars. Reed can be reached via CompuServe at 70714,3727.

Reed Jacobson
Jacobson GeniusWorks
PO Box 3632
Arlington, WA 98223

Contents at a Glance

Table of Contents

Table of Contents

Table of Contents

*Quick*Look Guide

Using the Object Browser, see Lesson 2 and Lesson 8

Using object collections, see Lesson 6

Using methods and properties see Lesson 6

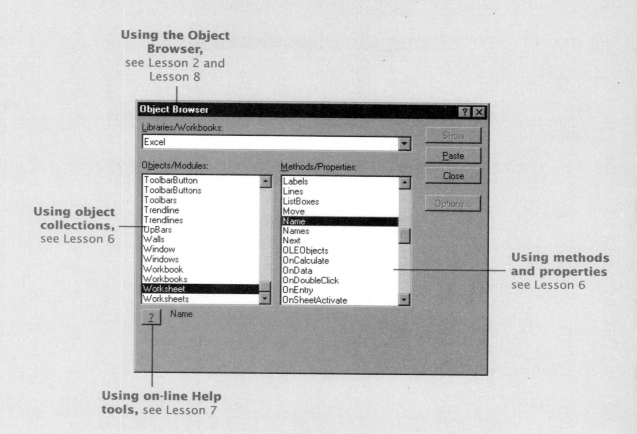

Using on-line Help tools, see Lesson 7

Running macros, see Lesson 1

Creating custom menus, see Lesson 5

Setting breakpoints, see Lesson 10

Recording macros, see Lesson 1

Watching the value of a variable, see Lesson 10

Stepping through macros, see Lesson 2

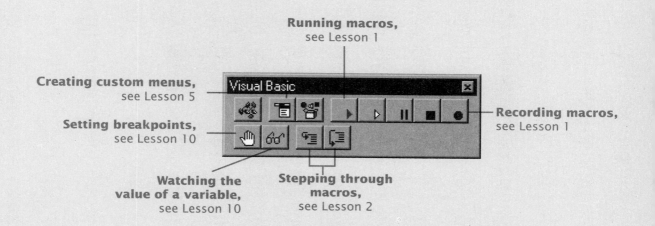

*Quick*Look Guide

Declaring variables,
see Lesson 10

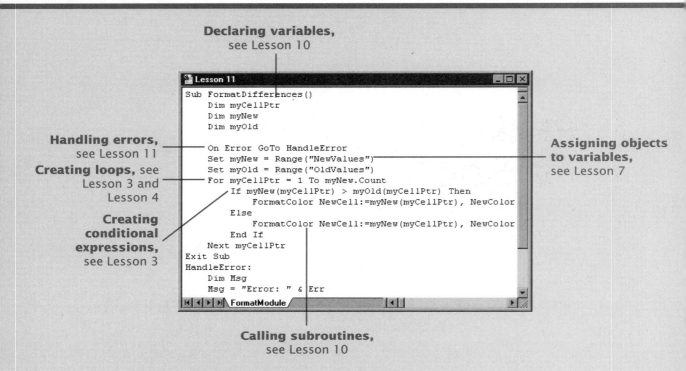

Handling errors,
see Lesson 11

Creating loops, see
Lesson 3 and
Lesson 4

**Creating
conditional
expressions,**
see Lesson 3

**Assigning objects
to variables,**
see Lesson 7

```
Sub FormatDifferences()
    Dim myCellPtr
    Dim myNew
    Dim myOld

    On Error GoTo HandleError
    Set myNew = Range("NewValues")
    Set myOld = Range("OldValues")
    For myCellPtr = 1 To myNew.Count
        If myNew(myCellPtr) > myOld(myCellPtr) Then
            FormatColor NewCell:=myNew(myCellPtr), NewColor
        Else
            FormatColor NewCell:=myNew(myCellPtr), NewColor
        End If
    Next myCellPtr
Exit Sub
HandleError:
    Dim Msg
    Msg = "Error: " & Err
```

Calling subroutines,
see Lesson 10

**Creating and modifying
PivotTables,**
see Lesson 7

**Creating and
modifying charts,**
see Lesson 9

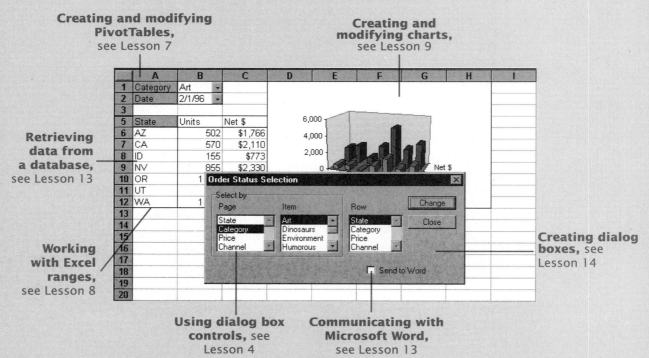

**Retrieving
data from
a database,**
see Lesson 13

**Working
with Excel
ranges,**
see Lesson 8

**Creating dialog
boxes,** see
Lesson 14

**Using dialog box
controls,** see
Lesson 4

**Communicating with
Microsoft Word,**
see Lesson 13

About This Book

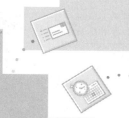

In "About This Book" you will learn:

- How to find your best starting point in this book based on your level of experience.
- What the conventions in this book mean.
- About different versions of Visual Basic.

Microsoft Excel is a powerful tool for analyzing and presenting information. One of the strengths of Excel has always been its macro language. Since Excel first appeared, it has always had the most extensive and flexible macro language of any spreadsheet program. The macro language in Excel for Windows 95 is really a development environment—Visual Basic for Applications.

Visual Basic for Applications is the programming engine for many of Microsoft's major application products, including Project and Access. Visual Basic for Applications is in many ways much simpler and easier to use—and at the same time more flexible and powerful—than Excel's earlier macro language.

When you start writing macros in Excel, you really need to learn two different tools. First, you need to learn how to work with Visual Basic. Everything you learn about Visual Basic will be true not only for Microsoft Excel, but also for other applications that incorporate Visual Basic. Second, you need to learn how to control Excel. The more you know about Excel as a spreadsheet, the more effective you can be at developing macros that control Excel. While this book focuses on Visual Basic as Excel's development environment, much of what you learn will help you to be more effective using the spreadsheet as well.

Finding the Best Starting Point for You

Learning everything you need to know about Visual Basic and also about how Excel works with Visual Basic can seem overwhelming. That's why you need this book. This book starts with simple, practical tasks and then takes you *step by step* on to advanced concepts and powerful applications.

The book is divided into five parts. Parts 1 and 2 teach practical skills without explaining underlying theoretical concepts. Parts 3 and 4 teach theoretical concepts, but in a very hands-on, experiential way. Part 5 puts the concepts to work to build a complete application.

Start by reading "Getting Ready," the next section in this book. Then find where you fit in the following table to determine where to start in the main body of the book.

If you are	Follow these steps
Experienced with Excel but new to macros	Start with the lessons in Part 1, "Automating Everyday Tasks." These lessons teach you how to record macros to produce effective results, without unnecessary conceptual explanations.
Experienced with Excel macros but new to Visual Basic	Skim the lessons in Parts 1 and 2, and then start working through the lessons in Part 3, "Exploring Objects," and Part 4, "Exploring Visual Basic." The lessons in Parts 3 and 4 teach the new concepts you will need for working with Excel objects using Visual Basic. They provide a solid foundation for the advanced practical skills presented in Part 5.
Experienced with Visual Basic but new to Excel	Skim Parts 1 and 2, work through the lessons in Part 3, skim the lessons in Part 4, and then work through the lessons in Part 5, "Building an Application." The lessons in Part 5 teach how to put Excel macros to work building solutions to serious business problems and assume an understanding of the concepts from Parts 3 and 4.

Using This Book as a Classroom Aid

If you're an instructor, you can use *Microsoft Excel/Visual Basic Step by Step* for teaching Microsoft Excel macros to beginning macro writers and for teaching specific concepts and techniques to experienced macro writers. You may want to select certain lessons that meet your students' needs and incorporate your own demonstrations into the lessons.

If you plan to teach the entire contents of this book, you should probably set aside four or five full days of classroom time to allow for discussion, questions, and any customized practice you may create.

Conventions Used in This Book

Before you start any of the lessons, you should understand the terms and conventions used in this book.

Typographic conventions

- Characters for you to type appear in **bold**.
- Important terms and the titles of books appear in *italic*.
- Names of keyboard keys appear in SMALL CAPITAL LETTERS.
- Samples of code appear in a monospaced font:

```
Sub MyFirstMacro()
```

Procedural conventions

Selected check box

Cleared check box

- Numbered lists (1, 2, 3, and so on) indicate steps for you to follow.
- Triangular bullets ( ) indicate single tasks for you to do.
- The word *select* means to highlight an item. For example, "Select range A1:E5" or "Select Microsoft Excel Workbook from the File Type list."
- With check boxes, *select the check box* means to put an *X* or check mark in the check box and *clear the check box* means to remove the *X* or check mark from the check box.

Other features of this book

Bold button

- You can perform many operations by clicking a button on a toolbar. When you can click a toolbar button, a picture of the button appears in the left margin of the book, as the Bold button does here.
- Text in the left margin provides tips, keyboard alternatives, and cross references to related topics.

Comparing Visual Basic with Older Excel Macros

The implementation of Visual Basic included in Excel for Windows 95 is virtually identical to that first introduced with Excel 5. Profound differences exist, however, between Visual Basic and the older "Excel 4" macros. If you have developed macros using the Excel 4 macro language, you may wonder about the differences between Visual Basic and Excel 4 macros.

The current version of Excel can run both Excel 4 and Visual Basic for Applications macros. Future versions of Excel will run Excel 4 macros, but new features of future versions may not be accessible from Excel 4 style macros.

- Excel 4 macro sheets are essentially worksheets. All Excel 4 macro commands are functions entered in individual cells. Visual Basic modules are not worksheets, even though they are kept in an Excel workbook.

- A single Excel 4 command must be entered into a single cell; you cannot split a long command into multiple lines. Visual Basic statements may be split into multiple lines.

- Visual Basic has true variables that can be restricted to certain data types and restricted to the current procedure or module. Excel 4 macros use ordinary Excel names as variables.

- Visual Basic code is compiled; an Excel 4 macro is interpreted when you run the macro. This makes Visual Basic much faster at executing loops and other traditional programming tasks. Excel 4 macros may, however, be faster when interacting heavily with Excel objects.

- Text strings in Excel are limited to 255 characters. This limit applies to both worksheets and Excel 4 macros. Visual Basic strings are not limited to 255 characters, except when transferring the text string to Excel.

- The Excel 4 macro language is used only by Microsoft Excel. Visual Basic belongs to the tradition of Basic languages, and Visual Basic for Applications is the language used to automate almost all major Microsoft applications.

- Because Visual Basic for Applications will be shared by all Microsoft applications, any improvements made to Visual Basic will become available to all applications. For example, if the code editor becomes easier to use in Microsoft Project, it will also be easier to use in Microsoft Excel.

- Excel 4 macros can use all Excel worksheet functions and operators, and they can manipulate Excel arrays in the same ways that Excel worksheets can. Visual Basic applications can use Excel worksheet functions but not Excel operators, and Visual Basic operators do not work with arrays.

- Excel 4 macros can refer directly to Excel named references and constants. Visual Basic applications require extra steps to access Excel named references and constants.

In brief, Visual Basic for Applications has many advantages relative to the older Excel 4 macro language, but it is still a new product. In future versions of Excel the benefits of Visual Basic for Applications will be even more significant. If you already know how to work with Excel 4 macros, you may want to continue to use Excel 4 macros for some tasks. If you do not already know Excel 4 macros, you will probably want to focus your attention on learning Visual Basic for Applications.

Comparing Versions of Visual Basic

The Visual Basic Programming System is available both as a separate, standalone product (the Standard, Professional, and Enterprise editions of Visual Basic, version 4) and as the Applications Edition, which is integrated with applications such as Microsoft Excel. If you are familiar with Visual Basic, you may wonder about the differences between the standalone editions of Visual Basic and Visual Basic for Applications.

■ The standalone editions of Visual Basic are available only for Microsoft Windows and MS-DOS. Visual Basic for Applications was written to be portable to other platforms, such as the Macintosh and Windows NT.

■ Visual Basic for Applications is tightly integrated with each host application. For example, it comes with an Object Browser that can help you find Visual Basic functions as well as Excel objects. Also, in Microsoft Excel, Visual Basic modules are stored directly in workbooks.

■ Procedures written with the standalone editions of Visual Basic must be compiled into a separate executable file. To control Excel from an application created by using one of the standalone editions of Visual Basic, you must run both Excel and the application. Procedures written with Visual Basic for Applications can be run as part of the Excel application, without a separate executable file.

■ With Visual Basic for Applications in Excel, you can create effective dialog boxes, but they are not as powerful as the forms in the standalone editions of Visual Basic.

■ The standalone editions of Visual Basic allow you to attach code to any of several events for each control on a form; Visual Basic for Applications currently supports only one event per control.

■ The standalone editions of Visual Basic can integrate custom controls that you can purchase or write; Visual Basic for Applications can use only the standard controls that come with the product.

■ The standalone editions of Visual Basic have some editing features that are not yet available in Visual Basic for Applications. For example, in the standalone version of Visual Basic, you can edit a module while stepping through the code, but in the version of Visual Basic implemented in Excel, you must halt the procedure in order to modify the code.

In summary, if you are developing an application to control Excel, or if you want to develop using Visual Basic on the Macintosh, you should use Visual Basic for Applications in Excel. If you must use custom controls or other features available only in the standalone versions of Visual Basic, you must use Microsoft Windows as your operating system, but you can still manipulate Excel objects using the concepts you will learn in this book.

Getting Ready

In "Getting Ready" you will learn how to:

- ■ Install and use the Step by Step practice files.
- ■ Make necessary modifications to the Typical Excel installation.

While completing the lessons in this book, you'll use the practice files on the accompanying disk to get hands-on practice with macros in Microsoft Excel. Install the practice files on your computer's hard drive, review the list of files, and then start learning Visual Basic!

Installing the Step by Step Practice Files

Included with this book is a disk named "Practice Files for Microsoft Excel/Visual Basic Step by Step." Some of the files on the disk contain sample data that you will use as you go through the lessons in this book. Other files are the finished result of the projects in the book.

Install the practice files

1 Start Microsoft Windows 95.

2 Remove the disk from the package inside the back cover of this book, and put the disk in drive A or drive B of your computer.

3 On the taskbar's Start menu, click the Run command.

4   In the Run dialog box, type **a:\setup** (or **b:\setup**, if you put the disk in drive B), and press ENTER.

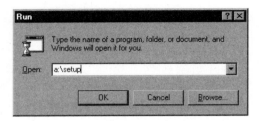

5   Follow the instructions on screen to complete the installation process.

The default name for the folder where you install the files is C:\ExcelVBA. You can choose a different folder name if you wish, but you should remember the folder name.

The installation program will also create a Favorites shortcut that you can use to switch to the folder containing the practice files. The name for the Favorites shortcut is Excel VB Practice. Lesson 1 will explain how to use the favorites shortcut to access the practice files. In some lessons, when retrieving data from the database file, you will need to use the actual folder name, not the name of the shortcut.

The ExcelVBA folder contains all the files you will use as you go through the lessons in this book. The text in each lesson explains how to use the practice files for that lesson. The Finished folder contains completed copies of the files you create in the lessons. The files in the Finished folder are not used in the lessons, but you may want to compare them with the files you create.

 NOTE   The installation program does not create any application programs. No new icons will appear on your desktop or in the Start menu. The practice files are files that you will use as you work through the lessons in the book.

Using the Practice Files

As you work through the lessons using the practice files, be sure to follow the instructions for saving the practice files and giving them new names. Renaming the practice files allows you to make changes, experiment, and observe results without affecting the original files. Keeping the practice files intact allows you to reuse the original file later if you want to repeat a lesson or try a new experiment.

In these lessons, you are the bookkeeper and financial analyst for the screen printing division of Miller Textiles. Your division designs, prints, and sells artistic transfers for T-shirts. Throughout these lessons, you will use macros to simplify tasks you do for the company.

Description of the Practice Files

These are the files you will use as you automate tasks during the lessons. You may not see the extensions for the files, depending on how you have configured Windows 95.

Filename	Description	Used in
Budget.xls	A workbook containing the annual budget for the division.	Lesson 1
Prices.xls	A workbook that contains a table with list and net prices for different grades of transfers.	Lesson 2
Orders.dbf	The Miller Textiles order history database. This file contains the monthly orders for different shirt designs. This file is stored in a format that can be accessed either by Excel or by the database drivers that come with Excel.	Lessons 2, 3, 5, 12, 13, and 14
Ord9603.txt	A text file containing the most recent month's order information.	Lesson 2
Lists.xls	The lists of categories, states, price groups, and distribution channels that appear in the order history database.	Lesson 13
Map.cgm	A worksheet containing a map of the region in which Miller Textiles does business.	Lesson 5

In addition, the Finished folder contains the workbooks for each lesson as they will look at the end of the lesson.

Customizing the Microsoft Excel Setup

When you install Excel using the Typical option, some components that are needed for this book are not installed. Before beginning the lessons in this book, please run the Excel setup program and add the following options:

"Online Help for Visual Basic" (under "Online Help and sample files," under "Microsoft Excel").

"Data Access" (under "Converters, Filters, and Data Access").

Automating Everyday Tasks

Part 1

Make a Macro Do Simple Tasks

Estimated time

40 min.

In this lesson you will learn how to:

- ■ Record and run a macro.
- ■ Make a macro always available.
- ■ Understand and edit simple recorded macros.
- ■ Run a macro by using a shortcut key or a toolbar button.

If you haven't yet installed the practice files that come with this book, refer to "Getting Ready" earlier in this book.

Have you ever lived with a squeaky door? Every time you open it, you're annoyed. "Oh, I really should put a drop of oil on that hinge." But you're in the middle of something, and the oil can is in the garage, and you'll do it as soon as you go back downstairs, but by the time you get downstairs you've forgotten about the hinge. Until next time. Grrr. If only that oil can were *where* you needed it, *when* you needed it.

Creating a convenience macro in Microsoft Excel is like putting oil on a squeaky door hinge. "Yes, I really should make a little macro to add that underline." Except that in Excel, the oil can isn't in the garage. It's called a *macro recorder* and it's part of Excel, ready whenever you are. All you have to do is use it. In this lesson, you'll learn how to use Excel's macro recorder to get those handy little macros written quickly and easily, even if you're in the middle of something else.

Start the lesson

> Start Excel. On the File menu click Open, and in the Open dialog box click the Look In Favorites button. Double-click the Excel VB Practice folder. Click the Budget file and click Open. Save the Budget file as **Lesson 1a**

3

The Macro Recorder

In some spreadsheet programs, a macro is a collection of keystrokes. For every key you press, you enter that keystroke into the macro. A keystroke macro can be easy to interpret because of the one-to-one correspondence between what you do on the keyboard and what you see in the macro. It doesn't take very long, however, before a keystroke macro becomes hopelessly illegible and inflexible.

The language you use to record macros in Excel—Visual Basic for Applications—is a real programming language. You will probably never find the limits of what you can do with Visual Basic. The trade-off for this power is that the language can be a little bit hard to understand right at first.

The macro recorder can help you get started creating macros and learning Visual Basic. You don't need to know anything at all about the language to turn on the recorder, work for a while, turn off the recorder, and then play back the resulting macro. But recording one long, extended macro rarely produces the results you want.

The best approach to learning Visual Basic is to use the macro recorder for simple tasks—you can get immediately usable results—and gradually learn more about the language, preferably with a good coach along the way.

That's precisely the approach this book takes. The lessons in Parts 1 and 2 of this book center around the macro recorder. Virtually everything you do in these lessons will consist of either recording a macro or making minor modifications to a recorded macro. The macro recorder is a great way to begin creating macros in Excel, and you can automate many tasks using nothing more than the techniques in these first few lessons. By the end of these lessons, you will be surprised at how much you can accomplish with the macro recorder. You will become comfortable with Visual Basic and Excel objects by performing real-world tasks, without worrying about technical concepts. You will learn to look at a clock and tell the time, without needing to know how the clock works internally.

Eventually, however, you may want the greater power that comes from understanding the concepts behind how Visual Basic and Excel work together. In Parts 3 and 4 you will take apart the clock and see what makes it work. Then in Part 5, you will build a completely new clock. You will deal once again with real-world problems, but you will rely less on the macro recorder and more on your knowledge of the underlying concepts.

The Best Macro Is No Macro

Before you create a macro to automate a task, always find out if Excel provides a built-in solution ready for you to use.

New Workbook button

For example, when you click the New Workbook button in Excel, you get a workbook that has 16 blank worksheets. Maybe you never use 16 worksheets. Maybe you really never use more than 4, and having those extra worksheets is really annoying. You could record a macro to delete the extra 12 worksheets. But don't. Change Excel's default instead.

Change the default number of worksheets

1 On the Tools menu click the Options command, and then click the General tab.

2 In the Sheets In New Workbook box, type **4** and click OK.

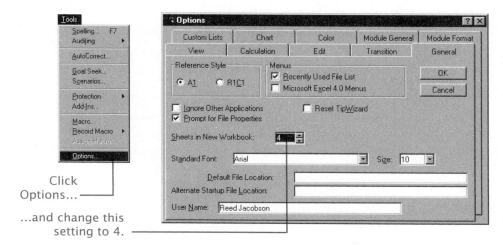

Click
Options...

...and change this
setting to 4.

Now whenever you click the New Workbook button, your new workbook will have only 4 sheets, and you didn't need a macro at all.

Which is not to say anything against macros. Macros are good, useful, and important. I want you to write lots and lots of macros. I want you to convince all your friends, coworkers, relatives, and casual acquaintances you pass on street corners to write lots and lots of macros (and, naturally, to buy lots and lots of copies of this book).

Watch the TipWizard

You may wonder how you can find out all of Excel's built-in conveniences. Sometimes it seems Excel has an endless stream of tricks that are impossible to learn. Even when you read or hear about new tips, those tips may not relate to tasks you are currently doing.

TipWizard button

The TipWizard can help you learn the shortcuts that are most likely to help with the tasks you do.

Excel watches every action you take. When you take an action that may have a more convenient alternative, the light bulb on the TipWizard button turns yellow. When you click the button, you see one or more tips related directly to the tasks you are doing—and none of these tips require any macros.

Creating a Simple Macro

Excel has a large collection of convenience tools readily available as shortcut keys and as buttons on toolbars. Sometimes the built-in convenience tool doesn't work quite the way you want. Enhancing a built-in tool is a good first macro to create.

Format currency with a built-in tool

On the Formatting toolbar, Excel has a button that formats the current selection as currency: the Currency Style button.

1 In the Lesson 1a workbook, select cells D3:F4 on the Budget96 worksheet.

2 Click the Currency Style button on the Formatting toolbar.

Excel reformats the selected cells as currency.

Currency Style button

	A	B	C	D	E	F	G
	Budget						
1	Summary		Rates	Jan-96	Feb-96	Mar-96	Qtr1
2	Projected Units			29000	30000	31000	90000
3	Projected Revenues			$71,000.00	$73,000.00	$75,000.00	219000
4	Projected Pre-tax Profit			$26,819.90	$27,057.90	$30,295.90	84173.7
5							
6	Variable Costs						
7	Ink		0.095	2755	2850	2945	8550

Click the Currency Style button to reformat the selection as currency.

The currency format Excel applies when you click the Currency Style button has two decimal places. Sometimes you want to display currency with two decimal places, perhaps in your checkbook. But other times you don't want two decimal places—perhaps your budget doesn't warrant that kind of precision. You may want to create a macro to format currency with no decimal places.

Record a macro to format currency

1 On the Budget96 worksheet, select cells D7:F8.

2 On the Tools menu, click the Record Macro, Record New Macro command.

A macro name can contain uppercase and lowercase letters, underscores and periods, but no spaces.

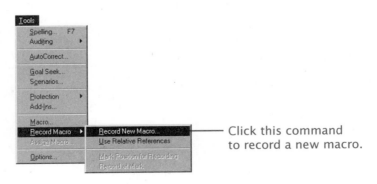

Click this command to record a new macro.

For details about number format codes, search Help for the phrase "format codes, number"

3   Replace the default macro name with **FormatCurrency**, and click OK.

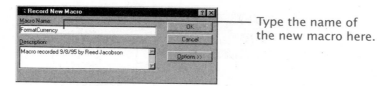

Type the name of the new macro here.

The word *Recording* appears in the status bar, and a Stop Recording toolbar appears. You are recording.

4   On the Format menu, click the Cells command, and then click the Number tab. Select Currency from the Category list. In the Decimal Places box, type **0** to change the number of decimal places to 0, and then click OK.

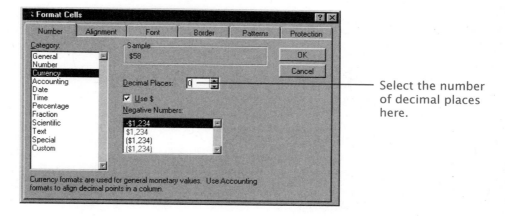

Select the number of decimal places here.

Excel formats the selected cells as currency without decimal places.

Stop Macro button

5   Click the Stop Macro button (or on the Tools menu, click Record Macro, Stop Recording) to stop the recorder.

That's it. You recorded a macro to format a selection with the currency format you want. Now you probably want to try out the macro to see how it works.

Run the macro

1   On the Budget96 worksheet, select cells D9:F10.

2   On the Tools menu, click Macro.

3 Click the FormatCurrency macro in the list, and click Run.

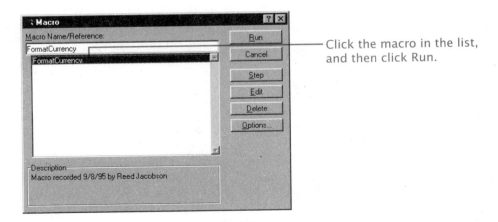

Click the macro in the list, and then click Run.

Your macro gives the selected cells your customized currency format. Running the macro from the Macro dialog box is not very much of a shortcut, though.

Assign a shortcut key to the macro

1 On the Tools menu, click Macro.

2 Click the FormatCurrency macro in the list, and click the Options button.

The Macro Options dialog box is like an extended version of the Record New Macro dialog box you saw before. In the Macro Options dialog box you can change certain attributes of a macro, including the shortcut key assignment.

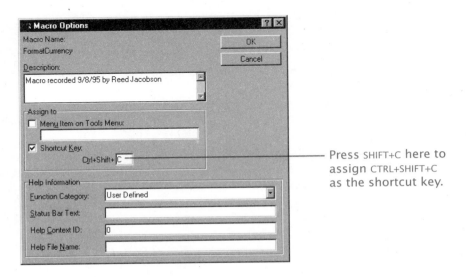

Press SHIFT+C here to assign CTRL+SHIFT+C as the shortcut key.

3 You want to assign CTRL+SHIFT+C as the shortcut key. Select the box to the lower right of the Shortcut Key check box and press SHIFT+C.

4 Click OK to return to the Macro dialog box, and then click Close to get back to the worksheet.

5 Select cells D11:F13, and press CTRL+SHIFT+C to run the macro.

Now you have successfully recorded, run, and modified a macro—all without seeing anything of the macro itself. Aren't you burning with curiosity to see just what you have created?

Look at the macro

When you created the Lesson 1a workbook, it had a single worksheet tab, Budget96, at the bottom of the workbook. Now there is a second tab, labeled Module1.

 Click the Module1 tab.

Click here to look at the macro.

A *module* sheet with no worksheet gridlines appears. (A module sheet is an Excel sheet that contains macros.) Your macro is on the Module1 sheet. Here's what it looks like:

```
'
' FormatCurrency Macro
' Macro recorded 9/8/95 by Reed Jacobson
'
'
Sub FormatCurrency()
    Selection.NumberFormat = "$#,##0"
End Sub
```

The five lines that start with apostrophes at the beginning of the macro are *comments*. The recorder puts in the comments partly to remind you to add comments as you write a macro. You can add to them, change them, or delete them as you wish without changing how the macro runs. Anything in any line that follows an apostrophe is a comment. On a color monitor, comments are green to help you distinguish them from statements that do something.

The macro is written in Visual Basic and follows standard Visual Basic rules. The macro itself begins with the word *Sub*, followed by the name of the macro. The word *Sub* is used because a macro is typically hidden, out of sight, like a *sub*marine. Or perhaps it stands for *Sub*routine, for reasons you will learn at the end of Lesson 2. The last line of a macro always consists of the words *End Sub*.

The Selection.NumberFormat statement does the real work. It is the body of the macro. The word *Selection* stands for "the current selection." The word *NumberFormat* refers to one of the attributes—or *properties*—of the selection. Read the statement from right to left, like this: "Let '$#,##0' be the number format of the selection."

NOTE Some people wonder why the word *NumberFormat* comes after the word *Selection* if you read Selection.NumberFormat as "number format of the selection." In an Excel worksheet, you do not use the English language convention of stating an action first and then the object. ("Copy these cells. Put the copy in those cells.") Instead, on an Excel worksheet you select the object first and then perform the action. ("These cells—copy. Those cells—paste.") Selecting the object first in the worksheet makes carrying out multiple actions more efficient.

Macro statements in Visual Basic work backwards, the same as actions do in an Excel worksheet. In a macro statement, you state what you're going to work on, and then you do something to it.

Make the macro always available

Your new shortcut key will format cells on any worksheet in the whole workbook. In fact, as long as Lesson 1a is open, you can use that shortcut on any worksheet in any workbook. When you close the Lesson 1a workbook, the shortcut key turns off. When you open the workbook, the shortcut key turns back on.

On the one hand, you should be happy that you can use your FormatCurrency macro on any worksheet as long as it's part of an open workbook. On the other hand, you may not want to keep the Lesson 1a workbook open all the time just so you can use this macro. Delete this macro and make a different version that will always be available.

1 Activate the module sheet by clicking the Module1 tab.

2 On the Edit menu click Delete Sheet, and click OK when asked for confirmation.

3 Select cells D16:F17.

4 On the Tools menu, click Record Macro, Record New Macro.

5 Replace the default name of the macro with **FormatCurrency**, and click the Options button.

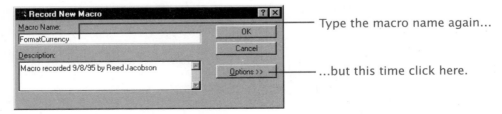

Type the macro name again...

...but this time click here.

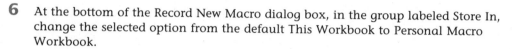

6 At the bottom of the Record New Macro dialog box, in the group labeled Store In, change the selected option from the default This Workbook to Personal Macro Workbook.

Excel remembers where you store new macros, even after it closes. If you later want to record a macro in the active workbook, you must use the Macro Options dialog box to change the Store In setting back to This Workbook.

When you click the Options button, the Record New Macro dialog box changes to an extended version that looks very much like the Macro Options dialog box you used to change the shortcut key assignment. While you're here, you might as well fix the description and the shortcut key.

7 In the Description box, replace the default description with **Assign custom currency format to the current selection**, and change the shortcut key to CTRL+SHIFT+C.

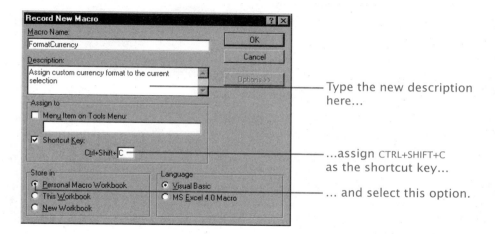

Type the new description here...

...assign CTRL+SHIFT+C as the shortcut key...

... and select this option.

8 Click OK to start recording.

9 Click the Cells command on the Format menu, select the Currency category, change the Decimal Places number format to 0, and click OK.

10 Click the Stop Macro button to quit recording.

Stop Macro button

11 Select cells D18:F19 and press CTRL+SHIFT+C to try out the re-recorded macro. (If Excel complains that it cannot find the original FormatCurrency macro, just click OK and press CTRL+SHIFT+C again.)

The macro works, but notice that the workbook does not have a Module1 tab at the bottom. It doesn't have any new tabs at all. Where is the macro now? Well, remember that the option in the dialog box did use the words *Personal Macro.* Maybe this new macro is just shy about personal matters.

Look at the Personal Macro Workbook

1   Click the Window menu.

Notice the Unhide command. The Unhide command is usually disabled, but now it is black.

2   Click the Unhide command.

The Unhide dialog box appears, listing all hidden windows.

The Unhide dialog box reveals to you the hiding place of the Personal Macro Workbook. Its name is Personal.xls, but the .xls extension is hidden unless you set Windows 95 to show extensions.

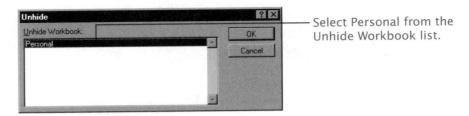

Select Personal from the Unhide Workbook list.

3   Click OK.

The Personal Macro Workbook appears. It has only one sheet, labeled Module1. This module sheet contains your FormatCurrency macro.

The Personal Macro Workbook is just like any other workbook. It typically contains only macro sheets, but you can put regular worksheets into it if you want. When you save the Personal Macro Workbook, Excel saves it as Personal.xls in the folder named XLStart in the folder where you installed Excel. Excel opens all files in the XLStart folder (except template files) when you start Excel, so the Personal Macro Workbook is always available.

Arrange the workbook windows

Before you record any more macros, change your screen to let you watch the macros grow as you record them. That way, you don't have to be patient and wait until you've finished recording to see how a macro is progressing. Put the Lesson 1a workbook, where you will carry out the actions, above the Personal Macro Workbook, where the macro will be growing.

1   On the Window menu, click Lesson 1a to activate the window containing the Budget96 worksheet.

2   On the Window menu click the Arrange command, select the Horizontal option, and click OK.

Excel arranges the Budget96 window above the module window, the window containing the Personal Macro Workbook.

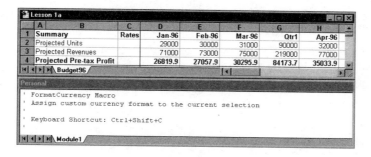

Now when you turn on the macro recorder and perform actions in the window on top, you can watch what the recorder is doing in the window on the bottom.

Changing Multiple Properties at Once

The FormatCurrency macro changes a single attribute of the current selection—the number format. In Excel macros, the word for an attribute is *property*. NumberFormat is a property of a cell. Sometimes when you record an action, the macro changes multiple properties at the same time.

Center text vertically with a command

Center button

Excel has a toolbar button that centers text horizontally in a cell: the Center button. But if the row height is taller than the text, you may want to center the text vertically in the cell as well as horizontally. Excel does not have a toolbar button that centers both horizontally and vertically, but you can record a macro that does. Start by carrying out the actions interactively, using menu commands.

1   Activate the Budget96 window.

2   Drag the bottom border of the row header for row 1 down until the row is about twice as high as before.

	A	B	C	D	E	F
1	Summary		Rates	Jan-96	Feb-96	Mar-96
	Projected Units			29000	30000	31000
2	Projected Revenues			$71,000.00	$73,000.00	$75,000.00

Drag here to increase row height.

3   Select cell D1.

The date is in the bottom right corner of the cell.

4   On the Format menu click Cells, and then click the Alignment tab.

The Alignment tab has several option groups: a Horizontal alignment group, a Vertical alignment group, an Orientation group, and a Wrap Text check box.

5 Select Center as the horizontal option and Center as the vertical option, and click OK to center the date in the cell.

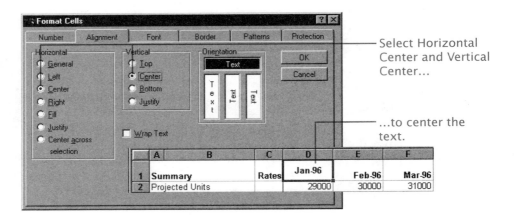

Select Horizontal Center and Vertical Center...

...to center the text.

Record a macro to center text

1 Select cell E1, and on the Tools menu click Record Macro, Record New Macro.

2 In the Record New Macro dialog box, replace the default macro name with **CenterBoth**, replace the default description with **Center both horizontally and vertically**, and click Options.

3 Change the shortcut key to CTRL+SHIFT+C.

The macro is already set to record to the Personal Macro Workbook. Excel remembers the setting for where to store the macro until you change it, even after you exit and restart Excel.

4 Click OK.

Excel displays a warning. CTRL+SHIFT+C is the same shortcut key you used for FormatCurrency. Excel displays this warning only if you try to assign a shortcut key that's already being used by another macro. You don't get a warning if you replace a built-in shortcut key.

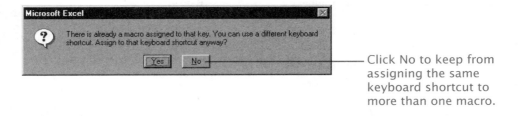

Click No to keep from assigning the same keyboard shortcut to more than one macro.

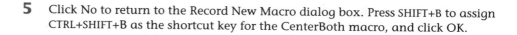

5 Click No to return to the Record New Macro dialog box. Press SHIFT+B to assign CTRL+SHIFT+B as the shortcut key for the CenterBoth macro, and click OK.

 IMPORTANT Assigning a shortcut key does not unassign the macro that was already assigned to that shortcut. When two macros have the same shortcut key, you cannot guarantee which macro will run when you press the shortcut key.

In the module window, you can see that the recorder immediately puts the comment lines and the Sub and End Sub lines into the macro.

```
' Keyboard Shortcut: Ctrl+Shift+B
'
Sub CenterBoth()
End Sub
```

6 On the Format menu, click Cells. In the Format Cells dialog box, click the Alignment tab. Select the two Center options and click OK.

The recorder puts several lines into the macro.

7 Click the Stop Macro button and look at the macro code in the module window.

```
'
' CenterBoth Macro
' Center text both horizontally and vertically
'
' Keyboard shortcut: Ctrl+Shift+B
'
Sub CenterBoth()
    With Selection
        .HorizontalAlignment = xlCenter
        .VerticalAlignment = xlCenter
        .WrapText = False
        .Orientation = xlHorizontal
    End With
End Sub
```

The macro shows four different property settings for the cell alignment. These relate directly to the groups of options you saw in the dialog box: Horizontal, Vertical, Wrap Text, and Orientation.

Each of the property settings affects an attribute of the current selection, just as the Style property setting does in the FormatCurrency macro. In the FormatCurrency macro, the property name is attached directly to the word *Selection* with a period, to show that the property affects the cells in the current selection. In this macro, each of the property names just hangs there.

15

The pair of statements *With Selection* and *End With* is called a *With structure*. It means that every time there is a period with nothing in front of it, pretend that the word *Selection* is there. The With structure makes the code easier to read because you can tell instantly that all the properties relate to the current selection. The With structure also makes the macro run faster because the macro has to figure out only once what the current selection is.

You could change the CenterBoth macro to the following code and it would produce exactly the same result.

```
Sub CenterBoth()
    Selection.HorizontalAlignment = xlCenter
    Selection.VerticalAlignment = xlCenter
    Selection.WrapText = False
    Selection.Orientation = xlHorizontal
End Sub
```

When you use the With structure, you can read the code as "With the current selection, let 'Centered' be the horizontal alignment, let 'Centered' be the vertical alignment, let...." When you don't use the With structure, you can read the code as "Let 'Centered' be the horizontal alignment of the selection. Let 'Centered' be the vertical alignment of the selection. Let...."

Eliminate unnecessary lines from the macro

In many dialog boxes, the macro recorder records all the possible settings, even though you might change only one or two of them. You can make your macro easier to understand if you eliminate unnecessary settings.

In this macro, you need to change only the HorizontalAlignment and VerticalAlignment property settings. You can delete the other lines from the macro.

1   Activate the module window and position the mouse pointer immediately to the left of the words *End With*. Click and hold down the mouse button.

2   Drag straight up until the pointer is on the line containing the word *WrapText*.

Delete unnecessary lines of code from the macro.

3   Press DELETE.

Test the macro

The macro is finished and ready to go. Now test it to find out whether it works.

1 Activate the Budget96 window and select cells F1:H1.

2 Press CTRL+SHIFT+B.

The macro centers the dates in all the selected cells.

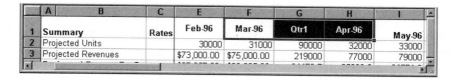

Now you have not only recorded a macro, you have also deleted parts of it. And it still works. Next you'll record a macro and make additions to it.

Editing a Recorded Macro

Each Excel workbook has tabs at the bottom to show the worksheets in the workbook. The sheet tabs share the same row of the screen as the horizontal scroll bar. If you do a lot of horizontal scrolling, you may want to remove the sheet tabs temporarily. First remove the tabs interactively with menu commands, and then record a macro to make the change.

Remove sheet tabs with a command

1 On the Tools menu click Options, and click the View tab.

2 Clear the Sheet Tabs check box at the bottom of the Window Options group.

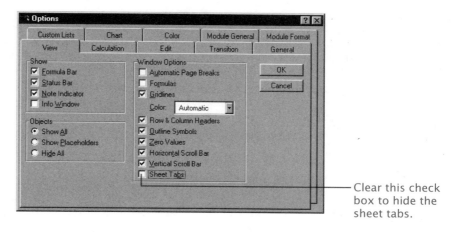

Clear this check box to hide the sheet tabs.

3 Click OK.

The sheet tabs are gone from the bottom of the window, so the scroll bar can expand to the whole width of the window.

4 Repeat step 1, and select the Sheet Tabs check box to turn the sheet tabs back on. Then click OK.

Sheet tabs are a property of the window. You can select the Sheet Tabs check box so that the value of the property is True and the window displays the tabs, or you can clear the check box so that the value of the property is False and the window does not display the tabs. Next, change the Sheet Tabs property setting with a macro.

Remove sheet tabs with a macro

1 On the Tools menu, click Record Macro, Record New Macro.

2 Replace the default macro name with **RemoveTabs** and click Options.

3 Set the shortcut key to CTRL+SHIFT+T, and click OK.

The recorder puts the shell of the macro (the comments and the Sub and End Sub lines) into the Personal Macro Workbook.

4 On the Tools menu click Options, click the View tab, clear the Sheet Tabs check box, and click OK.

The tabs disappear from the bottom of the window.

Stop Macro button

5 Click the Stop Macro button and look at the resulting code in the module window:

```
'
' RemoveTabs Macro
' Macro recorded 9/8/95 by Reed Jacobson
'
' Keyboard shortcut: Ctrl+Shift+T
'
Sub RemoveTabs()
    ActiveWindow.DisplayWorkbookTabs = False
End Sub
```

In Part 3 you will learn more about objects. This macro is very similar to the FormatCurrency macro. You can read it as "Let 'False' be the DisplayWorkbookTabs property of the active window." This time you're not changing the selection, but rather the active window. In both cases you are changing an *object*, an Excel element that you can control with macros. This time the object is not a cell, but a window.

Test the macro

1 Activate the Budget96 window.

2 On the Tools menu click Options, select the Sheet Tabs check box, and click OK to make the sheet tabs appear.

3 Press CTRL+SHIFT+T to make the tabs disappear.

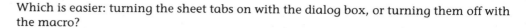

Which is easier: turning the sheet tabs on with the dialog box, or turning them off with the macro?

Toggle a property setting with a macro

You could record a second macro to turn the sheet tabs on, but somehow, letting a single macro *toggle* the setting seems more natural. Just change the macro to have it switch between the two property settings.

1 Activate the module window.

2 Select the words *ActiveWindow.DisplayWorkbookTabs* and press CTRL+C to copy them to the Clipboard.

```
Sub RemoveTabs()
    ActiveWindow.DisplayWorkbookTabs = False
End Sub
```

3 Double-click the word *False* later in the same line, and press CTRL+V to paste the words you copied.

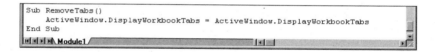

```
Sub RemoveTabs()
    ActiveWindow.DisplayWorkbookTabs = ActiveWindow.DisplayWorkbookTabs
End Sub
```

Putting the property name on the right side of the equal sign retrieves the current value for the property. But so far, all you've done is made the macro set the property to the same thing that it was before. Not particularly useful.

4 Click just after the equal sign. Press SPACEBAR, and then type **Not**

You should have a space on each side of the word *Not*.

This is what the macro should look like now:

```
Sub RemoveTabs()
    ActiveWindow.DisplayWorkbookTabs = Not ActiveWindow.DisplayWorkbookTabs
End Sub
```

5 Activate the Budget96 window, and press CTRL+SHIFT+T several times.

The macro reads the old value of the property, changes it to the opposite with the keyword *Not*, and assigns the newly inverted value back to the property.

Simplify the macro

The macro contains only one line, but that one line is rather long and a little hard to read. The DisplayWorkbookTabs property on the right applies to the same ActiveWindow object as the DisplayWorkbookTabs property on the left. Didn't Visual Basic have a *With* keyword that could eliminate the need to keep repeating the name of an object?

1 Activate the module window and position the insertion point right before the word *ActiveWindow* at the beginning of the line.

2 Type **With** and a space.

3 Move the insertion point to just before the first period and press ENTER to move the rest of the statement to the next line.

4 Press TAB to indent the new line.

5 Double-click the second occurrence of *ActiveWindow* and press DELETE, leaving the period and the property behind.

6 Move the insertion point to the end of the line, and press ENTER to create a new line.

7 Press BACKSPACE to align the insertion point with the beginning of the *With ActiveWindow* statement, and type **End With**

The final macro should look like this:

```
Sub RemoveTabs()
    With ActiveWindow
        .DisplayWorkbookTabs = Not .DisplayWorkbookTabs
    End With
End Sub
```
Module1

8 Activate the Budget96 window and press CTRL+SHIFT+T a few times to test the revised macro.

The new version of the macro is not remarkably different from the earlier one, but you may find it a little easier to see that both sides of the assignment relate to the same ActiveWindow object. Besides, you made some significant changes to the recorded macro and learned more about how the With structure works.

Rename the macro

This is a pretty nice macro, but now the name is wrong. This macro does not remove tabs anymore; it toggles the tab setting. You need to change the name of the macro from RemoveTabs to something that better matches its new functionality.

1   Activate the module window, and in the statement that begins with the word *Sub,* select the part of the macro name that says *Remove,* and replace it with **Toggle**

```
Sub ToggleTabs()
    With ActiveWindow
        .DisplayWorkbookTabs = Not .DisplayWorkbookTabs
    End With
End Sub
```
Module1

2   On the Tools menu, click Macro. The list reflects the new name of the macro.

3   Select ToggleTabs from the list, and click Run. The macro still works.

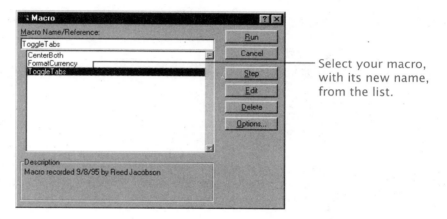

Select your macro, with its new name, from the list.

4   Delete (or fix) the comment line that told the old name of the macro. Comments do not automatically adjust when you rename the macro.

Aside from updating any comments, to rename a macro you just change the name in the line beginning with *Sub.*

Recording Actions in a Macro

You should see a pattern to creating a simple convenience macro: Try out an action interactively. Once you know how to do the task, start the recorder. Do the task with the recorder on. Stop the recorder.

So far, all the macros you have recorded have changed the settings of one or more properties of an object. Some actions that you can record do not change property settings. For example, copying and pasting cells do not change settings; they carry out tasks. Let's see what a macro looks like when you record simple actions.

Suppose you want to freeze the formulas of some cells in the Budget96 worksheet at their current values. First change the formulas to values using menu commands, and then create a macro that can change any formula to a value.

Convert a formula to a value interactively

1   Activate the Budget96 window, and select cell D4.

Notice the formula in the formula bar: =D3-D68.

You can also press CTRL+C to copy the current selection.

2   On the Edit menu, click Copy.

Copying the current selection to the Clipboard is an action. The act of copying does not display a dialog box.

3   Don't change the selection. On the Edit menu, click Paste Special. The Paste Special dialog box appears.

4   Select the Values option from the Paste group, and click OK.

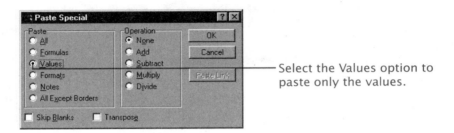

Select the Values option to paste only the values.

Excel pastes the value from the cell over the top of the existing cell, eliminating the formula that was in it. The moving border is still visible around the cell, indicating that you could paste the value again somewhere else if you wanted.

Pasting the value of the cell is an action just like copying the cell, but the act of pasting values action displays a dialog box.

5   Press ESC to get out of copy mode and clear the moving border.

Look at the formula bar: cell D4 now contains the value 26819.9.

As you carry out the copy and paste actions with the menus, notice that the Copy command does not bring up a dialog box. You see a moving border around the cells and a message in the status bar, but you don't need to tell Excel how to do the copying. The Paste Special command, on the other hand, does require additional information from you in order to carry out its job, so it displays a dialog box. Some actions in Excel need you to give additional information about how to carry out the action, and some don't.

Convert a formula to a value with a macro

Watch how the macro recorder handles actions that display a dialog box, compared to how it handles actions that don't.

1   On the Budget96 worksheet, select cell E4.

Notice the formula in the formula bar: =E3-E68.

2   On the Tools menu, click Record Macro, Record New Macro.

3   Replace the default name with **ConvertToValues** and click Options.

4   Set the shortcut key to CTRL+SHIFT+V, and click OK.

5   On the Edit menu, click Copy.

6   On the Edit menu click Paste Special, select the Values option, and click OK.

7   Press ESC to get rid of the moving border.

8   Click the Stop Macro button.

Stop Macro button

Look at the formula bar. Cell D4 now contains the value 27057.9. The recorded macro appears in the lower window.

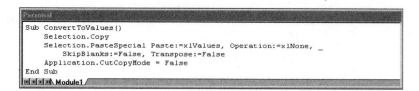

```
Sub ConvertToValues()
    Selection.Copy
    Selection.PasteSpecial Paste:=xlValues, Operation:=xlNone, _
        SkipBlanks:=False, Transpose:=False
    Application.CutCopyMode = False
End Sub
```

The basic structure of this macro is the same as that of the other macros you have seen in this lesson. The last line, for example, sets the value of the CutCopyMode property in much the same way that the ToggleTabs macro changed the DisplaySheetTabs property setting of the active window. The two lines that begin with *Selection*, however, are something new.

The words *Selection.Copy* look similar to the words *Selection.NumberFormat* from the FormatCurrency macro. In that macro, NumberFormat was a property of the selection and you were assigning a new value to the NumberFormat property. Copy, however, is not a property. You don't assign anything to Copy; you just do it. Actions for which you don't set the value of a property—that is, actions like Copy—are called *methods*.

When you execute the Copy command interactively, Excel does not ask you for any extra information. In the same way, when you execute the Copy method in a macro, you don't give any extra information to the command.

The word *PasteSpecial* is also a method in Excel. PasteSpecial is not a property that you assign a value to. The Paste Special command on the Edit menu does display a dialog box, but the dialog box does not show you properties to change; it just asks *how* to carry out the paste special action. When you execute the PasteSpecial method in a macro, you give the extra information to the method. The extra pieces of information you give to a method are called *arguments*.

Using a method with an object is like giving instructions to your nine-year-old son. With some instructions—like "Come eat"—you don't have to give any extra information. With other instructions—like "Go to the store for me"—you have to tell what to buy (milk), how to get there (on your bike), and when to come home (immediately). Giving these extra pieces of information to your son is like giving arguments to an Excel method. (You call them *arguments* because whenever you tell your son how to do something, you end up with an instant argument.)

23

The four arguments you give to PasteSpecial correspond exactly to the four option groups in the Paste Special dialog box. Each argument consists of a name for the argument (for example, Paste) joined to the argument value (for example, xlValues) by a colon and an equal sign (:=).

When you assign a new value to a property, you separate the value from the property with an equal sign, as in this statement:

```
ActiveWindow.DisplayWorkbookTabs = False
```

You read this statement as "Let 'False' be the DisplayWorkbookTabs property of the active window."

When you use a named argument with a method, you separate the method name from the argument name with a space, and you separate the argument name from the argument value with a colon and an equal sign. When you have more than one argument, separate each one from the next with a comma and a space, as in this statement:

```
Selection.PasteSpecial Paste:=xlValues, Operation:=xlNone
```

An argument looks a lot like a property, but an argument always follows a method name. A property is an attribute of an object. An argument is a special instruction to a method.

Make a long statement more readable

When one of the statements in a macro gets to be longer than about 70 characters, the macro recorder puts a space and an underscore (_) after a convenient word and continues the statement on the next line. The underscore tells the macro that it should treat the second line as part of the same statement. You can break long statements into as many lines as you want, as long as you always break the line where there is already a space. You can also indent related lines with tabs, to make the macro easier to read.

 In the ConvertToValues macro, put each argument of the PasteSpecial statement on a separate line, using a space and an underscore character at the end of each line except the last.

```
Sub ConvertToValues()
    Selection.Copy
    Selection.PasteSpecial _
        Paste:=xlValues, _
        Operation:=xlNone, _
        SkipBlanks:=False, _
        Transpose:=False
    Application.CutCopyMode = False
End Sub
```

Most of the macros in this chapter change the settings of object properties. This macro executes object methods. Properties and methods look very similar: both are separated from objects by periods. However, you assign new values to properties, and you execute methods, sometimes giving the method arguments along the way.

Adding a Macro to a Toolbar

Shortcut keys and toolbar buttons both make running macros more convenient. Shortcut keys can be faster—if you remember them—but toolbar buttons can be easier to remember and use. When you recorded the ConvertToValues macro, you created a shortcut key for it, but CTRL+SHIFT+V may be too hard to remember. You can create an easy-to-remember toolbar button for your macro.

Customize the toolbar

You can also use the right mouse button to open the Customize dialog box: click any toolbar, and then click Customize on the shortcut menu.

To add a custom button to a toolbar, you need to customize the toolbar. Amazingly enough, Excel has a Customize dialog box that allows you to work with toolbars.

1 Activate the Budget96 window. On the View menu, click Toolbars.

Open the Toolbars dialog box from the View menu to select different toolbar options.

2 Click the Customize button, and in the Customize dialog box, scroll down the Categories list to the bottom and click the Custom category.

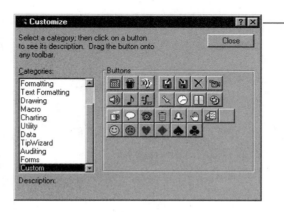

Open the Customize dialog box from the Toolbars dialog box to create your own custom toolbars.

Sort Descending button

3 Drag the Sort Descending button away from the Standard toolbar to make room for your new button. (While the Customize dialog box is displayed, you can click toolbar buttons without running them.)

4 From the collection of buttons in the Customize dialog box, click the one with the happy face and drag it up to the place where the Sort Descending button was.

5 As soon as you drag the new custom button up to the toolbar, Excel prompts you for a macro to assign to the button. Select ConvertToValues from the list, and click OK.

6 Click the Close button to close the Customize dialog box, select cell F4, and then click the new ConvertToValues happy button to convert the formula to a value.

Add status line text to a macro

One of the purposes of putting a custom button on a toolbar is to make the macro easy to remember and use. Most toolbar button pictures are a little hard to interpret, and a happy face does not immediately suggest converting to values. Each built-in Excel toolbar button displays a comment in the status line at the bottom of the screen. When you move the mouse pointer over a toolbar button, the status line tells you what the button does. You can assign a status line message to a custom button in much the same way that you assign a shortcut key.

1 On the Tools menu, click Macro.

2 From the list of macros select ConvertToValues, and click Options.

3 Near the bottom of the dialog box is a text box labeled Status Bar Text. Type **Convert formulas to values** in that box, and click OK.

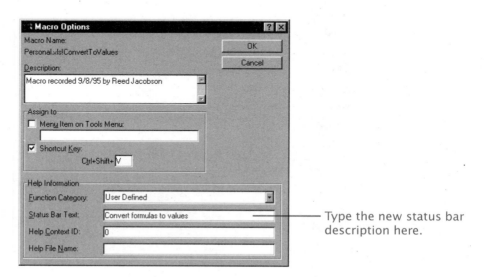

Type the new status bar description here.

4   Close the Macro dialog box.

5   Move the mouse pointer over the happy face button, and look at the status bar.

Change the picture on the toolbar button

Adding a status bar message helps you interpret what the toolbar button does, but the happy face still doesn't seem to have anything to do with converting formulas to values. You need to change the picture on the button.

Paste Values button

1   On the View menu click Toolbars, and then click Customize.

2   Select Edit from the Category list, and click the Paste Values button.

The built-in Paste Values button performs the same action as your ConvertToValues macro, except that it does not copy the selection first. The picture on the Paste Values button will serve as a good starting point for creating your picture, though.

3   Click Copy Button Image on the Edit menu, click the happy face button, and then click Paste Button Image on the Edit menu.

4   Use the right mouse button to click the new Paste Values button. Then click Edit Button Image on the shortcut menu.

The Button Editor dialog box appears, displaying an enlarged version of your button.

Create your own custom toolbar buttons with the Button Editor.

5   Click the blue color in the Colors palette, and then click the dots of the black border of the clipboard to change them to blue. This difference will remind you that this is the enhanced Paste Values button.

6   Click OK to return the revised image to your button, and click the Close button to remove the Customize dialog box.

Exit Microsoft Excel

You don't need to save changes to the Lesson 1a workbook, but you may want to save the macros you created in the Personal Macro Workbook to a different file.

1 Activate the Budget96 window, and on the File menu click Close. Click No when asked for permission to save changes.

2 Save the Personal Macro Workbook as Lesson 1b in the folder containing the sample files for this book, and then close the workbook. If the Properties dialog box appears, click OK.

3 On the File menu, click Exit to close Excel. (If you saved the Personal Macro Workbook during the course of the lesson, delete the Personal workbook from the XLStart folder in the folder where you installed Excel.)

Lesson Summary

To	Do this	Button
Turn on the recorder	On the Tools menu, click the Record Macro, Record New Macro command.	
Turn off the recorder	Click the Stop Macro button.	
Run a macro	On the Tools menu, click the Macro command, select the macro, and click Run.	
Add a shortcut key	In the Macro dialog box, click the Options button and enter the shortcut key.	
Attach a macro to a toolbar button	Use the right mouse button to click a toolbar, click Customize on the shortcut menu, and drag a button from the Custom category to a toolbar.	
Edit a toolbar button picture	Display the Customize dialog box, use the right mouse button to click the toolbar button you want to edit, and click Edit Button Image on the shortcut menu.	

For online information about	From the Excel Help menu, choose Contents, choose Getting Started with Visual Basic, and then
Recording macros	Select the topic "Recording and Running Macros"

Preview of the Next Lesson

In the next lesson you will learn how to combine multiple small macros to automate whole tasks. You will also learn more about how to find and fix problems when your macros don't work quite the way you want.

Make a Macro Do Complex Tasks

In this lesson you will learn how to:

**Estimated time
45 min.**

- Break a complex project into manageable pieces.
- Watch a macro run one statement at a time.
- Enter values into a macro while it is running.
- Record movements relative to the active cell.
- Create a macro that runs other macros.

Rube Goldberg was famous for intricate, involved contraptions in which a ball drops into a bucket, and the weight of the bucket lifts a lever that releases a spring that wakes up a cat, and so forth. Rube Goldberg contraptions are fun to look at. Milton Bradley has been successful for years with the Mousetrap game based on a Rube Goldberg concept. Boston's Logan International Airport has two massive, perpetually working Rube Goldberg contraptions in the lobby that entertain irritated travelers for hours.

Entertainment is one thing. Getting your job done is another. Sometimes the list of steps you have to go through to get out a monthly report can seem like a Rube Goldberg contraption. First you import the monthly order file and add some new columns to it. Then you sort it and print it and sort it a different way and print it again. Then you paste it onto the end of the cumulative order history file, and so forth. Each step has to be completed just right before the next one is started, and you start making sure you don't schedule your vacation during the wrong time of the month because you would never want to have to explain to someone else how to get it all done right. Right?

One good use for macros is putting together all the steps for a Rube Goldberg monthly report. This lesson will help you learn how to do it.

Start the lesson

 Start Excel, and save the blank default workbook as Lesson 2 in the folder that contains the practice files for this book. (Click Save As on the File menu, click the Look In Favorites button, double-click the Excel VB Practice folder, type **Lesson 2** as the filename, and click Save.)

Divide and Conquer

The secret to creating a macro capable of handling a long, intricate project is to break the project into small pieces, create a macro for each separate piece, and then glue the pieces together. If you just turn on the recorder, carry out four hundred steps, and cross your fingers hoping for the best, you have about a one in four hundred chance of having your macro work properly.

As the bookkeeper at Miller Textiles' Screen Printing division, you have an elaborate month-end project you would like to automate so that you can go on vacation next month. Each month, you get a summary report of orders for the previous month from the order processing system.

```
                              Miller Textiles
                       Order Summary for March 1996

  State     Channel      Category       Price   Qty     Dollars    List     Gross
  ========  ==========   ============   ======  ======  =========  =======  =========
  WA        Retail       Kids           Mid       9.00     40.50     4.50      40.50
                                        Low     143.00    434.06     3.50     500.50
                         Art            High     17.00     93.50     5.50      93.50
                                        Mid      23.00    103.50     4.50     103.50
                         Sports         High     26.00    143.00     5.50     143.00
                                        Mid       6.00     27.00     4.50      27.00
                                        Low       4.00     14.00     3.50      14.00
                         Seattle        High     13.00     71.50     5.50      71.50
                                        Mid       7.00     31.50     4.50      31.50
                                        Low      25.00     87.50     3.50      87.50
                         Dinosaurs      Mid      22.00     99.00     4.50      99.00
                                        Low      22.00     77.00     3.50      77.00
```

The report shows sales information for each state, channel, category, and price combination. The order processing system can export the report as a text file. You need to prepare the file, and add the new month's orders to a cumulative order history database.

This lesson will show you how to record the tasks that make up a large, complex project and then combine these small macros into one comprehensive macro. Along the way, you may learn some useful techniques for completing everyday tasks as well.

Activate the Visual Basic toolbar

Before you start creating the macros, take one small step that will make your work with macros much easier.

In Lesson 1, each time you wanted to record a macro, you had to go to the Tools menu, click the Record Macro command, and then click the Record New Macro subcommand. Each time you wanted to run a macro, you had to either set a keyboard shortcut or go to the Tools menu, click the Macro command, and then select the macro to run.

Excel has a special Visual Basic toolbar filled with buttons that are useful when working with macros. The Visual Basic toolbar contains two buttons that offer a much quicker solution when you want to record or run a macro.

The Visual Basic toolbar is typically *context-sensitive*: it appears when you activate a module sheet and disappears when you activate any other sheet. But if you display the Visual Basic toolbar when it would not normally appear, it becomes permanently visible.

1 Click any toolbar using the right mouse button.

  The toolbar shortcut menu appears, showing most of the available toolbars.

2 Select Visual Basic from the toolbar list.

  The Visual Basic toolbar appears. You can change the location and shape of this toolbar just as you can with any other Excel toolbar.

Now when you are ready to record a macro, just click the red circle. When you are ready to run a macro, click the green triangle.

NOTE To restore the Visual Basic toolbar to its original context-sensitive state, turn it off when a worksheet is active.

Task One: Opening the Report File

The orders for the most recent month, March 1996, are in the text file Ord9603.txt. The first task is to open the file, splitting it into columns as you do, and to move the file into the workbook with the macro.

Open the report file

 NOTE You may want to do steps 3 through 6 as a dry run before recording the macro.

Restore Window button

Record Macro button

Open button

1 If the Lesson 2 workbook window is maximized, click the Restore Window button.

2 On the Visual Basic toolbar click the Record Macro button, type **ImportFile** as the macro name, and click Options. In the extended dialog box, select This Workbook as the Store In option, and click OK.

3 Click the Open button, type **Ord9603.txt** in the File Name box, and click Open.

Step 1 of the Text Import Wizard appears.

4 The first three rows of the file contain the report title and a blank line, so change the Start Import At Row value to 4. The other default options in the Text Import Wizard are suitable for this file, so click Finish.

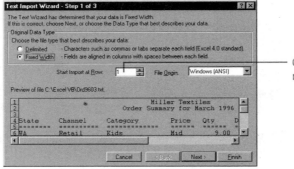

Change this number to skip rows at the top of the file.

The text file opens, with the columns split into Excel columns.

5 Drag up the bottom of the new window, so that you can see the tabs at the bottom of the Lesson 2 workbook. Then drag the tab for the Ord9603 worksheet down in front of the first tab of the Lesson 2 workbook.

Drag the Ord9603 tab from here...

...to here, to move the Ord9603 worksheet to the Lesson 2 workbook.

The Ord9603 worksheet moves to the Lesson 2 workbook, and the Ord9603.txt workbook disappears (because it lost its only worksheet, and a workbook cannot exist without at least one sheet).

NOTE   You will have several copies of the Ord9603 worksheet after you test this macro several times. Multiple copies will be useful as you develop the macros for the later project tasks. Because you already have a worksheet named Ord9603 in the workbook, new copies are automatically named Ord9603 (2), Ord9603 (3), and so forth.

6   Row 2 contains equal signs that you do not need. Select cell A2, click Delete on the Edit menu, select the Entire Row option in the Delete dialog box, and click OK.

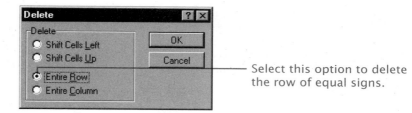

Select this option to delete the row of equal signs.

Stop Macro button

7   Select cell A1 and click the Stop Macro button to stop the recorder.

You should now have the imported file split into columns and stripped of extraneous rows.

Watch the ImportFile macro run

Rather than merely read the macro, you can both read it and test it as you watch it work. As you step through the macro, make notes of minor changes you may want to make to the macro.

Whenever you step through a macro, the Debug window appears over the top of the workbook. The Debug window lets you check the effects of the statements in your macro code. The lower half of the window, called the Code pane, displays the selected macro and allows you to see which statement will execute next. (The upper half, the Immediate pane, is introduced in Lesson 6.)

Run Macro button

1   Click the Run Macro button on the Visual Basic toolbar, select ImportFile from the Macro Name list, and click Step.

The Debug window appears on top of the workbook, with your code in the Code pane. A box around the statement highlights the statement that is ready to execute.

35

2 Drag the top left corner of the Debug window down and to the right so that you can see the Lesson 2 workbook behind it. You can also drag up the gray line that appears across the middle of the window to see more of your code.

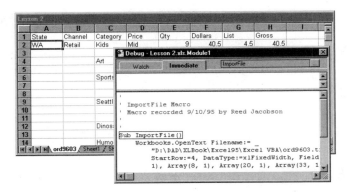

The highlighted statement is the first statement in the macro, the statement that contains the macro name:

```
Sub ImportFile()
```

3 Click the Step Into button to highlight the first statement in the body of the macro:

```
Workbooks.OpenText _
    Filename:="C:\ExcelVBA\Ord9603.txt", _
    Origin:=xlWindows, _
    StartRow:=4, _
    DataType:=xlFixedWidth, _
    FieldInfo:=Array(Array(0, 1), Array(8, 1), _
       Array(20, 1), Array(33, 1), Array(45, 1), _
       Array(53, 1), Array(64, 1), Array(73, 1))
```

Step Into button

Pressing F8 is the same as clicking the Step Into button.

In your recorded macro, the line divisions will differ from those in this example.

This long statement opens the text file. You can probably identify the argument that specifies the filename. The Origin and DataType arguments were default values in the first step of the Text Import Wizard. The StartRow argument is where you specified the number of rows to skip. The FieldInfo argument tells how to split the text file into columns. Be grateful that the macro recorder can create this statement so that you don't have to!

The macro recorder divides this long statement into several lines by putting a space and an underscore at the end of each partial line. However, it does not divide the statement at the most logical places. When you edit the macro, you should redivide the statement into meaningful lines (dividing before each new argument usually clarifies a statement). You can use the way the statement is divided above as a model.

This month, you opened the Ord9603.txt file. Next month, you will open the Ord9604.txt file. Make a note to change the macro statement to let you select the file you want to open.

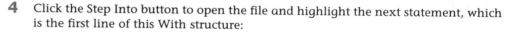

4 Click the Step Into button to open the file and highlight the next statement, which is the first line of this With structure:

```
With ActiveWindow
    .Width = 452.25
    .Height = 254.25
End With
```

These four statements were added when you moved the window out of the way. When you edit the macro, you will be able to delete these statements without harming the macro.

5 Click the Step Into button to step through the statements that moved the window. You will probably have more than four statements that change the size of the window. Make a note to delete all of them.

The next statement is now highlighted:

```
Sheets("Ord9603").Select
```

This statement makes the Ord9603 sheet into the active sheet, even though it was already the active sheet. (Macro recorders can't be too cautious, now.) You will be able to delete this statement later also.

6 Click the Step Into button to highlight the next statement:

```
Sheets("Ord9603").Move _
    Before:=Workbooks("Lesson 2.xls").Sheets(1)
```

This statement moves the new sheet into the macro workbook. But when you run this macro next month, the sheet will not be named Ord9603. It will be Ord9604. If you change Sheets("Ord9603") to ActiveSheet in the macro, it will work every month.

7 Click the Step Into button to move the worksheet and highlight the next statement:

```
Range("A2").Select
```

This statement selects cell A2 of the worksheet.

8 Click the Step Into button to select cell A2 and highlight the next statement:

```
Selection.EntireRow.Delete
```

Because the selected cell is A2, and this statement deletes the entire row of the selected cell, this statement deletes row 2.

9 Click the Step Into button to delete the row and highlight the next statement:

```
Range("A1").Select
```

This statement selects cell A1.

10 Click the Step Into button to select cell A1 and highlight the final statement of the macro:

```
End Sub
```

37

11 Click the Step Into button to end the macro and close the Debug window.

In summary, this is how you want to modify the macro:

■ Allow the user to decide which file to open.

■ Delete unnecessary statements.

■ Make the macro work with any month's file.

The next section will show you how to make these changes.

Generalize the macro

Excel provides a method that prompts the user to open a file, but doesn't actually open the file. Instead it returns the name of the file, which you can turn over to the OpenText method.

Run Macro button

1 Click the Run Macro button, select the ImportFile macro, and click Edit.

The Edit button in the Macro dialog box takes you to the macro.

2 Make the statement that begins with *Workbooks.Open* easier to read by dividing it into meaningful lines. Put a space and an underscore at the end of each partial line. Follow the example on page 36 in the preceding section.

3 Insert a new line immediately before the *Workbooks.OpenText* statement, and enter this statement:

```
myFile = Application.GetOpenFilename("Text Files,*.txt")
```

The Application.GetOpenFilename method displays the Open dialog box, just as if you had clicked Open on the File menu. The words in parentheses tell the method to display only text files: files ending with the .txt extension. (Be careful to type the quotation marks just as they appear above.) The word *myFile* at the beginning of the statement is a place to store the selected filename.

If the words Option Explicit appear at the top of your module sheet, delete them before continuing.

4 In the *Workbooks.OpenText* statement, select the entire filename, including the quotation marks, and delete it. In its place, type **myFile**

The first part of the statement should look like this when you finish:

```
Workbooks.OpenText _
    Filename:=myFile, _
    Origin:=xlWindows, _
    StartRow:=4, _
```

By the time this statement executes, the word *myFile* will contain the name of the file.

5 Delete the statements that resize the window, and also the statement that selects the Ord9603 sheet.

6 Change the words *Sheets("Ord9603").Move* to **ActiveSheet.Move**

When you're finished, the macro should look like this:

```
Sub ImportFile()
    myFile = Application.GetOpenFilename("Text Files,*.txt")
    Workbooks.OpenText _
        Filename:=myFile, _
        Origin:=xlWindows, _
        StartRow:=4, _
        DataType:=xlFixedWidth, _
        FieldInfo:=Array(Array(0, 1), Array(5, 1), _
            Array(20, 1), Array(38, 1), Array(44, 1),
            Array(53, 1), Array(64, 1), Array(73, 1))
    ActiveSheet.Move Before:=Workbooks("Lesson 2x.xls").Sheets(1)
    Range("A2").Select
    Selection.EntireRow.Delete
    Range("A1").Select
End Sub
```

7 Run the macro to make sure it works. It should display the Open dialog box (displaying only text files), and then open the file and move the worksheet to the Lesson 2 workbook.

TIP To run a macro from the module sheet, click anywhere in the macro and then click the Run Macro button. To step through a macro from the module sheet, click the macro and then click the Step Macro button. If the module sheet is active, pressing F5 is the same as clicking the Run Macro button.

Remember to save the Lesson 2 workbook.

That concludes the macro for the first task of your month-end processing project. By now you should have several copies of the Ord9603 worksheet in the Lesson 2 workbook. You are ready to move on to the next task.

Task Two: Filling in Missing Labels

When the order processing system produces a summary report, it enters a label in a column only the first time that label appears. Leaving out duplicate labels is one way to make a report easier for a human being to read, but for the computer to sort and summarize the data properly, you need to fill in the missing labels.

	A	B	C	D	E	F	G	H
1	State	Channel	Category	Price	Qty	Dollars	List	Gross
2	WA	Retail	Kids	Mid	9	40.5	4.5	40.5
3				Low	143	434.06	3.5	500.5
4			Art	High	17	93.5	5.5	93.5
5				Mid	23	103.5	4.5	103.5
6			Sports	High	26	143	5.5	143

Fill the blank cells with the missing labels.

You might assume that you need to write a complex macro to examine each cell and determine whether it is empty, and if so, what value it needs. Instead, you can use Excel's built-in capabilities to do most of the work for you. Because this part of the project introduces some powerful worksheet features, go through the steps interactively before recording the macro.

Select only the blank cells

Look at the places where you want to fill in missing labels. What value do you want in each empty cell? You want each empty cell to contain the value from the first nonempty cell above it. In fact, if you were to select each empty cell in turn and put into it a formula pointing at the cell immediately above it, you would have the result you want. The range of empty cells is an irregular shape, however, which makes the prospect of filling all the cells with a formula daunting. Fortunately, Excel has a built-in tool for selecting an irregular range of blank cells.

1 Select cell A1.

2 On the Edit menu, click Go To.

You can also press CTRL+G to display the Go To dialog box.

The Go To dialog box appears.

3 In the Go To dialog box, click the Special button.

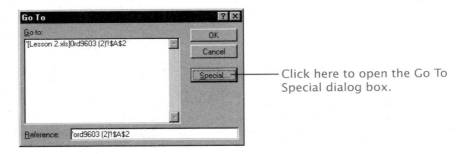

Click here to open the Go To Special dialog box.

*You can also press CTRL+STAR to select the current region (hold down the CTRL key while pressing the * [asterisk] key on the numeric keypad or SHIFT+8 on the regular key-board).*

4 In the Go To Special dialog box, select the Current Region option and click OK.

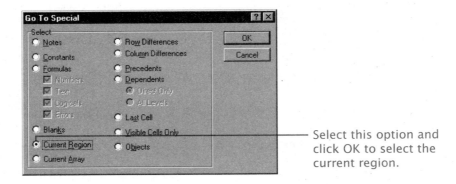

Select this option and click OK to select the current region.

40

Excel selects the *current region*—the rectangle of cells that includes the active cell and is surrounded by blank cells or worksheet borders.

5 On the Edit menu click Go To, and click the Special button.

6 In the Go To Special dialog box, select the Blanks option and click OK.

Excel selects only the blank cells from the selection. These are the cells that need new values.

	A	B	C	D	E	F	G	H
1	State	Channel	Category	Price	Qty	Dollars	List	Gross
2	WA	Retail	Kids	Mid	9	40.5	4.5	40.5
3				Low	143	434.06	3.5	500.5
4			Art	High	17	93.5	5.5	93.5
5				Mid	23	103.5	4.5	103.5
6			Sports	High	26	143	5.5	143
7				Mid	6	27	4.5	27
8				Low	4	14	3.5	14
9			Seattle	High	13	71.5	5.5	71.5

Excel's built-in Go To Special feature can save you—and your macro—a lot of work.

Fill the selection with values

You now want to fill each of the selected cells with a formula that points at the cell above. Normally when you enter a formula, Excel puts the formula into only the active cell. You can, however, if you ask politely, have Excel put a formula into all the selected cells at once.

1 With the blank cells selected and C3 as the active cell, type an equal sign (=) and press the UP ARROW key to point at cell C2.

The cell reference C2—when found in cell C3—actually means "one cell above me in the same column."

2 Press CTRL+ENTER to fill the formula into all the currently selected cells.

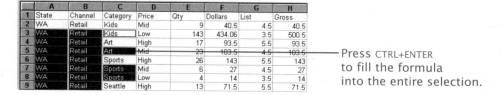

	A	B	C	D	E	F	G	H
1	State	Channel	Category	Price	Qty	Dollars	List	Gross
2	WA	Retail	Kids	Mid	9	40.5	4.5	40.5
3	WA	Retail	Kids	Low	143	434.06	3.5	500.5
4	WA	Retail	Art	High	17	93.5	5.5	93.5
5	WA	Retail	Art	Mid	23	103.5	4.5	103.5
6	WA	Retail	Sports	High	26	143	5.5	143
7	WA	Retail	Sports	Mid	6	27	4.5	27
8	WA	Retail	Sports	Low	4	14	3.5	14
9	WA	Retail	Seattle	High	13	71.5	5.5	71.5

Press CTRL+ENTER to fill the formula into the entire selection.

When more than one cell is selected, if you type a formula and press CTRL+ENTER, the formula is copied into all the cells of the selection. If you press ENTER without holding down the CTRL key, the formula goes into only the one active cell.

Each cell with the new formula points to the cell above it.

3 Press CTRL+STAR (CTRL+SHIFT+8) to select the current region.

4 Click Copy on the Edit menu. Then click Paste Special on the Edit menu, select the Values option, and click OK. Press ESC to get out of copy mode.

Now the block of cells contains all the missing label cells *as values*, so the contents won't change if you happen to re-sort the summary data. Select a different copy of the imported worksheet, and follow the same steps, but with the macro recorder turned on.

Record filling the missing values

1 Select a copy of the Ord9603 worksheet (one that does not have the labels filled in), or run the ImportFile macro again.

2 On the Visual Basic toolbar, click the Record Macro button, type **FillLabels** as the name of the macro, and click OK.

Record Macro button

3 Select cell A1 (even if it's already selected), press CTRL+STAR, click Go To on the Edit menu, click the Special button, select the Blanks option, and click OK.

4 Type =, press the UP ARROW key, and press CTRL+ENTER.

5 Press CTRL+STAR.

6 Click Copy on the Edit menu, click Paste Special on the Edit menu, select the Values option, and then click OK.

7 Click the Stop Macro button on the Visual Basic toolbar.

Stop Macro button

You've finished creating the FillLabels macro. Read it while you step through the macro.

Watch the FillLabels macro run

1 Select another copy of the imported worksheet, or run the ImportFile macro again.

2 Click the Run Macro button, select the FillLabels macro, and click Step.

Run Macro button

The Debug window appears, with the header statement of the macro highlighted.

3 Click the Step Into button to move to the first statement in the body of the macro:

```
Range("A1").Select
```

This statement selects cell A1. It doesn't matter how you got to cell A1—whether you clicked the cell, pressed CTRL+HOME, or pressed various arrow keys—because the macro recorder always records just the result of the selection process.

Step Into button

4 Click the Step Into button to select cell A1 and highlight the next statement:

```
Selection.CurrentRegion.Select
```

This statement selects the current region of the original selection.

5 Click the Step Into button to select the current region and move to the next statement:

```
Selection.SpecialCells(xlBlanks).Select
```

This statement selects the blank special cells of the original selection. (The word SpecialCells refers to cells you selected using the Go To Special dialog box.)

6 Click the Step Into button to select just the blank cells and move to the next statement:

```
Selection.FormulaR1C1 = "=R[-1]C"
```

For more information about R1C1 notation, select Answer Wizard from the Help menu, search for "Reference Style," and select the topic "How Microsoft Excel Identifies Cells."

This statement assigns *"=R[-1]C"* as the formula for the entire selection. When you entered the formula, the formula you saw was =C2, not =R[-1]C. The formula =C2 really means "get the value from the cell just above me"—as long as the active cell happens to be cell C3. The formula =R[-1]C also means "get the value from the cell just above me"—but without regard for which cell is active.

You could change this statement to *Selection.Formula = "=C2"* and the macro would work exactly the same—provided that the order file you use when you run the macro is identical to the order file you used when you recorded the macro, and the active cell happens to be cell C3 when the macro runs. If the command that selects blanks produces a different active cell, the revised macro will fail. The macro recorder uses R1C1 notation so that your macro will always work correctly.

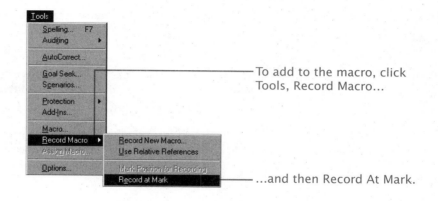

Resume Macro button

7 Click the Resume Macro button to execute the remaining statements in the macro:

```
Selection.CurrentRegion.Select
Selection.Copy
Selection.PasteSpecial Paste:=xlValues, Operation:=xlNone, _
    SkipBlanks:=False, Transpose:=False
```

These statements select the current region and then convert the formulas to values, just as you did in Lesson 1.

Append to the FillLabels macro

Notice that the status bar still says "Select destination and press ENTER or choose Paste" and the selection still has the moving border glittering around it. This means that Excel is still in copy mode. You could press ESC now to turn off copy mode, but you would probably prefer to append a statement to the macro to turn copy mode off each time you run the macro.

You can also record at the mark by holding down the SHIFT key as you click the Record Macro button.

Record Macro button

1 On the Tools menu, click Record Macro, Record At Mark.

To add to the macro, click Tools, Record Macro...

...and then Record At Mark.

Excel does not prompt you for a macro name. It just starts recording new statements.

2 Press ESC.

3 Select cell A1.

4 Click the Stop Macro button.

Stop Macro button

5 Click the Run Macro button, select the FillLabels macro, and click Edit to see the newly improved macro.

The macro now has two new statements at the bottom:

```
Application.CutCopyMode = False
Range("A1").Select
```

Run Macro button

These new statements turn off copy mode and select cell A1, just as you would expect.

Each time you stop the recorder, Excel leaves an invisible mark. If you click the Record At Mark command, the recorder restarts at the mark. This invisible mark enables you to turn the recorder off and on freely, even while creating a single macro.

Remember to save the Lesson 2 workbook.

You have completed the macro for the second task of your month-end project. Now you can start a new macro to carry out the next task—adding the dates.

Task Three: Adding a Column of Dates

The order summary report you are working with does not include the date in each row, since the text file includes numbers for only a single month. Before you can append these new records to the order history database, you will need to add the current month to each record.

Add a constant date

First you will create a macro that fills the range with the date *Mar-96*, by inserting a new column A and putting the date into each row that contains data.

Record Macro button

1 Select a worksheet that has the labels filled in, click the Record Macro button, type **AddDates** as the name of the macro, and click OK.

2 Select cell A1, and on the Insert menu click the Columns command.

Excel inserts a new column A, shifting the other columns over to the right.

3 Type **Date** in cell A1, and press ENTER.

4 Press CTRL+STAR to select the current region.

5 Click Go To on the Edit menu, click the Special button, select Blanks, and click OK to select only the blank cells. These are the cells where the dates should go.

6 Type **Mar-96** and press CTRL+ENTER to fill the date into all the cells.

Excel fills the date into all the rows.

Stop Macro button

7 Select cell A1, and click the Stop Macro button to stop the recorder.

Step through the macro

Run Macro button

Step Into button

1 With cell A1 selected, click Delete on the Edit menu, select the Entire Column option, and click OK.

2 Click the Run Macro button, select the AddDates macro, and click Step.

3 Click the Step Into button repeatedly to step through the macro.

This is what the macro should look like:

```
Sub  AddDates()
     Range("A1").Select
     Selection.EntireColumn.Insert
     ActiveCell.FormulaR1C1 = "Date"
     Range("A2").Select
     Selection.CurrentRegion.Select
     Selection.SpecialCells(xlBlanks).Select
     Selection.FormulaR1C1 = "Mar-96"
     Range("A1").Select
End  Sub
```

This macro is pretty straightforward. Notice that the statement that enters the word *Date* changes the formula of the active cell, whereas the statement that enters the actual date changes the formula of the entire selection. When you enter a formula using the ENTER key alone, the macro uses the word *ActiveCell*. When you enter a formula using CTRL+ENTER, the macro uses the word *Selection*. If the selection is only a single cell, then *ActiveCell* and *Selection* are equivalent.

The recorder always records putting a value into a cell by using the Formula R1C1 property—even if you enter a label—just in case you might have entered a formula.

Prompt for the date

Your recorded macro should work just fine if you always run it using the same month's data file. But the next time you actually use this macro, you will be working with April orders, not March orders. You need to change the macro so that it *asks* you for the date when you run it.

Run Macro button

1 Click the Run Macro button, select the AddDates macro, and click Edit.

2 Insert a new line just below the Sub AddDates() statement, and enter this new statement:

```
myDate = InputBox("Enter the date in MMM-YY format")
```

InputBox is a Visual Basic function that prompts for information while a macro runs. The words in parentheses are the message it displays. The word *myDate* is a place to store the date until the macro is ready to use it.

45

3 Select and delete the text "*Mar-96*" in the macro. Be sure to delete the quotation marks.

4 Type **myDate** where the old date used to be.

The revised statement should look like this:

```
Selection.FormulaR1C1 = myDate
```

5 Activate a worksheet that needs the date column added. (Delete the old date column, or run the FillLabels macro, as needed.)

If you click the Cancel button, the macro leaves the date cells empty. In Lesson 3, you will learn how to determine whether the user clicked the Cancel button.

6 Click the Run Macro button, select the AddDates macro, and click Run.

The macro prompts for the date and then inserts the date into the appropriate cells in column A.

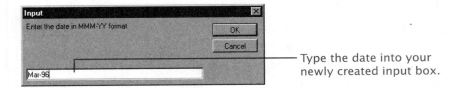

Type the date into your newly created input box.

TIP The InputBox function is a useful tool for making a macro work in slightly changing circumstances.

Remember to save the Lesson 2 workbook.

This completes your third task. Now you're ready to append the new data to the database.

Task Four: Appending to the Database

You may want to do steps 2 through 10 as a dry run before recording the macro.

Now that you have added monthly dates to the imported Ord9603 worksheet, it has the same columns as the order history database, so you can just copy the worksheet and append it to the first blank row below the database. Of course, you don't want to include the column headings.

Append a worksheet to a database

First you will copy the data (without the headings) from the Ord9603 worksheet. Then you will open the database, select the first blank cell below the database, rename the database range to include the new rows, and close the database file.

Record Macro button

1 Select one of the Ord9603 worksheets that has the labels filled and the dates added, click the Record Macro button, type **AppendDatabase** as the macro name, and click OK.

2 Select cell A1. On the Edit menu click the Delete command, select the Entire Row option, and click OK.

This deletes the heading row so you won't include it in the range you copy to the database.

3 Press CTRL+STAR to select the current region, and click Copy on the Edit menu.

4 On the File menu click Open, type **Orders.dbf** in the File Name box, and click Open.

The Orders.dbf database file opens with cell A1 selected. (The dates look different from those in your file but that is merely due to formatting differences.)

5 Press CTRL+DOWN ARROW to go to the last row of the database.

6 Press the DOWN ARROW key to select the first cell below the database. (It should be cell A3301.)

	A	B	C	D	E
3299	2/1/96	WA	Retail	Seattle	Mid
3300	2/1/96	WA	Retail	Sports	Mid
3301					
3302					

Select this cell, and then reactivate the Lesson 2 window.

7 On the Edit menu, click Paste to append the rows you previously copied, and then press ESC to remove the copy message from the status bar.

Orders

	A	B	C	D	E	F
3299	2/1/96	WA	Retail	Seattle	Mid	6
3300	2/1/96	WA	Retail	Sports	Mid	5
3301	Mar-96	WA	Retail	Kids	Mid	9
3302	Mar-96	WA	Retail	Kids	Low	143
3303	Mar-96	WA	Retail	Art	High	17

8 Press CTRL+STAR to select the entire new database range, including the newly appended rows.

NOTE When you open a dBase file in Excel, the range containing the actual database records is automatically named *Database*. When you save the updated Orders.dbf file as a dBase file, only the values within the range named Database are saved. Any other cell values in the file are discarded. In order to have the new rows saved with the file, you must enlarge the Database range name to include them.

9 On the Insert menu, click the Name, Define command. Type **Database** in the Names In Workbook box, and click OK.

IMPORTANT Do *not* select Database from the list of names. If you do, the range name will keep its current definition.

Now the entire database—including the new rows—is included in the Database range name and will be saved with the file.

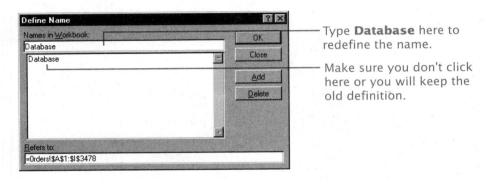

Type **Database** here to redefine the name.

Make sure you don't click here or you will keep the old definition.

10 On the File menu click Close, and click No when asked to save changes.

For now, you don't actually want to save the database with the new records back to the Orders.dbf file, because you will want to test the macro.

11 Select cell A1, and click the Stop Macro button to turn off the recorder.

Stop Macro button

Step through the AppendDatabase macro

Step through the macro to see it work, and make notes of any changes you should make.

1 Activate a worksheet with the labels filled and the dates added. (Run the ImportFile, FillLabels, and AddDates macros if necessary.)

2 Click the Run Macro button, select the AppendDatabase macro, and click the Step button. Look at the first five lines of the macro:

Run Macro button

```
Sub  AppendDatabase()
     Range("A1").Select
     Selection.EntireRow.Delete
     Selection.CurrentRegion.Select
     Selection.Copy
```

These statements are similar to statements you have seen in earlier macros.

3 Click the Step Into button five times to execute the first five statements in the macro.

Step Into button

In the Debug window, the Open statement should be highlighted:

```
Workbooks.Open    Filename:="C:\ExcelVBA\Orders.dbf"
```

This statement opens the database.

> **TIP** If you remove everything except Orders.dbf from the filename, the macro will look for the file in the current folder. That would be useful if you might move the project to a new folder.

4 Click the Step Into button to execute the Open statement and move to the next statement:

```
Selection.End(xlDown).Select
```

This statement is equivalent to pressing CTRL+DOWN ARROW. It starts with the active cell, searches down to the last non-blank cell, and selects that cell.

5 Click the Step Into button to select the last cell in the database and move to the next statement:

```
Range("A3301").Select
```

This statement selects cell A3301. That is the first cell below the database this month, but next month it will be wrong. This is the statement the recorder created when you pressed the DOWN ARROW key. What you wanted was a statement that moves one cell down from the active cell. You will need to fix this statement.

6 Click the Step Into button to select cell A3301 and move to the next statement. The next two statements work together:

```
ActiveSheet.Paste
Application.CutCopyMode = False
```

These paste the new rows into the database and remove the status bar message.

7 Click the Step Into button twice. The next two statements rename the Database range:

```
Selection.CurrentRegion.Select
ActiveWorkbook.Names.Add  Name:="Database",  RefersToR1C1:= _
       "=Orders!R1C1:R3478C9"
```

The first statement selects the current region, which is the correct range for the new database range. The second statement gives the name Database to the specific range R1C1:R3478C9 (A1:I3478). This is not what you want. You want the name Database to be assigned to whatever selection is current at the time the statement executes. You will also need to fix this statement.

8 Click the Step Into button twice to move to the statement that closes the workbook file:

```
ActiveWorkbook.Close
```

This statement closes the active workbook. If you have made changes to the workbook, it also prompts for whether to save the changes. You can change this so that it *always* saves changes or (while testing) *never* saves changes.

9   Click the Step Into button to close the database workbook. Choose No when asked if you want to save changes. Only two statements remain in the macro:

```
    Range("A1").Select
End Sub
```

10   Click the Step Into button twice to end the macro.

The macro works now only because you are running it under circumstances identical to those when you recorded it, with the same current month file and the same database file. Here is a recap of the changes you will need to make:

■   Select the first row under the database.

■   Give the name Database to the current selection.

■   Don't prompt when closing the database.

The next few sections will show you how to make these changes.

Record a relative movement

Take a closer look at the two AppendDatabase statements that find the first blank cell under the database. Imagine what will happen when you run this next month—when the database will have more rows.

The statement

```
Selection.End(xlDown).Select
```

will select the bottom row, but then the statement

```
Range("A3301").Select
```

will always select the absolute cell A3301 anyway.

When you select a cell, the macro recorder does not know whether you want the absolute cell you selected or a cell relative to where you started. For example, when you select a cell in row 1 to change the label of a column title, you always want the same absolute cell, without regard to where you started. But when you select the first blank cell at the bottom of a database, you want the macro to select a cell relative to where you started.

The macro recorder cannot automatically know whether you want to record absolute cell addresses or relative movements, but you can tell the recorder which kind of selection you want. Use the recorder to replace the offending statement in the macro with one that will work.

1   On the Tools menu, click Record Macro, Use Relative References.

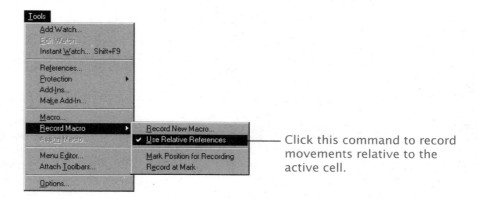

Click this command to record movements relative to the active cell.

This command changes the recorder so that it records all new cell selections *relative* to the original selection. Now you need to replace the statement that selects cell A3301 with one that makes a relative movement.

Run Macro button

2 Click the Run Macro button, select the AppendDatabase macro, and click Edit. Then select the entire row with the statement *Range("A3301").Select* and press DELETE.

Select this row, and press DELETE.

3 Don't move the insertion point. On the Tools menu, click Record Macro, Mark Position For Recording.

The Mark Position For Recording command moves the macro recorder's invisible mark to the beginning of the line with the insertion point. The Record At Mark command makes the macro start inserting new commands at the mark.

NOTE When you close and reopen a workbook, the invisible mark is lost. Excel disables the Record At Mark command, and the macro recorder creates a new module sheet for any new macros. If you want to record a new macro on an existing module sheet, click Mark Position For Recording to mark the location for new macros. When you record the new macro, it will appear on the sheet with the mark.

You want to record the action of moving down one cell, so you can record the macro from any cell, on any worksheet.

4 Activate any worksheet, and select any single cell.

5 On the Tools menu, click Record Macro, Record At Mark.

6 Press the DOWN ARROW key once to record a relative movement.

7 Click the Stop Macro button.

*Stop Macro
button*

8 On the Tools menu, click Record Macro, Use Relative References to clear the check mark next to the command.

This returns the macro recorder to the default of recording absolute cell addresses. Excel remembers the most recent setting until you exit Excel. Each time you open Excel, the setting is returned to the default: absolute references.

9 Activate the module sheet and look at the change.

The new statement you recorded should look like this:

```
ActiveCell.Offset(1,  0).Range("A1").Select
```

Lesson 8 discusses the Offset method in more detail.

This statement means "Select the cell below the active cell." It really does. At this point, you don't need to understand everything about how this statement works. Just trust the recorder. But you may wonder why the statement includes the words *Range("A1")* when it has nothing to do with cell A1. This statement calculates a new single-cell range shifted down one cell from the original active cell. The macro treats that new range as if it were the top left corner of an entire "virtual" worksheet and selects cell A1 of that imaginary worksheet!

You can use the macro recorder to insert new statements directly into the middle of a macro by using the Mark Position For Recording and Record At Mark commands. With the Use Relative References command you can control whether selections are absolute or relative to the current active cell. All these commands are located on the Record Macro submenu of the Tools menu.

Name the current selection

The statement in the macro that defines the Database range name contains a potentially serious problem:

```
ActiveWorkbook.Names.Add  Name:="Database",  RefersToR1C1:= _
    "=Orders!R1C1:R3478C9"
```

This statement sets the name Database to the range that the database occupies at the end of this month. If you don't change this statement before next month, April orders will be discarded from the database when you save it. This is a case where the macro recorder generates a complicated statement when a very simple one would work better.

➤ Replace the entire recorded statement with this one:

```
Selection.Name = "Database"
```

The word *Name* is a property of a range. By simply assigning a word in quotation marks as the value of the Name property you can name the range.

Save changes while closing a file

The statement that closes the database file looks like this:

```
ActiveWorkbook.Close
```

It triggers a prompt that asks you if you want to save changes to the file, because you have made changes to it since you opened it. Sometimes when you automate a process, you know that you always will (or won't) want to save changes. The Close method has an optional argument that allows you to specify whether to save changes. For now, while you are testing the macro, set the statement to *not* save the changes.

 Change the statement that closes the workbook to this:

```
ActiveWorkbook.Close    SaveChanges:=False
```

The SaveChanges argument answers the dialog box's question before it even gets asked. Once you have finished testing the macro and are ready to use it regularly, change the word *False* to **True**

Here's the final version of the AppendDatabase macro:

```
Sub  AppendDatabase()
      Range("A1").Select
      Selection.EntireRow.Delete
      Selection.CurrentRegion.Select
      Selection.Copy
      Workbooks.Open  Filename:="C:\ExcelVBA\Orders.dbf"
      Selection.End(xlDown).Select
      ActiveCell.Offset(1, 0).Range("A1").Select
      ActiveSheet.Paste
      Application.CutCopyMode = False
      Selection.CurrentRegion.Select
      Selection.Name = "Database"
      ActiveWorkbook.Close SaveChanges:=False
      Range("A1").Select
End  Sub
```

Remember to save the Lesson 2 workbook.

If you want, you can run the macro again now. It will work now the same as it did before, but it is also ready for next month, when the database will have more records.

You're almost finished. The only task left is to get rid of the imported worksheet.

Task Five: Deleting the Worksheet

You imported the text file worksheet so that you could fill in the labels and add a column of dates before appending the data to the database. Once the data is safely appended, you don't need the imported worksheet any more.

Create a macro to delete the active sheet

*Record Macro
button*

*Stop Macro
button*

1 Activate an expendable worksheet, click the Record Macro button, type **DeleteSheet** as the macro name, and click OK.

2 On the Edit menu click Delete Sheet, and click OK when asked to confirm.

3 Click the Stop Macro button to turn off the recorder.

4 Select another expendable worksheet, and step through the DeleteSheet macro:

```
Sub DeleteSheet()
    ActiveWindow.SelectedSheets.Delete
End Sub
```

The recorded statement refers to the "selected sheets of the active window" because it is possible to select and delete multiple sheets at the same time. (Hold down the CTRL key as you click several sheet tabs to see how you can select multiple sheets. Then click an unselected sheet—without using the CTRL key—to deselect the sheets.) Because you're deleting only one sheet, you could change the statement to *ActiveSheet.Delete* if you wanted, but that is not necessary.

The only problem with this macro is that it asks for confirmation each time you run it. When the macro deletes the imported sheet as part of the larger project, you would prefer not to be prompted.

Make the macro operate quietly

The Delete method doesn't have an optional argument that eliminates the confirmation prompt. You must add a new statement to turn off the warning.

1 Click the Run Macro button, select the DeleteSheet macro, and click Edit.

2 Insert a new line after the statement *Sub DeleteSheet()* and enter this statement:

```
Application.DisplayAlerts = False
```

DisplayAlerts is a property of the Excel application. When you set the value of DisplayAlerts to False, any confirmation prompts that you would normally see are treated as if you had selected the default answer. The DisplayAlerts setting lasts only until the macro finishes running; you do not need to set it back to True. However, you do need to be careful not to run this macro when the active sheet is something you care about.

*Run Macro
button*

*Remember to
save the Lesson
2 workbook.*

3 Select an expendable worksheet and run the DeleteSheet macro.

Assembling the Pieces

You have all the subordinate task macros ready for carrying out your complex monthly project:

■ ImportFile opens and parses the text file.

- FillLabels makes the file look like a database.
- AddDates distinguishes one month from another in the database.
- AppendDatabase adds the new rows to the bottom of the saved database.
- DeleteSheet cleans up the temporary worksheet.

Each piece is prepared and tested. Now you get to put them all together.

Create a shell macro

You will not record the macro that runs the other macros; you will build it "by hand."
You can, however, have the macro recorder create the shell of the macro for you.

Record Macro button

Stop Macro button

Run Macro button

1 On the Visual Basic toolbar click the Record Macro button, type **MonthlyProject** as the macro name, and click OK.

2 Click the Stop Macro button.

You didn't record any contents for the macro.

3 Click the Run Macro button, select the MonthlyProject macro, and click Edit:

```
Sub MonthlyProject()
End Sub
```

You will now make this macro run all the other macros in turn.

Make the macro run other macros

Object Browser button

You can also press F2 to display the Object Browser.

1 Insert a new line after the Sub MonthlyProject() statement and press TAB.

2 On the Visual Basic toolbar, click the Object Browser button.

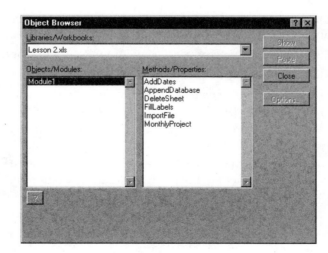

The Object Browser dialog box displays the module name on the left and the list of macros on the right. The list of macros is labeled Methods/Properties, but don't worry about that. For now, it's a list of macros.

3   Select the ImportFile macro name from the list on the right, click Paste, and then press ENTER.

The name of the InsertFile macro appears inside the MonthlyProject macro. You run one macro from another simply by including the name of the macro as a statement.

4   Click the Object Browser button, select FillLabels, click Paste, and then press ENTER.

5   Repeat step 4 for the AddDates, AppendDatabase, and DeleteSheet macros.

The final macro should look like this:

```
Sub  MonthlyProject()
     ImportFile
     FillLabels
     AddDates
     AppendDatabase
     DeleteSheet
End  Sub
```

The MonthlyProject macro will run each of the subordinate macros in turn. The subordinate macros are known as *subroutines*. (The reason you start macros with the word *Sub* is so that you can turn them into subroutines simply by running them from another macro.)

Step through the completed macro

Step Macro button

1   Click anywhere in the MonthlyProject macro, and then click the Step Macro button.

The Debug window appears, with a box around the Sub MonthlyProject statement.

Step Into button

2   Click the Step Into button twice.

The box moves to the *ImportFile* statement, and then to the first statement inside the subordinate macro. You are stepping *into* the subordinate macro.

3   Click the Step Into button repeatedly to execute each statement in the ImportFile macro. Stop when the FillLabels statement is highlighted.

When a macro like MonthlyProject runs other macros, the Step Into button steps through each statement of the main macro and can also step into the subordinate macros, or subroutines.

Step Over button

4   With the FillLabels statement highlighted, click the Step Over button.

The macro executes all the statements in the FillLabels subroutine without stepping through them. Finally it stops at the AddDates statement.

Pressing SHIFT+F8 is the same as clicking the Step Over button.

5 Use either the Step Into or the Step Over button to step through the rest of the MonthlyProject macro.

6 Run the MonthlyProject macro again, this time without stepping through it.

Hide the subordinate macros

When you open the Macros dialog box (by clicking the Run Macro button), you see the list of all the macros in the module. Most of the macros are really subroutines—they do not work properly unless they are run in the proper sequence. You can make those subroutine macros invisible to the Macros dialog box. Then the only way to run them is as part of the MonthlyProject macro.

1 Activate the module sheet and find the ImportFile macro. Immediately in front of the word *Sub* insert the word **Private** so that the statement looks like this:

```
Private Sub ImportFile()
```

Adding the word Private in front of the word Sub makes the macro invisible, except to another macro on the same module sheet. The macro doesn't appear in the Macros dialog box, and it won't accidentally run if you press F5 while the insertion point is in the macro.

Press CTRL+DOWN ARROW to move quickly to the next macro on the module sheet.

2 Insert the word **Private** at the beginning of the next three subroutine macros as well: FillLabels, AddDates, and AppendDatabase. You may prefer not to make the DeleteSheet macro private, so that you can use it either from another macro or directly from the Macro dialog box.

3 Run the MonthlyProject macro to make sure everything is still working properly.

4 Save the Lesson 2 workbook and exit Excel. You've worked hard and deserve a rest. Take the rest of the day off.

Lesson Summary

To	Do this	Button
Select blank cells in the current selection	Click the Go To command on the Edit menu, click the Special button, and select the Blanks option.	
Watch a macro execute one statement at a time	Select the macro name in the Macro dialog box and click Step. Click the Step Into button on the Visual Basic toolbar to execute the next statement.	
Prompt for a value while the macro runs	Use the InputBox function.	
Record movements relative to the active cell	On the Tools menu, click Record Macro, Use Relative References.	
Create a macro to run other macros	Type the names of the submacros into one main macro shell.	

For online information about	From the Excel Help menu, choose Contents, choose Getting Started with Visual Basic, and then
Editing Visual Basic macros	Select the topic "Recording and Running Macros"
Stepping through a macro	Select the topic "Debugging"

Preview of the Next Lesson

In this lesson, you learned how to break a complex project into pieces, record and test each piece, and then pull all the pieces together into a single macro. You ended up with a macro that does a lot of work, but it was a lot of work to make the macro. In the next lesson you will learn how to record a single simple macro and then get lots and lots of work out of it.

Make a Macro Do Repetitive Tasks

Estimated time

30 min.

In this lesson you will learn how to:

- Make decisions with a macro.
- Run a macro multiple times in a loop.
- Format exception cells with a macro.
- Interrupt a running macro.

Walk outside and stand in front of your car. Look down at the tread on the right front tire. See that little piece of gum stuck to the tread. Well, imagine you are that little piece of gum. Imagine what it feels like when the car first starts to move. You climb up, higher and higher, like a Ferris wheel. Whee! Then the pure thrill as you come back down the other side. Who needs Disneyland, anyway? But don't you think that just possibly by the five hundredth or the five thousandth or the five millionth revolution, you might start to get a little tiny bit bored? Thwack, thwack, thwack, thwack. It really could get old after a while.

Just about anything you do is interesting—the first few times you do it. Repetition, however, can bring boredom. When you start doing the same task over and over, you start wanting somebody—or something—else to do it. This lesson will teach you how to record repetitive tasks as Visual Basic macros, and then turn them into automatic machines that work relentlessly to improve your life.

Start the lesson

➤ Start Microsoft Excel and close all open workbooks, including hidden workbooks such as the Personal Macro Workbook. (Click the Unhide command on the Window menu or the File menu to find hidden workbooks.)

Creating a PivotTable

In your capacity as bookkeeper and financial analyst for Miller Textiles, you've been wondering how the various shirt design lines are doing in different geographical areas and at different prices. You have an order history database that contains the information you need to analyze.

In this lesson, you will use Excel's PivotTable Dynamic Views to show the order units by category. Then you will work through the PivotTable, highlighting cells that contain exceptionally high sales figures. First you will highlight the exceptions by hand, and then you will create Visual Basic macros that do more and more of the work for you.

Create a cross-tabulating PivotTable

1 On the File menu click Open, change to the folder containing the files for this book, type **Orders.dbf** as the file name, and click the Open button.

The order history database opens.

2 On the Data menu, click PivotTable.

In Lesson 5, you will learn how to use an external database directly as a source for a PivotTable.

Step 1 of the PivotTable Wizard appears, with the Microsoft Excel List Or Database option selected as the default. Even though the order history database is a dBase file, once you open it in an Excel workbook, it acts like an Excel database.

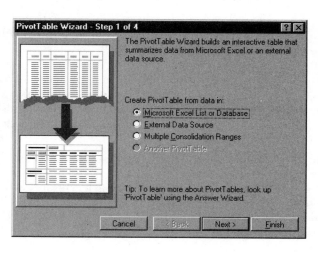

3 Click the Next button.

Step 2 of the PivotTable Wizard appears, with the name Database already entered as the default range. If the active workbook contains a range named Database, the PivotTable Wizard offers that range as the default.

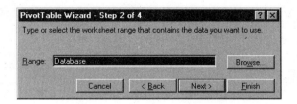

4 Click the Next button.

Excel takes a few seconds to read the data from the database, and then Step 3 of the PivotTable Wizard appears with a list of field names.

5 Drag the Price field tile to the Page area, drag the Category field tile to the Row area, drag the State field tile to the Column area, drag the Units field tile to the Data area, and click the Finish button.

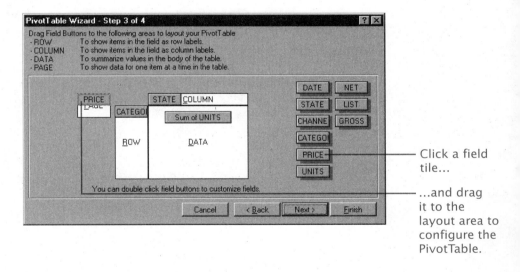

Click a field tile...

...and drag it to the layout area to configure the PivotTable.

After a few seconds, the PivotTable appears, with the different states across the top, the categories down the left column, the Price tile at the top, and the units displayed in each cell of the table. The Query And Pivot toolbar also appears, containing buttons for working with PivotTables.

	A	B	C	D	E	F	G	H	I	J
1	PRICE	(All)								
2										
3	Sum of UNITS	STATE								
4	CATEGORY	AZ	CA	ID	NV	OR	UT	WA	Grand Total	
5	Art	5292	28787	295	14275	53185	6080	26263	134177	
6	Dinosaurs	8192	16575	250	6160	10950	5990	27207	75324	
7	Environment	3356	14685	170	5070	35965	5345	22500	87091	
8	Humorous	1577	6970	290	1784	7466	8140	1423	27650	
9	Kids	3020	37733	226	11490	53288	2402	15067	123226	
10	Seattle	0	0	0	0	11375	0	58895	70270	
11	Sports	3904	7635	629	12855	7287	12111	2662	47083	
12	Grand Total	25341	112385	1860	51634	179516	40068	154017	564821	
13										

6 To make the worksheet name more meaningful, double-click the tab for the new PivotTable worksheet, type **Categories** as the name for the sheet, and click OK.

7 Use the right mouse button to click the tab labeled Orders, the sheet with the original database. Click Delete on the shortcut menu, and confirm the deletion.

Once the PivotTable has read the data from the original data source, it doesn't need the data source any more unless the data source changes and you want to refresh the data in the PivotTable.

8 On the File menu click Save As, type **Lesson 3** in the File Name box, select Microsoft Excel Workbook from the Save As Type list, and click Save. If the Summary Info dialog box appears, click OK.

Convert the PivotTable to percentages

This PivotTable displays a lot of information, but you still can't quickly see relationships among the different design categories. Part of the problem is that the variation in total units from state to state masks any patterns. Convert the PivotTable to display percentages so that you can compare the relationships more easily.

1 Select cell A3, the cell with the label Sum Of Units.

2 Click the PivotTable Field button on the Query And Pivot toolbar.

The PivotTable Field dialog box appears with information about the Sum Of Units field.

PivotTable Field button

3 Click the Options button to expand the dialog box.

4 In the Name box, select the word *Sum* and replace it with **Percent**

5 From the show Data As list, select the % Of Column option.

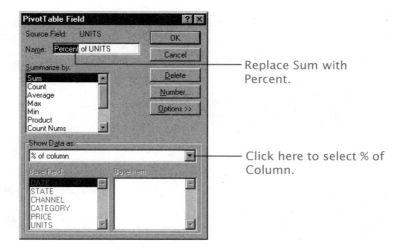

Replace Sum with Percent.

Click here to select % of Column.

6   Click the Number button, change the number of decimal places to zero, and click OK to return to the PivotTable Field dialog box.

7   Click OK to make the changes to the PivotTable.

IMPORTANT   Do *not* tell the PivotTable Wizard not to display the Grand Total row. The PivotTable needs the grand totals in order to calculate the percent-of-column values. If you don't display the Grand Total row, all the values in the table change to #NA.

Making Decisions with a Macro

Even with the numbers converted to percentages, the mass of data is so big that you still have a hard time deciphering relationships. Excel's formatting capabilities can be very useful. Change each cell in which the number is more than 20 percent of the total to yellow. Then the highlighted cells will show the top-selling categories for each state.

Highlight exceptions by hand

1   Select cell B5, the second value in the first column.

Since the value in this cell is 21%, this cell qualifies for a new color.

2   Click the arrow next to the Color button on the Formatting toolbar, and click the yellow color; it's in the sixth box in the top row of the color palette.

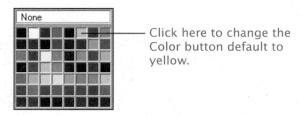

Click here to change the Color button default to yellow.

3   Scan down column B for the next cell that is greater than 20%. It is B6.

4   Select cell B6, and click the Color button. You don't have to open the palette any more, since yellow is now the default color for the Color button.

Color button

5   Find the next qualifying cell (C5) and format it. Find and format the next one after that (C9). Find and format the next one after that.

Formatting a cell to get a special visual effect is really fun—the first two or three times. But once you start repeating any action over and over, even one as delightful as formatting a cell, a certain amount of boredom does seem to creep in.

Make a macro format a single cell

Record a macro that simplifies your task just a little. Without any macro, you look at each cell in the column, decide whether it qualifies for the formatting, format it if it does, and then move down to the next cell. Start by recording a macro that formats a cell and moves to the next cell down. (At this stage, you still have to find each qualifying cell yourself.)

1   If the Visual Basic toolbar is not visible, use the right mouse button to click any toolbar, and click Visual Basic on the shortcut menu.

2   Click the arrow next to the Price page field and select Low from the list.

This changes the PivotTable to display only the units for low-price shirts. Changing the PivotTable clears the formatting you did to the cells.

3   Select cell B5, the first cell that should be formatted.

4   Click the Record Macro button, type **FormatCell** as the macro name, and click the Options button.

Record Macro button

5   Set CTRL+SHIFT+A as the shortcut key for the macro, select This Workbook as location for the macro, and click OK to start the macro recorder.

6   Click the Color button.

7 On the Tools menu, point to the Record Macro submenu. If the Use Relative References command does *not* have a check mark by it, click that command to select it. If Use Relative References already has a check mark, move the mouse pointer away from the menus, and press ESC until the Tools menu is no longer highlighted.

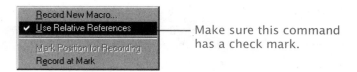

Make sure this command has a check mark.

8 Press the DOWN ARROW key once.

9 Click the Stop Macro button and then click the Module1 tab to activate the module sheet and look at the macro:

Stop Macro button

```
'
' FormatCell Macro
' Macro recorded 9/22/95 by Reed Jacobson
'
' Keyboard shortcut: Ctrl+Shift+A
'
Sub FormatCell()
    With Selection.Interior
        .ColorIndex = 6
        .Pattern = xlSolid
    End With
    ActiveCell.Offset(1, 0).Range("A1").Select
End Sub
```

This macro sets the interior of the current cell, the *Selection*, to a solid yellow color. Since yellow is the sixth item in the color palette, the macro sets *ColorIndex* to 6 to get yellow. After setting the color of the current cell, the macro moves down one cell, relative to the original active cell.

Format a cell with the macro

1 Activate the Categories worksheet.

2 Select cell C5, the next cell greater than 20%.

3 Press CTRL+SHIFT+A to run your macro.

Using this macro is slightly better, perhaps, than clicking the Color button, but you still have to find and select each qualifying cell manually.

Make the macro make a decision

When you color some cells yellow and leave other cells plain, you are making a decision. To automate this formatting task further, you need to get the macro to make the decision. The macro recorder cannot put decisions into your macro. You must add the decision yourself. You want the macro to decide whether the current cell qualifies for the color formatting.

After you rename a macro, the keyboard shortcut may try to run the old macro name. If this happens, simply press the shortcut key again to run the macro.

1   Activate the module sheet, double-click the word *FormatCell* in the Sub statement, and type **ChooseFormat** to change the name of the macro.

2   Move the insertion point to the end of the Sub statement, press ENTER, and then press TAB.

Your screen should look something like this:

Change the macro name to ChooseFormat...

...and insert a new line here.

3   Type **If ActiveCell > .2 Then** to decide whether the active cell is greater than 20%.

   TIP   If you type keywords—such as If, ActiveCell, and Then—in all lowercase letters, Visual Basic changes appropriate letters of the keywords to uppercase letters when you press the DOWN ARROW key to leave the line. Seeing the words change is a good confirmation that you spelled them correctly.

The next four statements—the statements that format the cell—should run only if the active cell is greater than 20%. If you indent them, you will be able to tell that they are controlled by the If statement.

4   Press the DOWN ARROW key to move down one line, press HOME to move to the beginning of the statement, and then press TAB. Repeat this step four times to indent each of the next four lines.

Indenting the statements reminds *you* that these statements will run only if the cell qualifies, but indenting does not tell the *macro* how to run.

5   Move the insertion point to the end of the End With statement. Press ENTER to create a new line, and press BACKSPACE to align the insertion point with the If statement.

6 Type **End If**

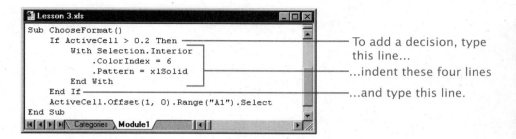

To add a decision, type this line...

...indent these four lines

...and type this line.

Now your macro will check the current cell, decide whether it qualifies for a color change, change the color if it does, and then select the next cell down. You want the macro to move down one cell whether or not it formats the current cell.

Watch the macro make a decision

Run Macro button

Step Into button

Resume Macro button

1 Activate the Categories worksheet and select cell D5, the first cell in the Idaho column.

Cell D5 qualifies for formatting, but cell D6 below it does not.

2 Click the Run Macro button, select the ChooseFormat macro, and click Step.

The Debug window opens over the Categories worksheet, with the ChooseFormat macro code in the Code pane.

3 Reduce the size of the Debug window so that you can see the worksheet.

The Sub ChooseFormat() line of the macro is highlighted.

4 Click the Step Into button to highlight the If statement.

5 Click the Step Into button again.

Because the value in cell D5, the selected cell, is greater than 20%, the macro steps down into the indented lines, to the With statement.

6 Click the Step Into button repeatedly until the end of the macro, or click the Resume Macro button to run the rest of the macro without stopping.

The active cell is now cell D6, which does not qualify for the formatting.

7 Once again, click the Run Macro button, select the ChooseFormat macro, and click Step.

8 Step through all the lines of the macro.

When the macro gets to the If statement, it jumps directly to the End If statement because the active cell is not greater than 20%.

9 Press CTRL+SHIFT+A repeatedly until you get to the end of the values in column D.

The macro takes care of the formatting decision for the active cell and then moves into position to run again. This macro is significantly more convenient (and reliable) than manually searching through the cells looking for numbers to format. But formatting the cells is still a repetitive task. Running the macro over and over seems like a task that could be automated.

Repeating an Action with a Macro

If you write a macro in such a way that each time it ends you can run it again, you can put the macro into a loop. Probably the most important requirement for putting a macro into a loop is that the macro gets everything ready for the next time around before it quits. The ChooseFormat macro does get everything ready for the next time around, so put it into a loop.

Make the macro run around in circles

You learned earlier that the macro recorder cannot put decisions into your macro automatically. In the same way, you have to add loops to your macro without the assistance of the macro recorder. That's OK. You can handle it.

1 Activate the module sheet, double-click the word *ChooseFormat*, and type **FormatLoop**

2 Move the insertion point to the end of the statement, press ENTER, and then press TAB.

Your screen should look something like this:

Change the macro name to FormatLoop, and insert a new line below it.

3 Type **Do**

The word *Do* tells the macro to start a loop.

You should indent each of the lines controlled by the Do statement to make the macro easy to read, just as you indented the lines controlled by the If statement.

4 Press the DOWN ARROW key to move down one line, move to the beginning of the line, and then press TAB. Execute this step a total of seven times to indent each of the seven lines controlled by the loop. (Indent everything except the End Sub statement at the end.)

Indenting the statements helps you remember that these statements are part of the loop, but you still have to tell the macro when to go back up to the top of the loop.

5   Move the insertion point to the end of the ActiveCell.Offset statement. Then press ENTER to create a new line, and press BACKSPACE to align the insertion point with the Do statement.

6   Type **Loop**

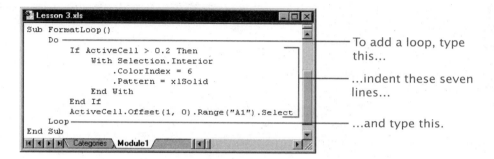

To add a loop, type this...

...indent these seven lines...

...and type this.

Now the macro will run over and over all by itself.

Watch the macro run around in circles

*Run Macro
button*

*Step Into
button*

*Resume Macro
button*

1   Activate the Categories worksheet and select cell E5, the first value in the Nevada column.

2   Click the Run Macro button, select the FormatLoop macro, and click Step to test the macro in the Debug window.

3   Click the Step Into button repeatedly to watch the macro run down to the Loop statement and then move back to the statement after the Do.

4   When you are bored with watching the macro loop, click the Resume Macro button to let the macro run without stepping.

    The macro quickly works through the rest of the cells—but then it just keeps on going and going. The macro really is running around in circles now!

5   Press ESC to halt the macro.

6   Click the End button in the dialog box that appears, and scroll back up to the top of the worksheet.

The loop does exactly what you told it to do. It runs the original part of the macro over and over, just like the magical brooms gone awry in the legend of the sorcerer's apprentice. This kind of loop is called an *infinite* loop. It keeps running until something like ESC stops it.

Make the macro stop gracefully

Your loop is like an albatross. It is beautiful, graceful, and powerful while it flies but looks like a clumsy, bumbling idiot when it lands. You need to tell your loop when to stop. How do *you* know when to stop? Well, you stop when you get to the bottom. But how do you know it's the bottom? It's the bottom when there's nothing else in the cells. So, you want the loop to keep going until the active cell has nothing in it.

1 Activate the module sheet, select the FormatLoop macro, and type **FormatColumn** as the new name for the macro.

2 Change the *Do* statement to **Do Until ActiveCell = " "**

A set of quotation marks matches an empty cell. Do not put a space between the quotation marks.

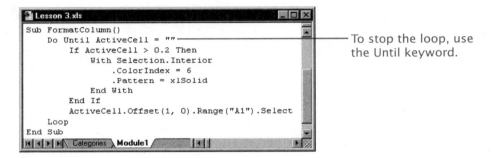

To stop the loop, use the Until keyword.

3 Activate the Categories worksheet, select cell F5—the top cell in the Oregon column—and press CTRL+SHIFT+A to run the macro.

The macro works down the whole column, and stops when it reaches the first blank cell at the bottom. Perfect.

4 Select cell G5, and press CTRL+SHIFT+A to run the macro again.

With this macro, you don't have to check each cell individually. Your job is reduced to selecting the top cell in each column and running the macro.

Make the macro find the next column

Moving the active cell up to the top of the next column is still somewhat bothersome. You can use the macro recorder to add the extra commands needed to move to the top of the next column.

1 Activate the module sheet, position the insertion point at the beginning of the End Sub statement, and click the Record Macro, Mark Position For Recording command on the Tools menu.

2 Activate the Categories worksheet and select the cell below the bottom of the last formatted column (cell G12), the cell where the macro stopped.

3   On the Tools menu, point to the Record Macro submenu. If the Use Relative References command does not have a check mark by it, click that command; otherwise, continue to step 4.

4   On the Tools menu, click Record Macro, Record At Mark.

5   Press the RIGHT ARROW key, and then press the UP ARROW key to get to the bottom value in column H (cell H11).

6   Hold down the CTRL key while you press the UP ARROW key to select the heading cell at the top of column H (cell H4).

7   Press the DOWN ARROW key to select the first cell in column H that contains a number (cell H5).

8   Click the Stop Macro button and activate the module sheet to look at the macro.

Stop Macro button

The recorder added three new lines to the bottom of your macro, just above the End Sub statement.

```
Sub FormatColumn()
    Do Until ActiveCell = ""
        If ActiveCell > 0.2 Then
            With Selection.Interior
                .ColorIndex = 6
                .Pattern = xlSolid
            End With
        End If
        ActiveCell.Offset(1, 0).Range("A1").Select
    Loop
    ActiveCell.Offset(-1, 1).Range("A1").Select
    Selection.End(xlUp).Select
    ActiveCell.Offset(1, 0).Range("A1").Select
End Sub
```

The first new line moves the active cell one up and one to the right. The second new line moves the active cell to the top of the column. The third new line moves the active cell down one, ready to run the macro again. The way the recorder creates relative selections may be a little hard to understand, but you didn't have to write them, so as long as they work, who's to complain?

Run the macro to go to the next column

1   Activate the Categories worksheet, change the Price page field to Mid, and select cell B5.

2   Press CTRL+SHIFT+A to run the macro.

The macro formats the eligible cells in column B and makes cell C5 the active cell.

3   Press CTRL+SHIFT+A to run the macro again, formatting the cells in column C.

Make the macro format the entire block

The FormatColumn macro now formats a whole column and leaves the worksheet ready to run the macro again. Because you can run the FormatColumn macro over and over, you can put it into a loop so that it formats the entire block with one push of a button. First, think about how you know when to stop running the FormatColumn macro. Once again, you stop when you get to a blank cell—this time when you get to a column that has a blank cell at the top.

1 Activate the module sheet, double-click the word *FormatColumn*, and type **FormatAll**

2 Insert the statement **Do Until ActiveCell** = "" as the first line in the macro.

3 Insert the statement **Loop** immediately before the End Sub statement in the macro.

4 Indent the 12 lines controlled by this loop.

The macro should look something like this:

```
Sub FormatAll()
    Do Until ActiveCell = ""
        Do Until ActiveCell = ""
            If ActiveCell > 0.2 Then
                With Selection.Interior
                    .ColorIndex = 6
                    .Pattern = xlSolid
                End With
            End If
            ActiveCell.Offset(1, 0).Range("A1").Select
        Loop
        ActiveCell.Offset(-1, 1).Range("A1").Select
        Selection.End(xlUp).Select
        ActiveCell.Offset(1, 0).Range("A1").Select
    Loop
End Sub
```

This macro is now able to format the entire block. Try it out.

Run the macro that formats the entire block

1   Activate the Categories worksheet, select cell B5, and press CTRL+SHIFT+A.

2   Change the Price page field to High, select cell B5, and press CTRL+SHIFT+A.

The macro formats all the appropriate cells in all the columns and then quits when it gets to the first blank column. You still, however, need to select the correct starting cell before you run the macro. Make the macro take care of that task, too.

Make the macro start at the beginning

1   Activate the module sheet and click anywhere in the first statement in the body of the macro (the statement that begins *Do Until*).

2   On the Tools menu, point to Record Macro, and then click Mark Position For Recording.

3   Activate the Categories worksheet and select any cell *other than* cell B5.

4   On the Tools menu, point to Record Macro, and then click Use Relative References to clear the check mark.

5   Again on the Tools menu, click Record Macro, Record At Mark to start the recorder.

6   Select cell B5.

7   Click the Stop Macro button to turn off the recorder.

8   Select any cell, change the Price page field to (All), and press CTRL+SHIFT+A to run the macro.

     The macro moves to cell B5 and formats all the cells.

Selecting cell B5 with the macro recorder set to use absolute references produces this statement at the beginning of the macro:

```
Range("B5").Select
```

By starting with a simple recorded macro and adding decisions and loops, you can make a powerful machine for eliminating repetition—and errors.

Lesson Summary

To	Do this
Run a block of statements only if a certain condition is true	Add If and End If statements around the block of statements.
Run a block of statements repeatedly	Add Do and Loop statements around the block of statements.
Indicate when to stop repeating a block of statements	Add an Until clause to the Do statement of a loop.
Stop a macro while it is running	Press ESC.

For online information about	**From the Excel Help menu, choose Contents, choose Getting Started with Visual Basic, and then**
Controlling how macro statements run	Select the topic "Using Loops and Conditional Statements"

Preview of the Next Lesson

In Part 1, you have learned how to create simple macros, complex macros, and repeating macros, all using the macro recorder. In Part 2, you will learn how to use some of Excel's tools for making macros easy to use. Some of the tools that make macros easy to use can also be used to make worksheets easy to use. For example, in Lesson 4 you will use dialog box controls to make a worksheet model easy for yourself and others to use.

Making Tools Easy to Use

Part 2

Use Dialog Box Controls

In this lesson you will learn how to:

■ Add dialog controls to a worksheet.

■ Link a list box to a worksheet range.

■ Link results from dialog controls to worksheet cells.

Microsoft Excel is a great program. Many people purchase Excel for use at work. Or at least the *excuse* people use for buying Excel is that they're going to use it at work. Do you want to know the real, ulterior reason 97.32 percent of Excel users have when they buy it?

You buy Excel, spend a lot of time learning how to use Excel, buy lots of books about Excel, even get a job somewhere so you can have an excuse for having Excel, just so that you can calculate loan payments for that new car you want. Try to deny it if you wish, but I know—absolutely, positively—that the car loan payment problem was the reason you bought Excel. All right, all right. Maybe I'm wrong. Maybe you *are* part of that incredible 2.68 percent of users who actually bought Excel so they could do something besides figure out their car payments. You bought it so you could figure out your *house* payment.

Now, say you have a friend who just bought Excel but doesn't really know how to use it very well yet. You want to help him out by building a little model so that he can immediately start calculating the payments for a used car he wants to buy. You want him to be able to try out several possible prices, interest rates, and repayment periods, but you want to minimize the chance for mistakes. Excel has some very powerful tools to help you make a nice model for your friend.

Start the lesson

➤ Start Excel with a new, fresh workbook, and save the workbook with the name Lesson 4 to the folder containing the practice files for this book.

Creating a Car Loan Calculator

When you interact with Excel, you do so through Excel's graphical user interface. A graphical user interface includes menus, dialog boxes, list boxes, scroll bars, buttons, and other graphical images. A graphical user interface makes a program easier to learn and also helps reduce errors by restricting choices to valid options.

Historically, creating a graphical user interface has been the domain of professional computer scientists. More recently, users of advanced applications could add graphical controls to custom dialog boxes. Now, with Excel, you can take advantage of dialog box-style controls directly on the worksheet, without doing any programming at all.

In this lesson, you will build a worksheet model to calculate a car loan payment amount, and you will add graphical controls to make it easy to use for a friend who is unfamiliar with worksheets. You won't create macros in this lesson, but you will become familiar with how dialog box controls work, which will be useful when you build a full-featured dialog box in Lesson 14.

Create a payment model

1 Type these labels into cells B2 through B7 of a blank worksheet: **Price**, **Down**, **Loan**, **Interest**, **Years**, and **Payment**

2 Type **$5,000** in cell C2 (to the right of Price), type **20%** in cell C3 (to the right of Down), type **8%** in cell C5 (to the right of Interest), and type **3** in cell C6 (to the right of Years).

3 In cell C4 (to the right of Loan), type **=C2*(1-C3)** and press ENTER.

The value 4000 appears in the cell.

4 In cell C7 (to the right of Payment), type **=PMT(C5/12,C6*12,C4)** and press ENTER.

The payment amount $125.35 appears in the cell. The red text color and the parentheses around the number in the worksheet indicate a negative number. You don't receive this amount, unfortunately; you pay it. This is the monthly payment amount for this hypothetical car. (If you want to change the monthly payment to a positive number, put a minus sign in front of the reference C4 in the formula.)

	A	B	C	D
1				
2		Price	$5,000	
3		Down	20%	
4		Loan	4000	
5		Interest	8%	
6		Years	3	
7		Payment	($125.35)	
8				

Make the model look nice

Since you're creating this model for your friend, you want to make the fonts a little larger and more inviting.

Font Size box

Format Painter button

Increase Decimal button

1 Select cell B2 and press CTRL+STAR to select all the cells in the model.

2 In the Font Size box on the Formatting toolbar, select 12.

3 On the Format menu, click Column, AutoFit Selection.

4 Select cell C2 (next to Price), and click the Format Painter button on the Standard toolbar. Then click cell C4 (the cell next to Loan) to give it the same format as cell C2.

5 Select cell C5 (next to Interest), and click the Increase Decimal button twice so that you can see fractional interest rates.

Now the model is easier to read.

	A	B	C	D
1				
2		Price	$5,000	
3		Down	20%	
4		Loan	$4,000	
5		Interest	8.00%	
6		Years	3	
7		Payment	($125.35)	
8				

Try out the model

1 Enter **$12,000** in cell C2. The loan amount should change to $9,600 and the payment amount should change to $300.83.

This simple model calculates monthly loan payments for a given set of input variables. You change the input variables to anything you like and the payment changes. You can even enter outlandish values.

2 Enter **$1,500,000** as the price of the car. This is a very expensive car. The payment formula bravely calculates the monthly payment, but you can't read it because it is too big.

3 Press CTRL+Z to change the price back to something more reasonable. (The monthly payment for the expensive car, in case you are interested, would be $37,603.64.)

One of the problems with this model is that it is too flexible. You can enter ridiculously large prices and ridiculously high interest rates. (Try 500%—I hope 500% is a ridiculous interest rate.) You can even enter, as the number of years, something totally useless, such as "Dog". The wide spectrum of choices available, only a few of which are meaningful, may confuse your friend as he uses the model.

Creating an Error-Resistant Loan Calculator

Excel has tools that enable you to make an error-resistant loan calculator. By restricting options to valid items, you can make your model less likely to produce erroneous results, and also much easier to use.

Make a list of cars

You know that your friend has been looking through the want-ads and has come up with a list of used cars he's thinking of buying. Put a list of the cars and their prices onto the worksheet as a reference.

1   Starting in cell K2, off out of the way, type this table of cars and prices into the worksheet, and adjust the column widths so that you can see all the values:

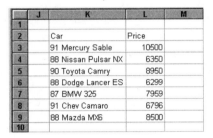

	J	K	L	M
1				
2		Car	Price	
3		91 Mercury Sable	10500	
4		88 Nissan Pulsar NX	6350	
5		90 Toyota Camry	8950	
6		88 Dodge Lancer ES	6299	
7		87 BMW 325	7959	
8		91 Chev Camaro	6796	
9		88 Mazda MX6	8500	
10				

2   Select cell K2 and press CTRL+STAR to select the entire block of cells.

3   On the Insert menu, click Name, Create. Select the Top Row check box, clear any other check boxes, and click OK. This gives the name Car to the list of cars and the name Price to the list of prices.

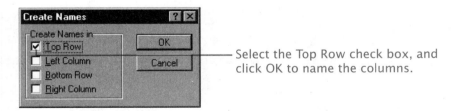

Select the Top Row check box, and click OK to name the columns.

You can drag the edges of the Forms toolbar to change its shape.

4   Use the right mouse button to click any toolbar, and click the Forms toolbar on the shortcut menu.

*Drop-Down
button*

5 Click the Drop-Down button and drag a rectangle from the top left corner of cell E2 to the bottom right corner of cell G2.

6 Double-click the new drop-down control to display the Format Object dialog box, and click the Control tab.

7 Type **Car** in the Input Range box, type **H2** in the Cell Link box, and click OK.

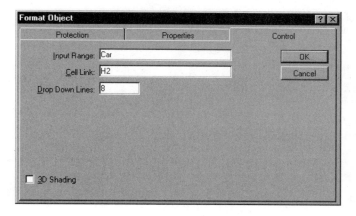

8 Press ESC to deselect the drop-down control.

9 Click the arrow next to the drop-down control, and select 90 Toyota Camry from the list.

The name for the Toyota appears in the drop-down control, and the number 3 appears in cell H2.

You just created an on-screen drop-down list box control. You linked the list box to the list of cars on the worksheet, and you linked the result of the list box to cell H2. Cell H2 displays the number 3 because 90 Toyota Camry is item number 3 in the list. If you type 4 in cell H2, the car in the drop-down control automatically changes to 88 Dodge Lancer ES. (If you try this, change the number back to 3.)

81

Retrieve the price from the list

1 Select cell C2.

2 Type **=INDEX(Price,H2)** and press ENTER.

The price of the Toyota—$8,950—appears in the cell. This formula finds the third item in the Price list because cell H2 contains the number 3.

3 Select the 87 BMW from the drop-down list of cars.

The number in cell H2 changes to 5 and the price changes to $7,959.

	A	B	C	D	E	F	G	H
1								
2		Price	$7,959		87 BMW 325		▼	5
3		Down	20%					
4		Loan	$6,367					
5		Interest	8.00%					
6		Years	3					
7		Payment	($199.52)					
8								

Now your friend will not accidentally try to find the payment for a million dollar car. He can just select various cars from the list—thinking in terms that are meaningful to him—and the price is guaranteed to be correct.

Restrict the down payment to valid values

Unfortunately, your friend can still enter an invalid down payment percentage—such as -50% or "Dog". You need to help him out.

Spinner button

1 Click the Spinner button on the Forms toolbar.

2 Drag from the top left corner of cell E3 down about half-way to the bottom and one-third of the way to the right of cell E4. The spinner control does not look good if it is too small.

Drag from here...

...to here, to create a spinner control.

3 Double-click the new spinner control.

4   Replace the default Maximum Value with **20**, type **H3** in the Cell Link box, and click OK.

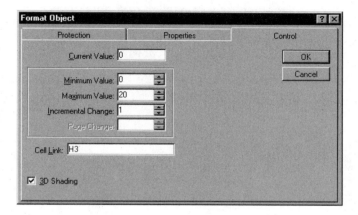

5   Press ESC to deselect the spinner control, and click the top and bottom parts of the control to see how the value in cell H3 changes within the range 0 through 20. Finish with the number 15 in cell H3.

6   Select cell C3, type =**H3/100**, and press ENTER.

The value 15% appears in the cell.

The spinner control can increment only in whole numbers, but the down payment needs to be entered as a percentage. Dividing the value in cell H3 by 100 allows the spinner control to use whole numbers and still allows you to specify the down payment as a percentage.

Make the spinner count by fives

Your spinner control now disallows invalid inputs like -50% and "Dog" but your friend might legitimately want to put more than 20 percent down on a car—50 percent, for example, or even 80 percent. In principle, he should be able to choose any whole-number percentage from 0% through 100%. But getting from 0% to 100% by clicking 100 times on a spinner control could be unpleasant. Incrementing 5 percent at a time is a good solution.

1   Hold down the CTRL key and click the spinner control to select it.

If you don't hold down the CTRL key, clicking the spinner control changes the value in cell H3.

2   Double-click the spinner control.

3   Replace the 20 in the Maximum Value box with **100**, type **5** in the Incremental Change box, and click OK.

4   Press ESC to deselect the spinner control.

Now you can try a wide variety of car model and down payment percentage combinations.

Restrict the interest rate to valid values

The next input value your friend might make a mistake with is the interest rate. The interest rate is similar to the down payment rate. Both are percentages. You probably want to allow interest rates to vary by as little as a quarter of a percent, and within a range from 0% through about 20%. Because you're allowing fractional percentages, you will have many more steps than with the down payment rate, so use a scroll bar control instead of a spinner control.

Scroll Bar button

1 Click the Scroll Bar button on the Forms toolbar.

2 Drag from the top left corner of cell E5 to the bottom right corner of cell G5.

Drag from here...

...to here, to create the scroll bar.

3 Double-click the new scroll bar control.

4 Type **0** in the Current Value box, type **2000** in the Maximum Value box, type **25** in the Incremental Change box, type **100** in the Page Change box, type **H5** in the Cell Link box, and click OK.

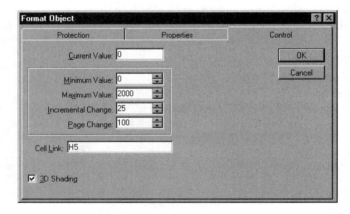

5 Press ESC to deselect the scroll bar control.

6 Try out the scroll bar control. If you click one of the arrows on either end, the number in cell H5 changes by 25. If you click between the box and the end, the number changes by 100 (the Page Change value).

7 Select cell C5, type **=H5/10000**, and press ENTER.

You divide by 100 to turn the number into a percent and by another 100 to allow for hundredths of a percent.

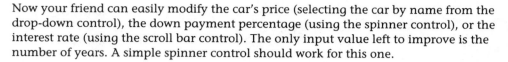

Now your friend can easily modify the car's price (selecting the car by name from the drop-down control), the down payment percentage (using the spinner control), or the interest rate (using the scroll bar control). The only input value left to improve is the number of years. A simple spinner control should work for this one.

Restrict the years to a valid range

1   Hold down the CTRL key and click the spinner control that's in cell E3. While continuing to hold down the CTRL key, drag a copy of the spinner control so that its top left corner is in the top left corner of cell E6.

Copying the control makes both controls exactly the same size.

2   Double-click the new spinner control.

3   Type **1** in the Minimum Value box, type **6** in the Maximum Value box, type **1** in the Incremental Change box, type **H6** in the Cell Link box, and click OK.

4   Select cell C6, type **=H6**, and press ENTER.

The completed model looks like this:

	A	B	C	D	E	F	G	H	I
1									
2		Price	$8,950		87 BMW 325			3	
3		Down	15%					15	
4		Loan	$7,608						
5		Interest	8.00%					800	
6		Years	4					4	
7		Payment	($185.72)						
8									

Now your friend can experiment with various scenarios as much as he wants without having to worry about typing invalid inputs into the model. In fact, he won't have to worry about typing anything into the model. He can do everything he wants by just clicking controls with the mouse. One of the greatest benefits of a graphical user interface is the ability to restrict choices to valid values. In an Excel worksheet, you can create a graphical interface without writing any code at all.

Protect the worksheet

The only remaining problem with your model is that your friend might forget to use the nice tools you have given him. For example, he might accidentally select the cell with the payment formula, type the payment he wants, and destroy the formula. You can protect the worksheet against accidental changes to formulas.

1   Select the cell range H2:H6, the cells linked to the controls.

2   On the Format menu click Cells, and then click the Protection tab.

Before you can protect the entire worksheet, you have to unlock these cells so that the controls will still be able to change them.

NOTE When you create a new worksheet, all the cells are already locked. You can still enter values into the cells, however. That is because locking a cell has no effect unless the worksheet is protected. Having locked cells is like having mice in your basement: you don't see them until you turn the light on.

3 Clear the Locked check box, and click OK.

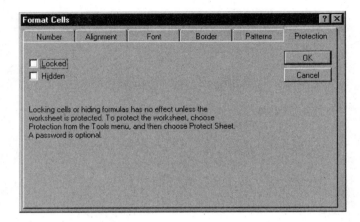

4 Select the cell range H2:L2. You want to hide the columns containing these cells.

5 On the Format menu, click Column, Hide.

Once you hide these columns, they won't be a distraction for your friend.

6 On the Tools menu, click Protection, Protect Sheet.

7 Accept the default options for the dialog box and click OK.

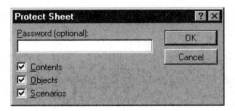

Now the worksheet model is ready to give to your friend. He doesn't need to know anything about formulas, worksheets, or entering values in a worksheet to use the model. I wish I could be there to see the happy look on his face when you give it to him.

8 Delete any unneeded sheets from the Lesson 4 workbook. (Click the tab for the first sheet you want to delete, hold down the SHIFT key while you click the tab for the last sheet you want to delete, click the Delete Sheet command on the Edit menu, and click OK when requested to confirm.)

9 Save and close the Lesson 4 workbook.

You have been very helpful to your friend, but if you don't hurry and get back to doing something for Miller Textiles, your boss will notice and then you won't have a job and then you won't have an excuse for playing with Excel any more. Hurry—back to work!

Lesson Summary

To	Do this
Add dialog box-style controls to a worksheet	Use the right mouse button to click any toolbar, and click the Forms toolbar on the shortcut menu. Click a control button and drag a place for it on the worksheet.
Select a control without running it	Hold down the CTRL key and click the control.
Copy an existing control	Hold down the CTRL key as you drag the control to a new location.
Link the value of a control to a cell	Double-click the control and type the cell address in the Cell Link box.
Link the list for a list box control to a worksheet range	Double-click the list box control and type the range name or address in the Input Range box.
Set limits for spinner and scroll bar controls	Double-click the control and type values in the Minimum Value and Maximum Value boxes.
Limit changes on a worksheet to selected cells	Unlock the cells you want to change (using the Protection tab in the Format Cells dialog box), and protect the worksheet (using the Protection, Protect Sheet command on the Tools menu).

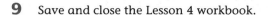

For online information about	**From the Excel Help menu, choose Contents, choose Getting Started with Visual Basic, and then**
Using dialog box-style controls on a worksheet	Select the topic "Creating Dialog Boxes" and then select "Adding Controls to a Sheet"

Preview of the Next Lesson

In this lesson, you used Excel's dialog box controls to make a worksheet model easy to use—without even writing any macros. In the next lesson, you will use dialog box controls to make easy-to-use macros for retrieving information from the order history database. Your macros will create a PivotTable and a chart, retrieving information directly from an external database without opening the database as an Excel worksheet.

Make an Enterprise Information System

Estimated time
45 min.

In this lesson you will learn how to:

■ Build a PivotTable with data from an external database.

■ Create a simple EIS application, with a graphical start-up screen.

■ Create a custom menu for your macros.

My grandmother used to use her sewing machine to embroider names on outfits for us. She had a powerful old sewing machine, with lots of pulleys and levers and loops. When she changed the thread, she had to poke the thread up and over and through what seemed like countless turns and spools and guides, even before getting to the needle. I still don't know how she managed embroidering the names. She would move levers and twist the fabric and the name appeared. She was very good, and the result was beautiful. Very few people could create embroidered names the way she did.

Now, even I can embroider names onto clothes. You flip the thread around a couple of guides and the machine is threaded. You type in the name, select the lettering style, and push another button to embroider the name. The machine sews in all directions so you don't have to turn the fabric. No longer do you have to be an expert to use a sewing machine.

In Microsoft Excel, you may be an expert at retrieving data from a database, producing a summary report, and creating a chart. Others in your organization, however, may not have the same expertise. The purpose of an Enterprise Information System (EIS) is to allow people from all parts of the enterprise to find the information they need—without having to become specialists at retrieving and formatting data. In this lesson, you will build a simple EIS application that anyone in the organization can use.

Creating a Simple Enterprise Information System

Even at work you sometimes need to create tools for others to use. One common request around Miller Textiles is for a simple way for people in the company to see how orders are doing for the various shirt categories in the different states. So you decide to build a rudimentary EIS application for them to use to browse the order history database.

Set up the database as a data source

In Lessons 2 and 3, you worked with the order history database by opening the database file directly in Excel. Excel is able to convert database files in DBF format (the file format originally defined by dBASE) directly to an Excel worksheet. When Excel opens a database file as a worksheet, it has to load the entire file into memory. That is fine for small databases with only a few thousand records, like your order history database, but as your database grows to hundreds of thousands, or even millions of records, you will undoubtedly manage the database with a specialized database program such as FoxPro or SQL Server.

You can connect to your small order history database as an external database using the same tools and techniques that you would use to connect to a large database. Then, as the company grows, your EIS application will continue to work without needing modification. Excel communicates with external databases using Open Database Connectivity (ODBC) drivers that you set up in the operating system. The first step in using the order history database as an external database is to set it up as an ODBC data source.

If the 32bit ODBC icon in Control Panel is not installed, run Excel Setup and add the Data Access component. Be sure to install the dBase driver so you can use the sample database.

1   In the Windows 95 Start menu, point to Settings and then click Control Panel.

One of the Control Panel icons is 32bit ODBC. This is the icon that allows you to manage ODBC data sources.

2   Double-click the 32bit ODBC icon to display the Data Sources dialog box.

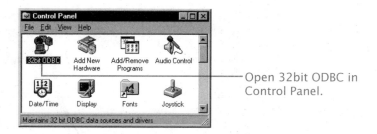

Open 32bit ODBC in Control Panel.

You can have data sources for single databases or for types of databases. Your list may or may not have sources already defined. You will set up a new data source specifically for the Miller Textiles databases.

3 In the Data Sources dialog box, click the Add button.

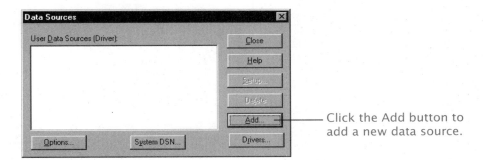

Click the Add button to add a new data source.

4 From the list of drivers that appears, select the one labeled Microsoft dBase Driver, and click OK to define a new data source using that driver.

The ODBC dBase Setup dialog box appears.

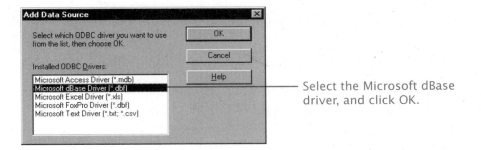

Select the Microsoft dBase driver, and click OK.

5 Type **Miller Textiles** in the Data Source Name box, and click the Select Directory button.

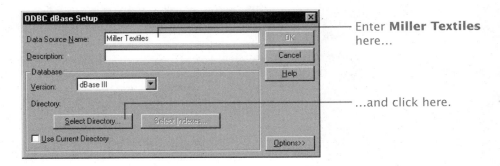

Enter **Miller Textiles** here...

...and click here.

6 Change to the folder that contains the sample files for this book.

The filename Orders.dbf should appear, grayed, on the left side of the dialog box.

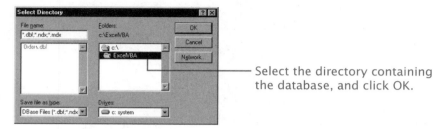

Select the directory containing
the database, and click OK.

7 Click OK to return to the ODBC dBase Setup dialog box, click OK to return to the Data Sources dialog box (where Miller Textiles now appears), and click Close to return to Control Panel.

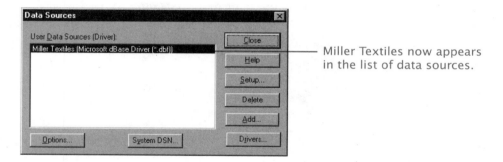

Miller Textiles now appears
in the list of data sources.

8 Close Control Panel, and activate Excel.

You have added the order history database as an ODBC data source in your Windows environment. Now you can use the Miller Textiles data source by name without specifying the location of the database files. If you move the database to a new location, or even change to a different database format, you only have to change the definition of the Miller Textiles data source.

Setting up a new data source may seem complicated at first, but giving a name to the data source can simplify the task of upgrading from a local database to a LAN-based client-server database, if you ever decide to make that change.

Look at the finished product

In this part of the lesson you will build an EIS for your associates at work. This will be a simple EIS, but it still requires a number of pieces to get it all to work. The pieces will make more sense if you have a vision of what you will end up with. Take a look at the finished product before you start building it yourself.

1 Start Excel.

2 On the File menu, click Open, change to the folder containing the sample files for this book and click the Finished folder, click the Lesson 5 file, and click Open.

The start-up screen for the EIS appears.

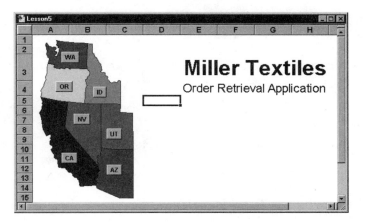

3 On the map, click the button for Oregon.

The screen flashes a bit and then you see the orders by category for Oregon, along with a simple chart.

Depending on your system configuration, your chart may look slightly different from this one.

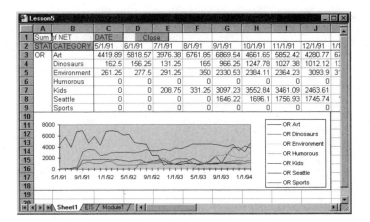

4 Click the Close button to return to the start-up screen.

Alternatively, you can retrieve the same order information by using the custom EIS menu.

5 On the EIS menu, click California.

You see the table and chart showing orders for California.

6 Click the Close button.

7 On the File menu, click Close to close the Lesson 5 file. Click No when asked to save changes.

This is not a sophisticated order history review tool. (You will learn how to make a more packaged application in Part 5.) But almost everything about this EIS was done using the macro recorder and other simple tools in Excel.

Make a start-up screen

Every good EIS must have a start-up screen. At first, you will just have a simple button on this screen, but later you will add the map so that you can let users click buttons on maps of the states.

New Workbook button

1 Click the New Workbook button to create a new workbook, change back to the folder containing the sample files for this book, and save the workbook as **Lesson 5**

2 Double-click the Sheet1 worksheet tab, type **EIS** as the worksheet name, and then click OK.

3 Click the Drawing button on the Standard toolbar to display the Drawing toolbar.

Drawing button

Create Button button

4 Click the Create Button button on the Drawing toolbar, and drag a button shape in the vicinity of cell F8.

5 In the Assign Macro dialog box that appears, click Cancel.

Canceling the Assign Macro dialog box does not cancel the creation of the button. It just closes the Assign Macro dialog box without assigning a macro to the button. You don't have a macro ready yet, so you will assign the macro later.

1 Start Excel.

2 On the File menu, click Open, change to the folder containing the sample files for this book and click the Finished folder, click the Lesson 5 file, and click Open.

The start-up screen for the EIS appears.

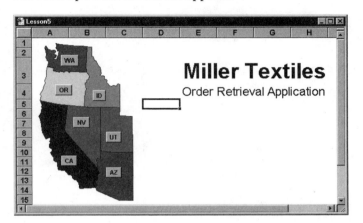

3 On the map, click the button for Oregon.

The screen flashes a bit and then you see the orders by category for Oregon, along with a simple chart.

Depending on your system configuration, your chart may look slightly different from this one.

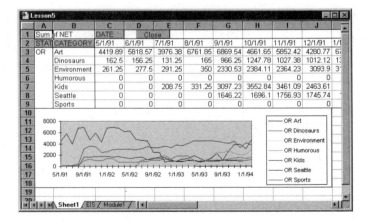

4 Click the Close button to return to the start-up screen.

Alternatively, you can retrieve the same order information by using the custom EIS menu.

93

5 On the EIS menu, click California.

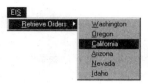

You see the table and chart showing orders for California.

6 Click the Close button.

7 On the File menu, click Close to close the Lesson 5 file. Click No when asked to save changes.

This is not a sophisticated order history review tool. (You will learn how to make a more packaged application in Part 5.) But almost everything about this EIS was done using the macro recorder and other simple tools in Excel.

Make a start-up screen

Every good EIS must have a start-up screen. At first, you will just have a simple button on this screen, but later you will add the map so that you can let users click buttons on maps of the states.

New Workbook button

1 Click the New Workbook button to create a new workbook, change back to the folder containing the sample files for this book, and save the workbook as **Lesson 5**

2 Double-click the Sheet1 worksheet tab, type **EIS** as the worksheet name, and then click OK.

Drawing button

3 Click the Drawing button on the Standard toolbar to display the Drawing toolbar.

Create Button button

4 Click the Create Button button on the Drawing toolbar, and drag a button shape in the vicinity of cell F8.

5 In the Assign Macro dialog box that appears, click Cancel.

Canceling the Assign Macro dialog box does not cancel the creation of the button. It just closes the Assign Macro dialog box without assigning a macro to the button. You don't have a macro ready yet, so you will assign the macro later.

6 With the new button still selected, type **Retrieve Orders**, and press ESC twice to deselect the button.

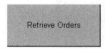

Now you are ready to retrieve the data and start building the application.

Launch Microsoft Query

You will learn more about Microsoft Query in Lesson 12.

For the EIS application, you will retrieve the data directly from an external database *without* opening the database file in Excel. You can use Excel's PivotTable Wizard to help you retrieve the data. The PivotTable Wizard uses Microsoft Query to enable you to identify the data you want. First practice creating a PivotTable without creating a macro, and then turn on the macro recorder while you build another one.

1 On the Data menu, click PivotTable.

2 Click the External Data Source option and then click Next.

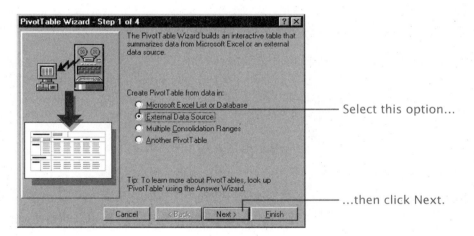

Select this option...

...then click Next.

Step 2 of the PivotTable Wizard appears.

3 Click the Get Data button.

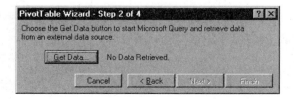

The Select Data Source dialog box appears on the screen.

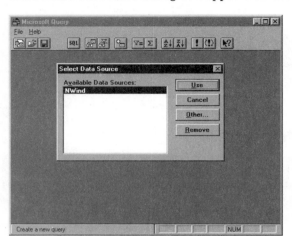

Even though you added Miller Textiles as an ODBC data source earlier, this list shows only the data sources previously used in Microsoft Query.

4   Click the Other button.

The Data Sources dialog box appears. The Miller Textiles data source is in this list.

5   Select Miller Textiles and click OK to return to the Select Data Source dialog box.

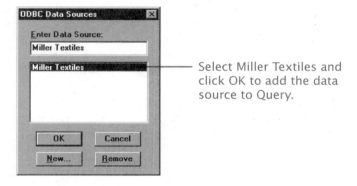

Select Miller Textiles and click OK to add the data source to Query.

Miller Textiles is now in the list of data sources for Query. The next time you use Query, Miller Textiles will already be in the list.

Create the query

1   In the Select Data Source dialog box, select Miller Textiles as the data source, and click Use.

2 In the Add Tables dialog box, select Orders.dbf as the table name, click Add, and then click Close.

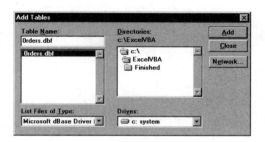

Query allows you to include more than one table in a query. For this query, you need only the one table.

3 In the list of fields, double-click Date, then double-click State, then double-click Category, and finally double-click Net.

As you double-click each field name, that name appears in the grid at the bottom.

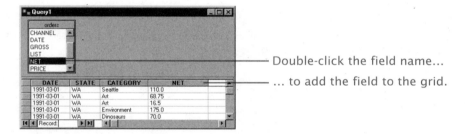

— Double-click the field name...

... to add the field to the grid.

4 Click the first cell under the State heading, the cell containing *WA*.

5 Click the Add Criteria button on the toolbar, to restrict the query to orders only from Washington.

Add Criteria button

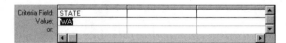

6 On the File menu, click Return Data To Microsoft Excel.

After a few seconds, you are back in Step 2 of the PivotTable Wizard, and the text next to the Get Data button changes to *Data Retrieved*.

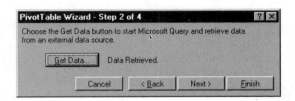

That's the process for retrieving data from an external database. Now you can continue creating the PivotTable from the retrieved data.

Create the PivotTable

You were in Step 2 of the PivotTable Wizard when you started Query to retrieve the data. Now you are back in Step 2, ready to continue creating the PivotTable.

1 In Step 2 of the PivotTable Wizard, click Next.

2 In Step 3 of the PivotTable Wizard, drag the Date field tile to the Column area, drag the State and Category field tiles to the Row area, and drag the Net field tile to the Data area.

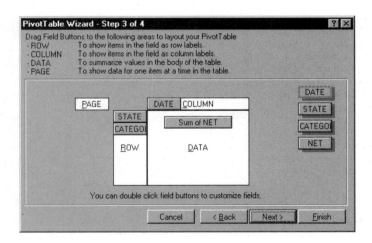

3 Click Next to accept the PivotTable layout.

4　In Step 4 of the PivotTable Wizard, clear the PivotTable Starting Cell box, clear both Grand Totals check boxes, and click Finish.

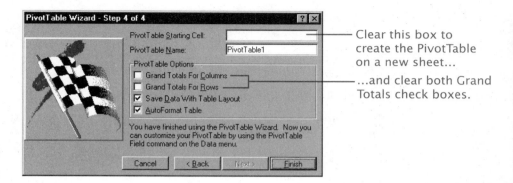

Clear this box to create the PivotTable on a new sheet...

...and clear both Grand Totals check boxes.

Even though you cleared the Grand Totals For Columns check box, the PivotTable has a row of totals at the bottom. These totals are really for the State field. Since you have data for only one state, the total by state seems to be a grand total. Get rid of it.

5　Double-click the State field tile, and when the PivotTable Field dialog box appears, select the None option in the Subtotals group and click OK.

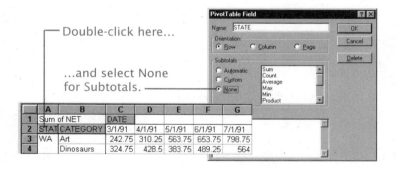

Double-click here...

...and select None for Subtotals.

You have now completed all the steps necessary to create a PivotTable from an external data source. When you repeat the steps to create a macro, you won't need to define a new data source.

Create a PivotTable with a macro

1　Delete the sheet containing the PivotTable. (On the Edit menu, click Delete Sheet, and click OK.)

2　If the Visual Basic toolbar is not visible, use the right mouse button to click any toolbar, and click Visual Basic on the shortcut menu.

Record Macro
button

3   Click the Record Macro button, type **MakePivot** as the name for the macro, and click OK.

4   On the Data menu, click PivotTable, select the External Data Source option, and click Next.

5   Click the Get Data button to launch Query.

6   Repeat the steps from the "Create the query" and the "Create the PivotTable" sections earlier in this lesson.

7   Click the Stop Macro button to stop the recorder.

Stop Macro
button

You now have a macro that will access the external database and create a PivotTable displaying monthly orders by category.

Assign the macro to the button

Before testing the macro, assign it to the button on the EIS worksheet to make it easier to run.

1   On the Edit menu, click Delete Sheet and confirm that you do want to delete the worksheet.

You should be back on the EIS worksheet.

2   Use the right mouse button to click the Retrieve Orders button, and click Assign Macro on the shortcut menu.

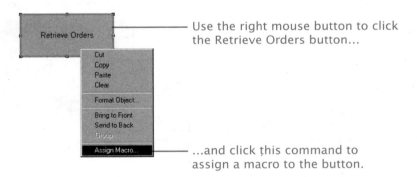

Use the right mouse button to click the Retrieve Orders button...

...and click this command to assign a macro to the button.

3   Select MakePivot from the list (hard choice, isn't it?), and click OK.

4   Click cell A1 to deselect the button, and then click the Retrieve Orders button to test the macro.

5   Delete the new PivotTable worksheet to get back to the EIS worksheet.

Now you can produce a new PivotTable of Washington state orders at the click of a button. Of course, Washington *is* the most important state—even if you sell more designs elsewhere—but there is a slight possibility that some of your associates at Miller Textiles might conceivably want to look at orders for a different state. In order to modify the macro, you have to look at it.

Look at the MakePivot macro

Before you look at the macro that creates the PivotTable, I want to tell you some bad news and some good news. The bad news is that the macro looks terrible. It is almost completely indecipherable. The good news is that you don't need to decipher it. All you have to do in order to make the macro retrieve data for any state you want is to follow the steps that I will show you.

 Activate the Module1 sheet and look at the macro.

 NOTE The macro on your screen might look slightly different from the macro here because some of the lines on the screen are too long to fit on a single printed page in a book. You don't need to read the macro that closely anyway, though, so don't worry about it.

```
Sub MakePivot()
    ActiveSheet.PivotTableWizard SourceType:=xlExternal, SourceData:= _
        Array("DSN=Miller Textiles", _
        "SELECT Orders.DATE, Orders.STATE, Orders.CATEGORY, Orders.NET
            FROM C:\ExcelVBA\Orders.dbf Orders
            WHERE (Orders.STATE='WA')"), _
        TableDestination:="", TableName:="PivotTable2", RowGrand _
        :=False, ColumnGrand:=False
    ActiveSheet.PivotTables("PivotTable2").AddFields RowFields:=Array( _
        "STATE", "CATEGORY"), ColumnFields:="DATE"
    ActiveSheet.PivotTables("PivotTable2").PivotFields("NET"). _
        Orientation = xlDataField
    ActiveSheet.PivotTables("PivotTable2").PivotFields("STATE"). _
        Subtotals = Array(False, False, False, False, False, False, _
        False, False, False, False, False, False)
End Sub
```

You can probably figure out that all the statements have something to do with PivotTables. In Lessons 7 and 12, you will work directly with PivotTables. For now, all you need to do is make the macro prompt the user for a state. You want to touch as little as possible, while still learning how to customize recorded statements like this.

Make the macro prompt the user for a state

When you created the PivotTable, the entire request for external data was sent to Query as a single long text string. The characters *WA* were in the middle of that text string because you used Washington as the sample state. Now you need to replace those characters with a state code that changes each time you run the macro.

1 Put the insertion point at the end of the Sub MakePivot() statement, press ENTER, and then press TAB. You are now ready to type a new line in the macro.

2 Type **myState = InputBox("Enter State Code")** and press ENTER to get a new blank line.

3 On the Edit menu, click Find.

4 Type **WA** in the Find What box, select the Match Case check box and the Find Whole Words Only check box, and click Find Next.

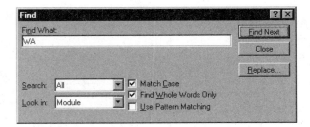

When you created the original query, you used WA as the sample state code. Now you need to find where that state code appears in the mass of Visual Basic code.

5 Click Close to dismiss the Find dialog box.

The Find command found the text *WA* in the phrase *(Orders.STATE='WA')* which is in the middle of a long quoted text string.

You need to replace the text *WA* with the myState variable that you created at the beginning of the macro. Since the constant is in the middle of a text string, you have to close the text string, add your variable, and then continue the text string.

6 With WA selected, type " and type a space; type & and type another space; type **myState** and type a third space; type & and type a fourth space; and type "

The phrase should now be *(Orders.STATE= '" & myState & "')* Think of this as the variable myState, bracketed by ampersands to "add" it to the rest of the statement, with quotation marks on each end to close and then to continue the original text string.

7 Activate the EIS worksheet, click the Retrieve Orders button, and enter **CA** when prompted for a state name.

The macro produces a new PivotTable, this time with California orders.

 NOTE If the macro fails with the error *Variable not defined*, go to the top of the module sheet and delete the *Option Explicit* statement. Then click Options on the Tools menu, click the Module General tab, clear the Require Variable Declaration check box, and click OK. (You will learn about Option Explicit in Lesson 10.)

8 Delete the new PivotTable worksheet.

The macro recorder records all the instructions for creating the PivotTable, including the criteria for retrieving the records. As long as you are careful about starting and stopping text strings, you can replace constants in the macro with variables without having to understand very much about the PivotTable macro statements themselves.

Try canceling the macro

Try running the macro again, pretending you are a naive user who has never seen it before.

1 Click the Retrieve Orders button.

The input box prompting you for the state code appears. You are not sure what you should put in for a state code.

2 You don't want to risk entering the wrong value, so click the Cancel button.

The macro does not stop, as you might expect. It continues, blinking and clicking and making you very nervous. Finally, a strange, malicious-looking dialog box with several buttons appears.

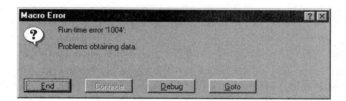

3 Click the End button. (Remember that it is the End button you click to stop the macro from running any more. You will see the word *End* again later.)

Thankfully, the macro stops. You hope you didn't hurt anything. You certainly never want to use this macro again.

Of course, you don't want your associates to feel like that. You need to fix the macro.

Make the macro quit when canceled

1 Activate the module sheet.

2 In the blank line you inserted right after the statement that prompts the user for the state code, type **If myState = "" Then End**

Add this statement to make the Cancel button.

If a user of the macro clicks Cancel—or just clicks OK without entering a state code—the myState variable ends up with nothing in it. If there is nothing in the variable, you want to stop the macro. The *End* statement stops the macro, just as clicking the End button in the error dialog box did.

3 Run the macro again, and click Cancel in the input box to see the macro quit.

Adding a Close Button to the Application

Each time you run the macro, it creates a new worksheet for the new PivotTable, but the macro does not get rid of any old worksheets. You can't just delete the worksheet as part of the MakePivot macro, because the worksheet would disappear before the users had a chance to see the information they requested. You need to give them a Close button to delete the worksheet. First, make a macro to delete the worksheet, and then make a macro that actually puts a Close button onto the EIS worksheet.

Create a macro to delete a worksheet

1 Select a blank, expendable worksheet. (If you don't have one handy, insert one.)

Record Macro button

2 Click the Record Macro button, replace the default name for the macro with **DeleteSheet**, and click OK.

3 On the Edit menu, click Delete Sheet, confirm that you want to delete the worksheet, and click the Stop Macro button.

Stop Macro button

4 Activate the module sheet and scroll to the bottom to see the macro:

```
Sub DeleteSheet()
    ActiveWindow.SelectedSheets.Delete
End Sub
```

The macro prompts you and then deletes the selected worksheet. You can make the macro delete the worksheet without asking for confirmation.

Make the DeleteSheet macro work quietly

> Below the Sub DeleteSheet() statement, insert the statement
> **Application.DisplayAlerts = False**

You will learn more about the Application object in Lesson 9.

The DisplayAlerts property of the application determines whether Excel displays alert messages. If you set the DisplayAlerts property to False, the macro will not prompt the user when it deletes the worksheet.

The finished macro should look like this:

```
Sub DeleteSheet()
    Application.DisplayAlerts = False
    ActiveWindow.SelectedSheets.Delete
End Sub
```

Now you can run the macro to quickly—and quietly—delete any selected worksheet.

Assign the DeleteSheet macro to a button

1 Activate another blank, expendable worksheet.

Create Button button

2 Click the Create Button button on the Drawing toolbar, and while holding down the ALT key drag a new button that covers cell D1. Holding down the ALT key when you move or size an object makes the object borders snap to the edges of the worksheet cells.

3 In the Assign Macro dialog box that appears, select DeleteSheet as the macro name, and click OK.

4 With the new button still selected, type **Close** and press ESC twice to deselect the button.

5 Click the button.

It worked—the worksheet is gone, without a whisper. Great job! Three cheers!

Uh-oh. The button is gone too.

Make a macro to make a button

If the button for deleting the worksheet disappears along with the worksheet, you obviously need an easier way to make the button.

1 Activate another expendable worksheet.

2 Click the Record Macro button, type **AddDeleteButton** as the name for the macro, and click OK.

Record Macro button

3 Repeat steps 2 through 4 in the preceding section, "Assign the DeleteSheet macro to a button."

4 Click the Stop Macro button.

Stop Macro button

5 Activate the module sheet and scroll to the bottom to look at the macro:

```
Sub AddDeleteButton()
    ActiveSheet.Buttons.Add(144, 0, 48, 12.75).Select
    Selection.OnAction = "DeleteSheet"
    Selection.Characters.Text = "Close"
    With Selection.Characters(Start:=1, Length:=5).Font
        .Name = "Arial"
        .FontStyle = "Regular"
        .Size = 10
        .Strikethrough = False
        .Superscript = False
        .Subscript = False
        .OutlineFont = False
        .Shadow = False
        .Underline = xlNone
        .ColorIndex = xlAutomatic
    End With
    Range("A1").Select
End Sub
```

The most complex part of this macro is the With structure (the statements from *With* through *End With*). Actually, those statements are there just in case you want to add extra formatting to the button. Because you used the default settings for the button, you can delete everything from the With statement through the End With statement. You can also leave the macro as it is. The extra statements won't hurt anything.

Now you can add a Close button to any worksheet just by running this macro.

Add the Close button with the MakePivot macro

The MakePivot macro creates a new worksheet with a new PivotTable. The best time to add the Close button to the worksheet is when you create it. Since the MakePivot macro and the AddDeleteButton macro do two separate tasks, leave them as two separate macros, and add a third macro that runs both of them as subroutines. You could use the recorder to create this new macro, but you are probably comfortable enough with Visual Basic now to just type it in yourself.

1   At the top of the module sheet, type **Sub RetrieveOrders** and press ENTER.

A Sub statement always ends with open and close parentheses. If you press ENTER without typing the parentheses, Visual Basic adds them for you.

2   Press TAB, type **MakePivot** and press ENTER.

3   Type **AddDeleteButton** and press ENTER.

4   Press BACKSPACE, type **End Sub** and press ENTER.

That's your main macro that calls two subroutine macros. Here's the whole macro:

```
Sub RetrieveOrders()
    MakePivot
    AddDeleteButton
End Sub
```

Now you can try out the whole application.

Try out the RetrieveOrders macro

Your RetrieveOrders macro will now prompt the user for the state code, create the PivotTable, and add the Close button. Try it out. First change the Retrieve Orders button on the EIS worksheet to run the RetrieveOrders macro.

1   On the EIS worksheet, use the right mouse button to click the Retrieve Orders button, and click Assign Macro on the shortcut menu.

2   Select RetrieveOrders, click OK, and then press ESC to deselect the button.

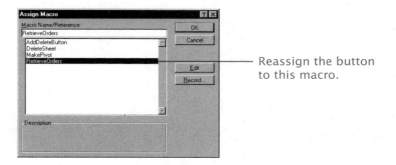

Reassign the button to this macro.

3   Click the Retrieve Orders button and type a state code (**WA, OR, ID, CA, NV, UT**, or **AZ**).

The macro retrieves the data, builds the PivotTable, and adds the Close button.

4   Click the Close button to delete the PivotTable worksheet.

Adding a Chart to the Application

Big blocks of tabular numbers are hard for most people to decipher. You want to add a chart to the EIS application so that your associates can more easily interpret whether orders are improving.

Chart the PivotTable

1   On the EIS worksheet, click the Retrieve Orders button and enter **WA** as the state code. Do *not* click the Close button to delete the worksheet.

Record Macro button

2 Click the Record Macro button, type **MakeChart** as the name of the macro, and click OK.

3 Select cell A1, the top left cell in the PivotTable, and press CTRL+STAR (CTRL+SHIFT+8) to select the entire PivotTable.

4 Click the Reference area to the left of the formula bar, type **ChartRegion** as the name for the range, and press ENTER.

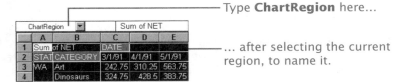

Type **ChartRegion** here...

... after selecting the current region, to name it.

NOTE Some states have more dates or more categories than other states. For example, Washington orders start much sooner than Idaho orders. When you create the sample chart, you are using Washington orders, but later you will want your macro to create a chart of Idaho orders. Even though you don't need to name the range to create a chart, giving a name to the range will simplify the process of making the macro work with different states.

ChartWizard button

5 Click the ChartWizard button and drag a place for the chart from the top left corner of cell A10 to bottom left corner of cell K18.

6 In the ChartWizard, click Next in Step 1, double-click Line for the chart type in Step 2, double-click option 2 as the format in Step 3, and click Finish in Step 4.

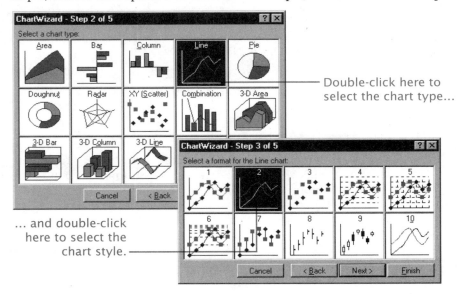

Double-click here to select the chart type...

... and double-click here to select the chart style.

7 Press ESC to deselect the chart.

8 Click the Stop Macro button.

Test the MakeChart macro

You need to try out the MakeChart macro to see if it works properly.

1 Click the Close button to close the Washington state PivotTable.

2 Click the Retrieve Orders button, type **NV** as the state code, and click OK.

3 When the PivotTable is ready, click the Run Macro button, select MakeChart from the list, and click Run.

The macro should create the chart, but the chart doesn't look right. The lines stop about halfway across the chart.

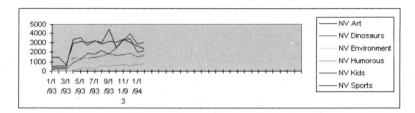

4 Click the chart to select it, and press DELETE. You can try creating the same chart again after looking at the macro.

5 Activate the module sheet and scroll to the bottom to see the MakeChart macro:

```
Sub MakeChart()
    Range("A1").Select
    Selection.CurrentRegion.Select
    ActiveWorkbook.Names.Add Name:="ChartRegion", RefersToR1C1:= _
        "=Sheet8!R1C1:R9C38"
    ActiveSheet.ChartObjects.Add(0, 114.75, 420.75, 114.75).Select
    Application.CutCopyMode = False
    ActiveChart.ChartWizard Source:=Range("A1:AL9"), Gallery:=xlLine, _
        Format:=2, PlotBy:=xlRows, CategoryLabels:=1, SeriesLabels _
        :=2, HasLegend:=1
    Range("A1:AL9").Select
End Sub
```

You may not understand everything in every statement of the macro, but you can get a general sense of what it is doing: "Select cell A1, select the current region, define the name ChartRegion, create a chart, turn off copy mode (who knows why), adjust the chart with the settings from the ChartWizard, and select range A1:AL9 on the worksheet."

109

Make the chart plot the current selection

Notice in the ChartWizard method that the macro recorder created the chart pointing at a specific range of cells: A1:AL9. That was the range for the Washington state PivotTable. Since you haven't been selling designs in Nevada as long as you have in Washington, the chart extends way past the current data.

Fortunately, when you recorded the macro, you had the foresight to define the name ChartRegion right after selecting the current region of the table. Unfortunately, the statement that adds the name seems to use a specific cell address range also. The range Sheet8!R1C1:R9C38 in the statement with the Add method is equivalent to the range A1:AL9 in the statement with the ChartWizard method.

Instead of giving the name ChartRegion to the same range each time you run the macro, you need to make the name ChartRegion refer to the current selection. To make a name refer to the current selection, you assign the name to the Name property of the selection.

Once the name ChartRegion refers to the correct range, you can change the ChartWizard method to use the ChartRegion range.

1   Delete the entire statement *ActiveWorkbook.Names.Add Name:="ChartRegion", RefersToR1C1:= "=Sheet8!R1C1:R9C38"*.

2   In place of the deleted statement, type **Selection.Name = "ChartRegion"**

This statement sets the name of the current selection to ChartRegion. The size of this named range can change depending on the number of months and categories for a particular state.

3   After the word *Range* in the statement with the ChartWizard method, select the reference A1:AL9, and delete it. (Do not delete the quotation marks.)

4   In place of the reference, type **ChartRegion**

The first part of the statement now looks like this:

```
ActiveChart.ChartWizard Source:=Range("ChartRegion")
```

With these two changes, the ChartWizard will create a chart based on the current selection.

5   Activate the worksheet with the Nevada PivotTable, click the Run Macro button, and run the MakeChart macro.

Run Macro button

The chart lines should fill the whole chart.

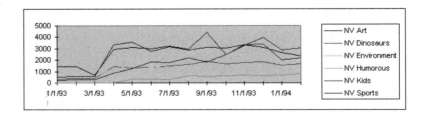

6 Click the Close button to remove the worksheet.

Giving a name to the selection and then using that defined name is the easiest way to get the ChartWizard to create a chart from the current selection. At least, that's the easiest way to do it until you understand more about Excel objects and references, which you will learn about in Part 3. Once you understand how Excel objects really work, you can simplify many of these recorded macros. (Just a little sales pitch for the next few lessons.)

Add the MakeChart macro to the EIS button

You will learn more about working with charts in Lesson 9.

You want the chart to appear whenever a user clicks the Retrieve Orders button, so add the MakeChart subroutine to the RetrieveOrders macro.

1 Activate the module sheet, scroll to the top, and insert the statement **MakeChart** after the MakePivot statement.

2 Activate the EIS worksheet, click the Retrieve Orders button, enter a state code, and watch the magic.

Linking the Application to a Map

Your RetrieveOrders macro can do a lot. Simply by clicking a button and typing a state code, a user of your macros can see the orders for a state, both as tabular data and as a chart. But what if one of your associates types an invalid state code, or accidentally types *AX* for Arizona instead of *AZ*. The PivotTable will not be able to retrieve the data from the database, and the macro will halt with an error.

You can prevent the problem of entering an invalid state—and at the same time create a more appealing start-up screen—by allowing the user to click a button on a map of a state to retrieve the orders for that state.

Add a map to the start-up screen

1 Activate the worksheet named EIS and select cell A1.

2 On the Insert menu, click Picture, and in the Picture dialog box click Map and then click Insert.

3 Click the arrow next to the Zoom Control box on the Standard toolbar, and then click Selection.

The window zooms out until you can see the whole map.

Zoom Control box

4 Hold down the SHIFT key and drag the bottom right corner of the map up and to the left until the bottom of the map lines up with row 17 of the worksheet.

When you hold down the SHIFT key while you resize an object, the object maintains the same height and width ratio. You want the map to remain in proportion after you shrink it.

5 Get rid of the border on the picture: on the Format menu, click Object, click the Patterns tab, set the Border option to None, and click OK.

6 Enter **Miller Textiles** in cell E3, and then enter **Order Retrieval Application** in cell E4.

7 Change the zoom back to 100%, change the font size of cell E3 to 28 points, and change the font style to bold. Then change the font size of cell E4 to 16 points.

Center Across Columns button

8 Select the range E3:H4, and click the Center Across Columns button to center the labels on the right side of the screen.

9 Get rid of the gridlines on the worksheet: on the Tools menu click Options, click the View tab, clear the Gridlines check box, and click OK.

Your screen should look like this:

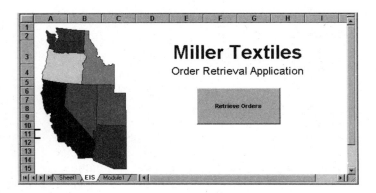

Now your EIS start-up screen looks very nice. Next you need to add buttons to each of the states so that a user can retrieve orders for a state by clicking a button. But before you can add buttons that run macros, you need to create macros for the buttons to run.

Make the macro fill in the blank

Currently, you have one RetrieveOrders macro that prompts the user for a state code. You don't want your associates to have to remember and type in the state codes; you want the macro to fill in the state code. Start by changing the RetrieveOrders macro to fill in the state code for Washington.

1 Activate the module sheet and scroll to the RetrieveOrders macro.

2 Change the name of the macro from RetrieveOrders to **RetrieveWA**

3 At the end of the MakePivot statement, type a space, and then type **myState:="WA"** (type both a colon and an equal sign).

The finished statement should be *MakePivot myState:="WA"*

You can give arguments to built-in Excel commands by adding the argument name, a colon, and an equal sign, and then the value of the argument. In the same way, you can give arguments to your own subroutine macros. Read this statement like this: "With 'WA' as my state, make pivot."

4 Inside the parentheses at the top of the MakePivot macro, type **myState**

112

The finished statement should be *Sub MakePivot(myState)*

In Lesson 10 you will learn more about using arguments with subroutines.

You always have to put parentheses at the end of a Sub statement so that the parentheses will be ready if you ever want to add arguments to the subroutine. The name you put inside the parentheses is the link between the value in the subroutine and the value back in the RetrieveWA macro. You must spell the name inside the parentheses (*myState*) exactly the same way you spell the argument name in the statement that calls the subroutine (*MakePivot myState:="WA"*).

5   Delete the statement myState=InputBox("Enter State Code")

You don't need to prompt the user for a state code any more.

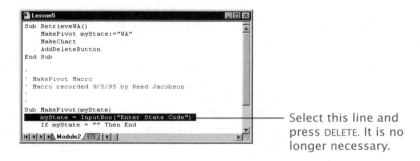

Select this line and press DELETE. It is no longer necessary.

Put a button on the map

1   Activate the EIS worksheet, use the right mouse button to click the Retrieve Orders button, and click Assign Macro on the shortcut menu.

2   Select RetrieveWA from the list and click OK.

3   Type **WA** as the new label for the button.

4   Press ESC to stop typing, which reselects the button.

5   On the Format menu, click Object, click the Alignment tab, select the Automatic Size check box, and click OK to shrink the button to fit the label.

6   Use the Font Size control on the Formatting toolbar to change the font size on the label to 8 points.

The label shrinks and the button shrinks with it.

7   While the mouse pointer is an arrow, drag the button on top of the map of Washington state and press ESC to deselect the button.

The button disappears because you created the button before you created the map. The button is behind the map.

8   Click the map to select it, and on the Format menu, click Placement, Send To Back.

9   Click the WA button to try out the macro, and click Close after you have finished perusing the resulting information.

Make seven macros for seven states

1 Activate the module sheet, and select the entire RetrieveWA macro.

2 Press CTRL+C to copy the RetrieveWA macro.

Select the entire macro, and press CTRL+C to copy it.

3 Press the UP ARROW key and then the DOWN ARROW key to change the selection to a single insertion point.

4 Press CTRL+V six times to paste six copies of the RetrieveWA macro onto the module sheet.

5 Put the insertion point at the beginning of the second RetrieveWA macro, and click Replace on the Edit menu.

6 Type **WA** in the Find What box, type **OR** in the Replace With box, clear any selected check boxes, and click the Find Next button to select the next occurrence of the letters *WA*.

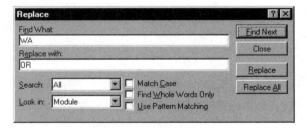

7 Click the Replace button twice to replace two occurrences of *WA* with *OR*.

8 Type **CA** in the Replace With box and click the Replace button twice. Replace the state code two times in each of the remaining macros, using **NV**, **AZ**, **UT**, and **ID** as the Replace With values.

9 Press ESC to dismiss the Replace dialog box.

You now have seven very simple macros, each of which runs the MakePivot macro with the appropriate state code and then runs the MakeChart and AddDeleteButton subroutines.

Link seven buttons to seven macros

Now you just need to add buttons to the other states to run the individual state macros.

1   Activate the EIS worksheet.

2   Hold down the CTRL key and drag a copy of the WA button to the middle of the map of Oregon. Do not release the CTRL key until after you release the mouse button. Repeat this step five times, dragging a copy of the button onto the map of each remaining state.

3   Use the right mouse button to click the button on the map of Oregon, and click Assign Macro on the shortcut menu.

4   Select RetrieveOR from the list of macros, click OK, and then type **OR** as a new label for the button.

5   Repeat steps 3 and 4 to assign and relabel each of the remaining state buttons.

Creating separate macros and separate buttons for each of the states can make running the macro much more intuitive. Your associates will be less likely to make mistakes and more likely to say nice things about you for creating such an easy-to-use application.

Adding the Application to a Menu

A big, splashy start-up screen with a big map and lots of buttons is easy to understand and use: just point at the state you want and click. The problem with big, splashy start-up screens with big maps and lots of buttons is that they take up the whole screen. What if one of your associates wants to be able to take a look at the orders at any time, even when working with another worksheet in Excel? If you create a custom menu for your application, that associate will be able to review the orders anytime.

Add macros to a menu

Menu Editor button

1   Activate the module sheet and click the Menu Editor button on the Visual Basic toolbar.

The Menu Bars list should display Worksheet as the default menu bar.

2   In the Menus list, select (End Of Menu Bar) at the bottom of the list—notice that the Caption box is grayed out—and click Insert.

An empty line appears in the Menus list—and notice that the Caption box is now available.

3   In the Caption box, type **EI&S** (but do not press ENTER).

NOTE   The ampersand in a caption tells Excel where to put the underline for the keyboard accelerator character. The keyboard accelerator character allows you to choose a menu item with the keyboard by typing ALT and then the underlined letter. The letters *E* and *I* are already used (for Edit and Insert, respectively) so use *S* as your accelerator character.

---

4 Select the (End Of Menu) label in the Menu Items list and click Insert.

EIS now appears in the Menus list.

5 In the Caption box, type **&Retrieve Orders**

6 Select the (End Of Menu) label in the Submenu Items list and click Insert.

Retrieve Orders now appears in the Menu Items list.

7 Type **&Idaho** in the Caption box, select RetrieveID from the Macro list, and click Insert.

8 Repeat step 7 for each of the other six states, starting from the bottom of what you want the final list to be. When you are finished, click OK.

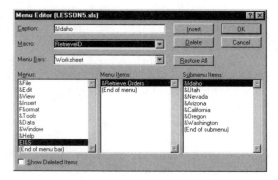

Your menu is finished and operational. Look on the menu bar, to the right of the Window menu. What? You don't see it? You're sure?

Try out the menu bar

When you add a new menu to a menu bar, you typically add the menu to the Worksheet menu bar. If the active sheet is a module sheet or a chart sheet, you won't see the new menu.

1 Activate the EIS worksheet.

With a worksheet active, the EIS menu appears, with the *S* appropriately underlined.

2 On the EIS menu, click Retrieve Orders, Nevada.

The macro runs, retrieving Nevada's orders.

3 Click Close.

4 Click the New Workbook button.

The EIS menu is still visible. The workbook containing the macro does not have to be active for the menu to work.

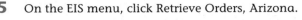

5 On the EIS menu, click Retrieve Orders, Arizona.

The macro works just as well with a different workbook active. The workbook containing the macro just has to be open for the new menu to work.

Your application is finished. It may not be as full-featured as some EIS applications you can imagine, but *you* created it! Give it to your associates. I can't wait to hear them ooh and aah.

Lesson Summary

To	Do this	Button
Set up an external data source	Double-click the 32bit ODBC icon in Control Panel, select the database driver, and add the data source.	
Assign a macro to an existing button in a worksheet	Use the right mouse button to click the existing button, and then click Assign Macro on the shortcut menu.	
Make a macro stop	Enter the End statement in the macro.	
Insert a variable in a text string	Replace the constant in the text string with *"& Variable &"*.	
Prevent statements in a macro from displaying a warning message	Use the statement *Application.DisplayAlerts = False.*	
Make a chart of the current selection	Make the macro, assign a name to the selection, and then use the name of the range as the value of the ChartWizard method's Source argument.	
Give the name NewName to the current selection	Use the statement *Selection.Name = "NewName".*	
Import a picture from a file to a worksheet	On the Insert menu, click Picture and select the picture file.	
Attach a macro to a menu command	Click the Menu Editor button on the Visual Basic toolbar, type a caption for the menu item, and select a macro from the Macro list.	![button icon]

For online information about	From the Excel Help menu, choose Contents, choose Getting Started with Visual Basic, and then
Buttons and other worksheet controls	Select the topic "Creating Dialog Boxes"
Menus and custom menu commands	Select the topic "Customizing Menus and Toolbars"

Preview of the Next Lesson

In the lessons of Part 2, you have learned how to use graphical user interface tools to make worksheet models and macro applications easy to use. When you have needed macros, you have still largely utilized the macro recorder to build the macros.

If you want to create macros that are faster, more flexible, and easier to read, however, you need to understand more about how Excel and Visual Basic work together. In the lessons of Part 3, you will learn what Excel objects are and how to work effectively with them.

Exploring Objects

Part

3

Explore Object Collections

Estimated time
30 min.

In this lesson you will learn how to:

■ Manipulate collections of workbooks and worksheets.

■ Manipulate individual workbook and worksheet items.

■ Manipulate module sheets and other sheet types.

■ Use properties and methods with objects.

Think back on your third grade classroom. Your wooden frame desk, decorated with decades of crudely carved names, was fourth from the front, over in the last row next to the windows. Remember those big stairs down to the main floor, with that magnificent banister you would always watch for a chance to slide down? The main hallway was papered with drawings clustered around each classroom door. Each door led to a classroom, and each classroom was filled with kids.

A Microsoft Excel workbook is a lot like a school. The cells in a worksheet appear in rows and columns like students in a classroom. Worksheets are grouped into workbooks, like classrooms in a school. And Excel can have several open workbooks, just as a city can have several schools. Just as you were able to move around freely in the rooms and halls of your old elementary school, you will soon be able to move around freely in Excel objects with your macros.

Visual Basic interacts with Excel by working with Excel objects. Everything in Excel that Visual Basic can control—workbooks, worksheets, cells, menus, text box controls—all these are *objects*. In order to control Excel from Visual Basic effectively, you must understand what objects are and how they work in Excel.

Start the lesson

➤ Open Excel with a clean, blank workbook. If you have other workbooks open, such as the Personal Macro Workbook, close them. (To find any hidden workbooks, click Unhide on the Window menu.)

What Is an Object?

The easiest way to understand objects in Excel is to compare them to objects in the real world. In the real world, cities, schools, classrooms, and students are all objects. A city is dotted with schools, a school is lined with classrooms, a classroom is packed with students—and all the students are arranged in tidy rows of tidy desks, smiling happily and listening attentively to the kind, wise, firm, but patient teacher. Well, maybe not *all* the desks are tidy.

Objects come in collections

Look around you. The world consists of objects in collections, which are in turn objects in other collections: rooms in apartments in buildings in complexes, flowers in beds in yards in neighborhoods, rocks on crags on mountains in ranges, children in households in extended families in clans. Each object—each city, each student, each flower, each mountain, each family—is an individual item, yet each also belongs to a collection of similar objects, and each collection of objects is itself an individual item within a larger collection.

If you're a city official thinking about the collection of School objects, you may refer to the collection of schools as a group: "All the schools have asbestos problems." Or you may refer to an individual school: "We need to replace the light fixtures at Jefferson Elementary School."

When you do refer to an individual school, you may refer to the school by name: "Jefferson Elementary School, as you may know, was named for the esteemed author of the Declaration of Independence." Or you may refer to it by its position in the collection: "The first school built in our city, back in 1887, is the one I attended as a child." Or (if you are conducting a driving tour) you may refer to the individual school by pointing: "Notice the classic architecture of this magnificent school building."

An Excel workbook is like a school. Just as you can have more than one school in a city, you can have more than one workbook open in Excel. Each workbook is individual and unique, yet each is a Workbook object. You can refer to the entire collection of open workbooks as a group ("Close all the open workbooks"), or you can refer to individual workbooks. If you refer to an individual workbook, you can specify the workbook by name ("Open the Lesson 1 workbook"), by position ("What is the first workbook in the list of recently opened files?"), or by pointing ("Save the active workbook").

A worksheet in a workbook is like a classroom in a school, and worksheet cells are like students in a classroom, arranged in neat little rows and columns. Excel also has other collections of objects: menu items in menus in menu bars, columns in a series in a layer in a chart, items in fields in rows in a PivotTable. You can refer to each collection,

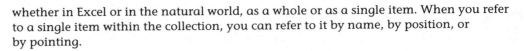

whether in Excel or in the natural world, as a whole or as a single item. When you refer to a single item within the collection, you can refer to it by name, by position, or by pointing.

Objects have properties

Do you see that little boy in Mrs. Middlefields's class—the one in the third row, the fourth seat over? He's about four feet seven inches tall. His hair is short. The color of his shirt is blue. His name is Jared. And his eyes are closed.

The boy's height, hair length, shirt color, name, and eye state are *properties* of that one particular Student object. The little girl sitting behind him also has Height, HairLength, ShirtColor, Name, and EyeState properties, but the *values* of her properties are different. The boy is a different object from the girl, but each is a Student object.

The boy's desk is also an object, a Desk object. A Desk object has a Height property, as does a Student object, but a Desk object does not have a HairLength property. Likewise, a Student object does not have a Manufacturer'sName property, as a Desk object does. Because the boy and the desk have different lists of properties, they are different types, or *classes*, of objects. Because the boy and the girl share the same list of properties—even though they have different values for the properties—they both belong to the same class of object. They both belong to the Student *object class*. Sharing the same list of properties is what makes two objects belong to the same object class.

Just as Jared is an object—a *Student* object—Mrs. Middlefield's entire collection of students is also an object—a *Students* object. The *Students* collection has its own properties; the properties of the collection are not the same as the properties of the individual objects contained within it. For example, you don't really care about a HairLength property of the entire collection of students. Would that be total hair length or average hair length? But a collection object does have properties of its own. For example, the number of students in the collection is a property of the Students object. Because Mrs. Middlefield's collection of students has a different list of properties than Jared's property list, Students is a different object class from Student. But because Mr. Osgood's Student collection and Mrs. Middlefields' Student collection have the same list of properties—even though they may have different values for the properties—both collections belong to the same Students object class. The Students object class is different from the Student object class because the two object classes have different lists of properties.

Some properties are easy to change. You could perhaps change Jared's EyeState property with a good, sharp rap with a ruler on his desk. (And of course, he can change the property right back after you look the other way.) You might even change Jared's name to Gerard temporarily for French language instruction. But changing Jared's height, weight, eye color, or gender probably falls outside the scope of a normal school activity.

Excel objects have properties too. A workbook has an author. A worksheet has a name. A cell has a width, a height, and a value. A menu has a caption. A collection of worksheets has a count of the worksheets in the collection. Changing some of the properties—such as the name of a worksheet or the height of a cell—is easy. Changing other properties—such as the count of cells on a worksheet—probably falls outside the scope of a normal macro activity.

Objects have methods

Look, Mrs. Middlefield is telling the class to stand up. She's leading them in a stirring rendition of "Row, Row, Row Your Boat." Student objects can sing songs. Singing a song is an activity. Student objects also do other activities. Student objects eat. Student objects draw pictures. One student may sing, or eat, or draw well, and another student may sing, or eat, or draw badly, but they both share the ability to do the action. Desk objects, on the other hand, do not sing songs or eat or draw pictures. Desk objects may squeak, perhaps, whereas Student objects generally don't. In the same way that different classes of objects have different lists of properties, they also have different lists of activities they can do. The activities an object can do are called *methods*. Objects that belong to the same class can all do the same methods.

A collection object has a list of methods separate from the list of methods that belongs to the individual items in it. One of the most important methods for most collections is adding a new item to the collection. When a new student moves into the class, you are executing the Add method on the Students object, not on an individual Student object. When the construction bond passes and the school gets a new wing, you are executing the Add method on the Classrooms object. You don't add the new classroom to an individual classroom; you add it to the collection of classrooms.

Another important method for a collection is selecting a single item out of the collection. If Mrs. Middlefield wants to communicate with Jared so that she can ask him to sing a solo, she will establish a communication link with him by calling his name, "Jared." The action of singling out an individual Student object and establishing a communication link with that individual is a method of the Students collection.

Most Excel collection objects have an Add method for adding a new item to the collection, and they all have an Item method for establishing a link to an individual item in the collection. Excel worksheet objects also have a Calculate method for causing all the cells to recalculate, and Excel charts have a ChartWizard method that quickly changes various attributes of a chart.

Sometimes the distinction between a method and a property is vague. When Jared opens his eyes, is he carrying out the OpenEyes method (an action), or is he assigning a new value to his EyeState property? Here are some concepts that may help:

Methods can change properties   Some methods do change properties. When Jared carries out the Fingerpaint method, the action happens to change his Shirt Color property. When he goes home and carries out the WashClothes method, the ShirtColor property changes back (with perhaps a few residual stains). Likewise, in Excel, the ChartWizard *method* can change several *properties* of the chart.

Properties can involve actions   Setting a property does sometimes involve some kind of action. When you change the classroom's WallColor property, you do get out the paint rollers and the ladders and start working, but you are more concerned about the finished attribute of the wall than about the action that changed the attribute. In Excel, hiding a worksheet is setting a property (because the worksheet is still there and you may want to change the property back). But closing a file is a method because there's no trace of the file left in memory after you are done.

> **NOTE** Most of the time you don't need to worry about the difference between properties and methods. Excel has on-line tools to help you find the methods and properties for objects, and you may not need to know which is which. For example, you can turn on the macro recorder, carry out a task, and then modify the code that the macro recorder produced—without ever really knowing whether Excel used a property or a method for any given action.

In summary, an individual item is an object from one object class, while a collection of those items is an object from a different object class. A single item from one collection can contain an entire collection of other objects. For example, a single school from the district's collection of schools can contain an entire collection of classrooms. Each object belongs to an object class that has a unique list of properties and methods. Many different individual objects (Student objects) can belong to a single object class (the Student object class), in which case they all share the same list of properties and methods, while retaining their own individuality. In these lessons in Part 3, you will learn how to work with many kinds of Excel objects.

Understanding Workbooks

Workbooks are the major structural unit in Excel. You can learn much about how objects and collections work in Excel by experimenting with workbooks.

In Lesson 9, you will learn how to convert experiments from the Immediate pane to a macro.

Excel also has a powerful tool to help you experiment with objects, properties, and methods: the Immediate pane of the Debug window. You can use the Immediate pane to explore Workbook objects. The Immediate pane is a place to do experiments without writing macros. Everything you do in the Immediate pane is lost when you close Excel.

Add a new workbook

1 If the Visual Basic toolbar is not visible, use the right mouse button to click any toolbar, and click Visual Basic on the shortcut menu.

2 Click the Insert Module button to create a new module.

3 On the View menu, click the Debug Window command.

InsertModule button

The Debug window appears. This is the same window that appears when you step through a macro.

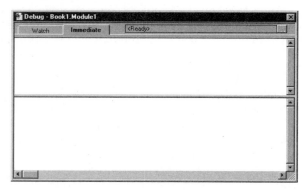

4 Resize the Debug window so that you can see the workbook behind it, and click the top half of the Debug window. If your window is maximized, restore it.

The top half of the Debug window is called the Immediate pane (as long as the tab labeled Immediate is selected).

5 In the Immediate pane, type **Workbooks.Add** and press ENTER.

A new workbook appears on top of the first workbook. The Add method added a new workbook to the collection, and you watched it happen.

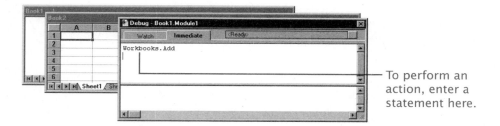

To perform an action, enter a statement here.

 NOTE In the Immediate pane, you type macro statements and see the effect immediately. The Immediate pane is an effective tool for finding out immediately what happens when you execute a statement.

6 Press the UP ARROW key to put the insertion point back in the *Workbooks.Add* statement, and press ENTER.

The Add method creates another Workbook object.

To reexecute a statement in the Immediate pane, put the insertion point anywhere in the line and press ENTER.

The word *Workbooks* is a link to the Workbooks object—the collection of workbooks currently open in Excel. The word *Add* is a method of the Workbooks object that adds a new item to the collection. A method follows an object, separated by a single period (*object.method*). Most collections in Excel have an Add method for adding new items to the collection.

Count the workbooks

You have now used a method—the Add method—with a Workbooks object. The Workbooks object also has properties. One of the properties—the Count property—tells you how many items are in the collection. The Count property returns a value. You can display that value in the Immediate pane.

1   In the Immediate pane, type **?Workbooks.Count** and press ENTER.

The number 3 (or however many workbooks are currently open) appears.

In the Immediate pane, when you type a question mark followed by anything that returns a value, that value appears on the next line. Because the Count property returns a number value, you can display that value using the question mark.

2   Press the UP ARROW key to get back to the *Workbooks.Add* statement, press ENTER to add a new workbook, and then press ENTER again in the *?Workbooks.Count* statement to see the new count of workbooks.

The count should now be 4 (or one greater than whatever it was before).

The word *Count* is a property. You attached the Count property to its object with a period in the same way that you attached the Add method to its object.

When you execute the Add method, you don't put a question mark in front of it because the Add method returns an object rather than a value. You can see the effect of the Add method by looking at the screen. When you use the Count property, you want to find out the value of the property. Putting a question mark in front of the property name displays the property's value.

 NOTE   You cannot change the number of workbooks by changing the Count property. You must use the Add method to add a new workbook to the collection. A property for which you cannot assign a new value, but can only look at, or read, the current value, is called a *read-only* property.

Close the workbooks

The Add method works on the Workbooks object by adding one item to it. The Workbooks object has an additional method—the Close method—that can close the entire collection.

1   Type **Workbooks.Close** and press ENTER. Click No when asked to save changes.

All the open workbooks disappear. Using the Close method on the Workbooks object closes the entire collection. The Close method closes everything so fast that you may want to see it work again.

2   Reexecute the *Workbooks.Add* statement three or four times to create a few new workbooks.

3   Reexecute the *?Workbooks.Count* statement to see how many workbooks are in the collection.

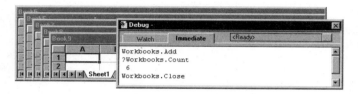

4   Reexecute the *Workbooks.Close* statement to close all the workbooks.

Doesn't that give you a great sense of power? One keystroke and all those workbooks are utterly annihilated.

5   Reexecute the *?Workbooks.Count* statement to see how many workbooks are in the collection.

The number 0 appears because you destroyed all the workbooks.

Add and Close are both methods of the Workbooks object. Count is a property of the Workbooks object. The Add and Close methods indirectly change the value of the Count property—they are, in fact, the only ways you can change the Count property. The Count property is *read-only*.

Refer to a single workbook

Closing the entire Workbooks collection all at once is a powerful experience, and might even possibly, occasionally, be useful, but usually you want more control over which workbooks disappear. To close a single workbook, you need to specify a single item out of the Workbooks collection.

1   Run the *Workbooks.Add* statement at the top of the Immediate pane several times to create a few new workbooks.

Press CTRL+END to move quickly to the bottom of the Immediate pane.

2   Scroll to the bottom of the Immediate pane.

3   Type **?Workbooks.Item(1).Name** and press ENTER.

The name of the first workbook—the first of the current set of workbooks to be opened (probably something like Book12)—appears.

Reading from right to left, you can paraphrase this statement as: "The name of the first item in the workbooks collection is what?"

- *Name* is a property of a single workbook. Because Name is a property, you can display its value by using the question mark at the beginning of the statement. The Name property is not available for a Workbooks object because a collection of workbooks doesn't have a name.

- *Item* is a method. Like the teacher establishing a communication link by addressing an individual student, the Item method creates a link to an individual item in a collection. The Item method requires a single argument: the position number of the item you want.

- *Workbooks* establishes a link to the entire collection of workbooks—the Workbooks object. Once you have a link to the Workbooks object, the word *Item(1)* switches the link to the specified item within the collection—a Workbook object. Once you have a link to a Workbook object, the Name property returns the name of that object.

 NOTE Retrieving a single item from a collection is so common that you can leave out the word *Item* (and its accompanying period) and put the parentheses right after the name of the collection. The statement *?Workbooks(1).Name* accomplishes the same task as the statement *?Workbooks.Item(1).Name*. The macro recorder, Excel's Help files, and most people all use the shorter form. However, if you find that you consistently forget to use a plural for the collection method name, you may want to use the Item method explicitly for a while.

4 Type **Workbooks(1).Close** and press ENTER.

The first workbook disappears.

5 Reexecute the *?Workbooks.Item(1).Name* statement.

The name of the new first workbook appears. (If the first workbook was Book12 before, the new first workbook is probably Book13.)

6 Reexecute the *Workbooks(1).Close* statement to close the new first workbook in the collection.

The word *Workbooks* has two meanings in Excel. On the one hand, *Workbooks* is the name of an object class, the Workbooks object class; it is a noun, a "thing." On the other hand, *Workbooks* is also the name of a method that establishes a link to the collection of open workbooks; it is a verb, an "action." You cannot put the actual Workbooks object "thing" into your macro. (The Workbooks object is inside Excel; you can see it on your computer screen.) What you put into your macro is the verb, the Workbooks "action" that establishes a link to the Workbooks "thing."

Once the Workbooks method establishes a link to the Workbooks object, you can "talk" to the object using methods and properties from the list that a Workbooks object understands. You can use the Count property to look at the number of items in the collection. You can use the Add method to add a new item to the collection. You can use the Close method to close the entire collection of workbooks. *Count*, *Add*, and *Close* are three of the words that a Workbooks object can understand.

A Workbooks object can also understand the Item method. The Item method is an "action" that establishes a link to an individual Workbook "thing." Excel does not have a Workbook method to link to a single Workbook object. You use the Item method of the Workbooks object—or use the shortcut form and put parentheses directly after the Workbooks method—to establish the link to an individual object.

Once the Item method establishes a link to an individual Workbook object, you can "talk" to the object using methods and properties that a Workbook object understands. You can use the Name property to look at the workbook's name. You can use the Close method to close the one workbook.

Each collection object in Excel shares the same name as the method that establishes a link with that object. The Workbooks object shares its name with the Workbooks method. The Workbooks method establishes a link with the Workbooks object. As you learn more about objects, you will see that the Worksheets object shares its name with the Worksheets method, the Windows object shares its name with the Windows method, the Charts object shares its name with the Charts method, and so forth.

In Visual Basic code, you never refer to an individual item from a collection by leaving the letter *s* off the name of the collection. For example, you never refer to an individual workbook in a macro by using the word *Workbook*. Every collection object class has an Item method that you use to establish a link to an individual item in the collection.

Refer to a workbook by name

So far when you have used the Item method to establish a link to an individual workbook, you have specified the workbook you want by number—by indicating its position in the collection. A workbook's position number is determined by the order in which you open the workbooks. But you can also refer to an item in a collection by its name.

1   If you are running out of workbooks, scroll back to the top of the Immediate pane and execute the *Workbooks.Add* statement a few more times.

2   Scroll to the bottom of the Immediate pane.

    Pick the name of one of the workbooks, preferably one in the middle of the stack, perhaps a workbook named Book17.

3   Type **Workbooks("Book17").Activate** and press ENTER.

    The workbook you specified moves to the top of the stack of workbooks. The word *Activate* is a method that a single Workbook object understands.

You can refer to a workbook either by name or by position number. If you use the name, you must put it in quotation marks. If you use the position number, you must *not* use quotation marks.

4   Type **Workbooks("Book17").Close** and press ENTER to close the workbook.

5   Reexecute the *Workbooks("Book17").Close* statement.

Excel displays an error message because the workbook with that name no longer exists. When you refer to an item in a collection by name, you always get the same item—as long as it still exists.

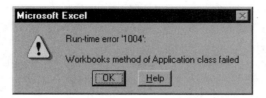

6   Click OK to remove the error message.

You can use either the name or the position number to refer to an item in a collection. If you use the position number, you may get a different item each time you use the Item method; if you use the name, you'll get an error if the item no longer exists.

Refer to a workbook by pointing

Suppose you want to refer to the top workbook on the stack, but you don't know its name or its position number. Because it is the active workbook, you can refer to it by pointing.

➤   On a blank row at the bottom of the Immediate pane, type **ActiveWorkbook.Close** and press ENTER.

The top workbook on the stack disappears.

The word *ActiveWorkbook* in this statement establishes a link directly to the active workbook, bypassing the Workbooks object. If the first workbook opened happens to be the active workbook, you could substitute *Workbooks(1)* to establish a link to the same Workbook object as *ActiveWorkbook*. Once you have a link to the workbook, you can look at its name or close it. Once you have a link to any object, the process by which you established that link is not important.

Change a workbook property value

Both the Count property of a Workbooks object and the Name property of a Workbook object are *read-only* properties. You can look at the value returned by the property, but you cannot change it. A workbook has other properties, *read-write* properties, whose values you can change as well as look at.

1   In the Immediate pane, type **?ActiveWorkbook.Saved** and press ENTER.

The word *True* appears because the workbook hasn't had any changes made to it.

131

NOTE When you close a workbook, Excel uses the value of the Saved property to decide whether to prompt you to save changes. If the value of the Saved property is True, Excel does not prompt you; if it is False, Excel does prompt you.

Normally, you change the Saved property to False by changing the contents of a cell, and you change the Saved property to True by saving the workbook. You can, however, change the Saved property directly.

2   Type **ActiveWorkbook.Saved = False** and press ENTER.

Nothing seems to have happened, but you just changed the value of the property.

3   Reexecute the *?ActiveWorkbook.Saved* statement to see the new value for the property.

The word *False* appears. Now Excel thinks that the worksheet has unsaved changes in it.

4   Reexecute the *ActiveWorkbook.Close* statement.

Because you set the Saved property to False, Excel asks if you want to save changes.

5   Click the Cancel button to leave the workbook open.

6   At the bottom of the Immediate pane, type **ActiveWorkbook.Saved = True** and press ENTER.

7   Reexecute the *ActiveWorkbook.Close* statement.

The workbook closes without a whisper.

If you write a macro that modifies a workbook and you want to close the workbook without saving changes (and without displaying a warning prompt), make the macro change the Saved property of the workbook to True.

The Saved property is a *read-write* property. You can display its current value, and you can also change its value.

Look at the return value of the Close method

Normally, you execute a method and you change or retrieve the value of a property. Methods do return values, however, and you may want to see the value that a method returns. For example, when you use the Close method on a workbook, the effect of the method is to close the workbook, but the method also returns a value to the macro.

1   If you are running out of workbooks, scroll back to the top of the Immediate pane, execute the *Workbooks.Add* statement several more times, and then scroll to the bottom of the Immediate pane.

2   Type **?ActiveWorkbook.Close** and press ENTER.

The active workbook closes, and the word *True* appears after the statement.

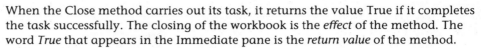

When the Close method carries out its task, it returns the value True if it completes the task successfully. The closing of the workbook is the *effect* of the method. The word *True* that appears in the Immediate pane is the *return value* of the method.

If the Close method cannot accomplish the desired effect, it produces a different return value.

3   Type **ActiveWorkbook.Saved = False** and press ENTER.

This makes Excel think the current active workbook has been changed.

4   Type **?ActiveWorkbook.Close** and press ENTER. Click Cancel when asked if you want to save changes.

The word *False* appears after the statement. This time, the Close method did not complete the task of closing the workbook, so it returns the value False. You can often look at a method's return value to find out whether it completed its task.

All methods always return something. Some methods (like Close) return either True or False, depending on whether they are successful at their task. Some methods (like Activate) always return True because if they do not accomplish the desired effect, the macro refuses to continue. Some methods (like Item) establish a link to an object and return that link so that you can use methods and properties to communicate with the object.

Quit Microsoft Excel

You have done a lot of experimenting using the Immediate pane. Before you continue, close Excel. You can close Excel directly from the Debug window.

➤   In the Immediate pane, type **Application.Quit** and press ENTER. Click No if prompted to save changes to any workbooks.

In this section, you learned how to use the Add and Close methods on a Workbooks object, and you learned how to use the Activate and Close methods on a Workbook object. You saw how to look at the values of the Count property of a Workbooks object, and of the Name property of a Workbook object. You also saw how to change the value of the read-write Saved property of a Workbook object.

You learned how to use the Workbooks method to establish a link to the Workbooks object, how to use the Item method of the Workbooks object to switch the link to a single Workbook object, and how to use the ActiveWorkbook property to set a link directly to the active Workbook object.

Along the way, you learned how to use the Immediate pane of the Debug window to look at the values of properties, set the values of read-write properties, watch the effect of executing methods, and display the return values of some methods.

Understanding Worksheets

Worksheets come in collections just as workbooks do. By manipulating worksheets in the Immediate pane, you will see some similarities—and also some differences—between different classes of collections.

Add a new worksheet

Insert Module button

1   Start Excel and display the Visual Basic toolbar.

2   Click the Insert Module button to add a new module, and then delete all the other sheets in the workbook. (To delete the other sheets, click the Sheet1 tab, scroll through the sheet tabs until you can see the last worksheet, hold down the SHIFT key, and click the last worksheet tab. Click Delete Sheet on the Edit menu, and click OK to confirm.)

3   With the Module1 sheet active, click Debug Window on the View menu. Resize the Debug window so that you can see the sheet tab in Workbook1.

4   In the Immediate pane, type **Worksheets.Add** and press ENTER.

   A new worksheet appears before Module1.

You add a new worksheet to the current workbook the same way you add a new workbook to Excel: with the Add method. The name *Worksheets* is used for both the Worksheets object and the Worksheets method. When you enter the word *Worksheets* into your code, you are using the Worksheets method, which establishes a link to the Worksheets object that exists inside Excel somewhere. You never enter an object name directly into your code; you always enter a method or property that establishes a link to the object.

5   Reexecute the *Worksheets.Add* statement three times so that you have a total of four worksheets (plus one module sheet) in the workbook.

6   Type **?Worksheets(1).Name** and press ENTER to display the name of the first worksheet.

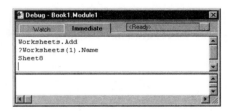

In the same way that you use the Item method (in either its long or its short form) on a Workbooks object to establish a link to a single Workbook object, you use the Item method on a Worksheets object to establish a link to a single Worksheet object. Once you have the link to a Worksheet object, you can use Worksheet object properties, such as Name.

The name of a work*book* is a read-only property: you have to save a file to change its name. The name of a work*sheet* is a read-write property: you can change the name directly.

7   Type **Worksheets(1).Name = "Input Values"** and press ENTER.

The name of the worksheet changes.

As with workbooks, you can refer to a single worksheet by name, by number, or by pointing. Now that the first worksheet has the name *Input Values*, the expressions *Worksheets("Input Values")*, *Worksheets(1)*, and *ActiveSheet* can all establish a link to the same Worksheet object.

Look at the result of the Add method

Earlier in this lesson, you saw that the Close method returns either True or False depending on whether it achieves the desired effect. The Add method also has an effect: it creates a new item in the collection. But the Add method does not return True or False. The Add method returns a link to the newly created object. You can use that link the same way you use the link created by the Item method or by the ActiveSheet property.

➤   In the Immediate pane, type **?Worksheets.Add.Name** and press ENTER.

A new worksheet appears in the workbook, and the default name of the new worksheet, possibly Sheet9, appears in the Debug window.

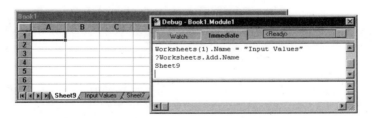

The Add method has an effect: it creates the new worksheet. It also returns a link to the new object. If you don't use the link immediately—as part of the same statement—the link is discarded. If you then want to communicate with the new worksheet, you must reestablish a link using the ActiveSheet property or the Item method. Usually, you don't bother using the link returned by Worksheets.Add because using ActiveSheet to establish a new link is as easy as shouting "Jared" to get a slumbering student's attention.

Copy and move a worksheet

1 Type **Worksheets("Input Values").Copy** and press ENTER.

A new workbook appears in front of the original workbook, containing a copy of the Input Values worksheet.

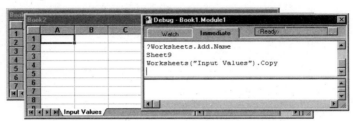

The word *Copy* is a worksheet method. If you don't tell the Copy method where to put the copy of the worksheet, it creates a new workbook for the copy.

2 Type **Workbooks(1).Activate** to put the original workbook back on top.

3 Type **Worksheets("Input Values").Copy Before:=Worksheets(2)** and press ENTER to create a copy of the Input Values worksheet.

You can tell the Copy method where to put the copy by using the Before argument. Use a link to a single Worksheet object as the value of the Before argument. (The Copy method also has an After argument that you can use instead of the Before argument to specify a location for the copy.)

4 Type **Worksheets(2).Name = "Variant Values"** and press ENTER to change the name of the new worksheet.

A worksheet does not have to be active for you to change its properties. All you need is a link to the Worksheet object you want to change.

5 Type **Worksheets("Variant Values").Move Before:=Worksheets(1)** and press ENTER to move the second worksheet to the first position.

Move is another method that applies to a worksheet. You must give the Move method either a Before argument or an After argument. When you use the name of an argument, you separate the argument name from the argument value with a colon and an equal sign (:=).

6 Type **Workbooks(2).Worksheets(1).Name = "Old Values"** and press ENTER.

The name of the worksheet in the second workbook changes. (The second workbook is the one that you created in step 1 when you copied the worksheet without giving it a location.)

You can manipulate an object in a workbook that's not active in the same way that you manipulate an object in the active workbook. You just specify the workbook name when you establish a link to the object.

Manipulate multiple worksheets

When you were exploring workbooks, you closed all the workbooks at the same time using the statement *Workbooks.Close*, and you closed a single workbook from the collection using the statement *Workbooks(1).Close*. Most of the time when working with a collection, you want to use either the entire collection or a single item from the collection. Sometimes, however, you want to create a subcollection: a new collection that includes some, but not all, of the items in the original collection.

1 Type **Worksheets(3).Select** and press ENTER to select the third worksheet in the workbook, the Input Values worksheet.

The Select method allows you to select a new worksheet within the workbook.

2 Type **Worksheets(Array(1,3,4)).Select** and press ENTER to select the first, third, and fourth worksheets.

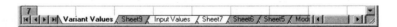

Array is a function that lets you treat multiple values as one. With the Array function, you can select more than one worksheet at the same time. (When you are not in a macro, you select multiple worksheets by holding down the CTRL key and clicking the sheet tabs.)

3 Type **Worksheets(3).Activate** and press ENTER to activate the third worksheet in the workbook, the Input Values worksheet, while leaving all three worksheets selected.

When you select more than one worksheet, one of the worksheets is on top as the active worksheet. All three worksheets are selected, but only one is active. You use the Activate method to specify which worksheet should be the active worksheet. If only one worksheet is selected, the Select method and the Activate method act the same way: they select and activate a single worksheet. You can execute methods or set properties for the entire subcollection of worksheets at once.

4   Type **?Worksheets(Array(1,3,4)).Count** and press ENTER.

The number 3 appears. When you select items from a collection with the Array function, the selected items form a new collection.

5   Type **ActiveSheet.Select** and press ENTER to select only a single worksheet.

Select a type of sheet

So far, you have worked exclusively with the Worksheets collection. Excel workbooks can also contain other types of sheets. The other types of sheets in a workbook have their own collections.

1   Type **Modules.Add** and press ENTER to add a new module sheet.

Modules, like worksheets, are contained in a workbook, but modules are a different collection from worksheets, and they have their own Modules object. Using the Add method on the Modules object adds a new module to the workbook.

2   Type **?Modules.Count** and press ENTER.

A count of only the modules in the workbook appears. The Modules collection object is similar to the Worksheets collection object: you can add a module, count the modules, hide modules, or establish a link to a single module. The Module item object is similar to the Worksheet item object: you can copy one, move one, delete one, or give a new name to one.

3   Type **?Sheets.Count** and press ENTER.

The total count of worksheets and module sheets appears.

Sheets is a method that establishes a link to a Sheets object. The Sheets object is a special collection that includes worksheets, modules, chart sheets, and dialog sheets. Use the Sheets object if you want to refer to all the sheets regardless of type.

In addition to worksheets and modules, Excel workbooks can contain chart sheets and dialog sheets. Each type of sheet has its own collection object: the Worksheets object, the Modules object, the Charts object, the DialogSheets object. Each of those objects has a method of the same name, which you use to establish a link to the collection. As a result, you can establish a link to all the sheets in the workbook, to all the sheets of one type, or to one or more individual sheets.

Quit Microsoft Excel

➤ In the Immediate pane, type **Application.Quit** and click No when asked to save changes to any workbooks.

Lesson Summary

To	Do this
Create a new workbook	Use the statement *Workbooks.Add*.
Add a new worksheet to the active workbook	Use the statement *Worksheets.Add*.
Close the active workbook	Use the statement *ActiveWorkbook.Close*.
Give the name NewSheet to the first worksheet in a workbook	Use the statement *Worksheets(1).Name = "NewSheet"*.
Select multiple worksheets	Use the Array function to specify items from the collection. For example, use the statement *Worksheets(Array(1,3)).Select*.
Quit Excel	Use the statement *Application.Quit*.

For online information about	**From the Excel Help menu, choose Contents, choose Getting Started with Visual Basic, and then**
MS Excel Objects	Select the topic "Understanding Visual Basic"
Working with Workbooks and Worksheets	Select the topic "Working With Workbooks and Worksheets"

Preview of the Next Lesson

In this lesson, you have seen how collections, properties, and methods work with worksheets. Collections, whether worksheets, modules, or workbooks, all work in basically the same way. The fact that all collections work consistently will be useful to you as you learn how to work with Excel objects.

In the next lesson, you will learn how to use Excel's online Help to find the methods and properties of an object. In the process, you will learn how to work with some of the most exciting objects in Excel: the objects that support PivotTables.

Understanding PivotTables

In this lesson you will learn how to:

- Build a PivotTable.
- Manipulate fields and items in a PivotTable.
- Use online Help to learn about Excel objects.

Since the turn of the century, one of the mainstays of medical technology has been x-ray photography. One of the problems with x-ray photographs, however, is that you can only look at a photograph from the angle at which it was taken. If the bones or organs are badly aligned, the photographs may not properly reveal the problem. In 1974, the British company EMI Ltd. made use of the money they had made selling Beatles records to develop computerized axial tomography (CAT) scan technology, which does not suffer from the blind spots of conventional x-rays.

A database report is like an x-ray photograph. It is an image, but it is a static image. If the rows and columns are not defined properly, the person reviewing the report may miss important relationships. A PivotTable is like a CAT scan. It is a multi-dimensional view of the data that enables you to find the most meaningful perspective on the data.

Building PivotTables

In Lesson 6 you learned about the Workbook and Worksheet objects, with the corresponding Workbooks and Worksheets collections. Each object class—Workbook, Worksheet, Workbooks, Worksheets—has its own list of methods and properties that you can use to manipulate objects belonging to that class. In this lesson you will see how this pattern of collections and items, methods and properties, works with an important and powerful group of objects, the objects that support PivotTables. Along the way, you will learn how to use Microsoft Excel's powerful Help tools to get instant information about Excel objects.

Learn about PivotTables in Help

If Visual Basic Help is not available, rerun Excel Setup and select the Visual Basic Help option.

1   Start Excel. On the Help menu, click Microsoft Excel Help Topics, and click the Contents tab.

2   Scroll to the bottom of the list of topics, select the heading Microsoft Excel Visual Basic Reference, and click Open.

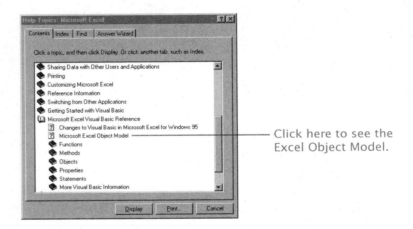

Click here to see the Excel Object Model.

3   Select the topic Microsoft Excel Object Model and click Display.

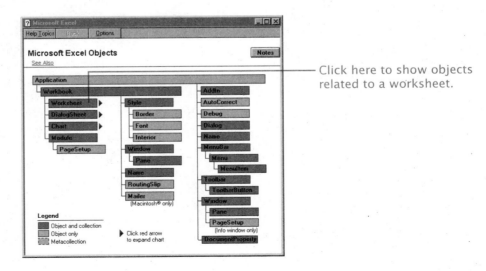

Click here to show objects related to a worksheet.

A diagram of Excel's object model hierarchy appears. At the top is the Application object. In Lesson 9, you will learn more details about the Application object. Under the Application object are boxes for the Workbook and the Worksheet object classes that you learned about in Lesson 6. These boxes are dark blue because they each have a corresponding collection object class that is not shown on the diagram.

4 Click the red triangle next to the Worksheet object box.

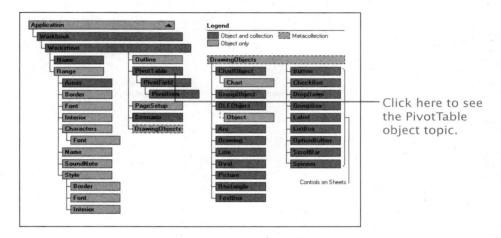

Click here to see the PivotTable object topic.

Objects that are not related to worksheets disappear from the diagram, and additional worksheet objects appear in their stead. One family of objects on a worksheet is the set of objects that support PivotTables: PivotTable, PivotField, and PivotItem. Each of these objects is colored dark blue on the diagram, so each has a corresponding collection object: PivotTables, PivotFields, and PivotItems.

5 Click the PivotTable box.

The word Accessors *in a Help topic refers to methods and properties that can* access—*or return a pointer to—the object being described.*

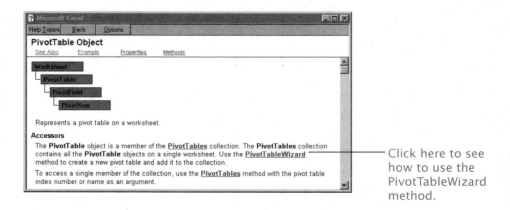

Click here to see how to use the PivotTableWizard method.

143

The PivotTable Object topic appears. The topic explains that to create a new PivotTable, you use the PivotTableWizard method, which both creates the PivotTable and adds it to the PivotTables collection.

6   Click the underlined word *PivotTableWizard* to jump to the PivotTableWizard Method topic.

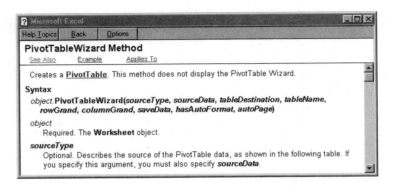

The topic explains that the PivotTableWizard method must come after a Worksheet object, which is required, and can use several arguments, all of which are optional.

Armed with this information, you can now create a PivotTable in the Immediate pane, using the data from the Orders.dbf database.

Create a default PivotTable

Open button

1   Click the Microsoft Excel button on the Windows taskbar to return to Excel.

2   Click the Open button on the Standard toolbar, change to the folder containing the sample files for this book, and then click Cancel.

3   Insert a module sheet into a new workbook, click Debug Window on the View menu to display the Debug window, and resize the window to fill the right half of the screen.

4 In the top half of the Debug window, the Immediate pane, type **Workbooks.Open "Orders.dbf"** and press ENTER to open the database workbook.

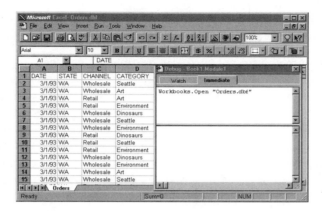

In a few seconds, the database appears. The active sheet in the database workbook is a worksheet. In order to use the PivotTableWizard method, you must first specify a Worksheet object. The ActiveSheet property returns a pointer to the currently active worksheet, so you can use that in front of the PivotTableWizard method.

5 In the Immediate pane, type **ActiveSheet.PivotTableWizard** and press ENTER.

The status bar displays the message *Reading Data* for a few seconds, and then a PivotTable appears.

If the Query And Pivot toolbar appears, close it.

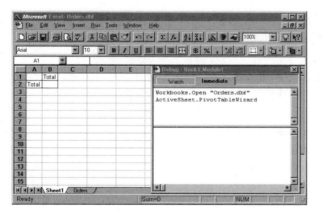

Congratulations! You have just used Visual Basic commands to create a PivotTable. Aren't you proud of yourself?

Save a pointer to a PivotTable

The PivotTable you created is called a PivotTable object. You will be working with that PivotTable object quite a bit. Every time you work with the PivotTable object, you must establish a link, or a pointer, to that object. Before enhancing the PivotTable, take a few minutes to learn more about how Visual Basic works with objects and pointers to objects.

1   In the Immediate pane, type **?TypeName(ActiveSheet)** and press ENTER.

The word *Worksheet* appears because the ActiveSheet property returns a pointer to an object that belongs to the Worksheet object class. The function *TypeName* tells you the *name* of the *type* of an object, when you put a pointer to the object inside the parentheses.

2   Type **?TypeName(ActiveSheet.PivotTables)** and press ENTER.

The word *PivotTables* appears, because the PivotTables method returns a pointer to the collection of PivotTables on the specified worksheet. Even if the collection contains only one — or even zero — items, it is still a collection.

3   Type **?TypeName(ActiveSheet.PivotTables(1))** and press ENTER.

The word *PivotTable* appears, because you can point to an individual PivotTable from the PivotTables collection in the same way that you can point to an individual workbook in the Workbooks collection.

Each of these three expressions returns a pointer to an object. You can store each of those pointers in variables, so that you can then use the variables in the same way that you would use the expression that gave you the pointer in the first place. You store an object pointer in a variable in the same way that you store an ordinary value in a variable, except that you add the keyword *Set* at the beginning of the statement.

4   Type **Set mySheet = ActiveSheet** and press ENTER.

5   Type **?TypeName(mySheet)** and press ENTER.

The word *Worksheet* appears, just as when you used the TypeName method with the ActiveSheet property directly.

6   Type **Set myTables = mySheet.PivotTables** and press ENTER.

You can use the object variable *mySheet* anywhere that you could have used the expression *ActiveSheet* that you assigned to *mySheet*.

7   Type **?TypeName(myTables)** and press ENTER.

The word *PivotTables* appears, because the variable *myTables* now contains a pointer to the collection of PivotTables.

8   Type **Set myPivot = myTables(1)** and press ENTER.

The expression *myTables* is now completely equivalent to the expression *ActiveSheet.PivotTables*. You can even refer to a single item from the collection assigned to the variable.

9 Type **?TypeName(myPivot)** and press ENTER.

The word *PivotTable* appears. You can now use *myPivot* in any context where you need a pointer to a PivotTable object. Rather than assign each intermediate object pointer to a variable, you could use the statement *Set myPivot = ActiveSheet.PivotTables(1)* to assign the PivotTable to a variable.

 TIP The PivotTableWizard method returns a pointer to the PivotTable it creates, so you can store the pointer in a variable at the time that you create the PivotTable. Use the statement *Set myPivot = ActiveSheet.PivotTableWizard* to both create the PivotTable and assign the variable, all in one step.

If someone says to assign an object to a variable, it really means to assign the pointer to an object.

Assigning an object to a variable has a couple of benefits. For one thing, Excel does not have to figure out how to reestablish a link to the object, so it's faster to use an object variable in place of an expression that points to an object. For another thing, variable names are usually shorter than object expressions, so you don't have to do as much typing.

Learn about PivotFields in Help

I don't know quite how to tell you this, but your PivotTable looks somewhat, well, anemic. You may want to see some data, perhaps even some headings in the PivotTable. To make the PivotTable look like a PivotTable, you manipulate PivotFields. See what Help has to say about PivotFields.

1 Click the button for Microsoft Excel Help on the Windows taskbar.

The PivotTableWizard Method topic should still be visible.

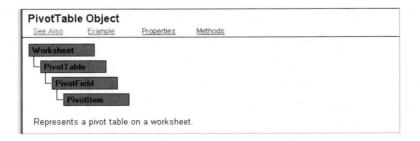

2 The word *PivotTable* in the first sentence is underlined. Click it to return to the PivotTable Object topic.

147

The diagram shows how the PivotField collection relates to the PivotTable collection.

3 Click the PivotField box.

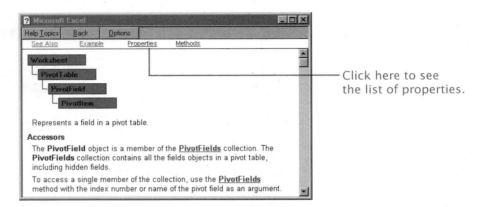

Click here to see the list of properties.

To manipulate a PivotField object, you change the object's properties.

4 Click the underlined word *Properties* at the top of the PivotField object topic.

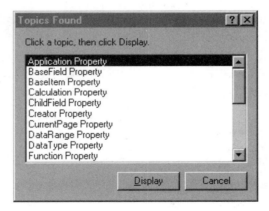

The list of PivotField properties appears. The PivotField object class has 22 properties. In this lesson, you will learn about the most useful ones.

5   Select the *Orientation* property from the list and click Display.

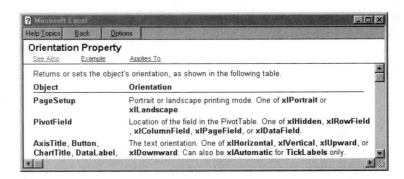

The Orientation property behaves differently depending on which object it belongs to. For a PivotField object, it controls the "location of the field in the PivotTable." Try it out.

Manipulate PivotFields

1   Return to Excel and, in the Immediate pane, type **myPivot.PivotFields("Units").Orientation = xlDataField** and press ENTER.

The label *Sum of UNITS* appears, and a number appears in the body of the PivotTable.

	A	B	C
1	Sum of UNITS	Total	
2	Total	564821	
3			

The PivotFields collection contains one item for each of the seven fields in the database. You refer to a single item from the collection in the standard way, by name or by number. In this case, it's easier to remember the name of the Units field than to recall where it happens to fall in the database. Assigning *xlDataField* to the Orientation property summarizes the data in that field.

2   Type **myPivot.PivotFields("State").Orientation = xlRowField** and press ENTER.

	A	B	C
1	Sum of UNITS		
2	STATE	Total	
3	AZ	25341	
4	CA	112385	
5	ID	1860	
6	NV	51634	
7	OR	179516	
8	UT	40068	
9	WA	154017	
10	Grand Total	564821	
11			

Row headings appear, dividing the sum of units into appropriate buckets, along with a new grand total. You can probably guess how to use the items from the Price field as column headings.

3   Type **myPivot.PivotFields("Price").Orientation = xlColumnField** and press ENTER.

	A	B	C	D	E	F
1	Sum of UNITS	PRICE				
2	STATE	High	Low	Mid	Grand Total	
3	AZ	3723	9009	12609	25341	
4	CA	11122	31504	69759	112385	
5	ID	193	493	1174	1860	
6	NV	17859	13325	20450	51634	
7	OR	32866	73521	73129	179516	
8	UT	4605	15216	20247	40068	
9	WA	29771	72744	51502	154017	
10	Grand Total	100139	215812	248870	564821	
11						

You can also add a second row heading field.

4   Type **myPivot.Pivotfields("Channel").Orientation = xlRowField** and press ENTER.

	A	B	C	D	E	F	G
1	Sum of UNITS		PRICE				
2	STATE	CHANNEL	High	Low	Mid	Grand Total	
3	AZ	Retail	783	2869	3789	7441	
4		Wholesale	2940	6140	8820	17900	
5	AZ Total		3723	9009	12609	25341	
6	CA	Retail	6152	5229	10414	21795	
7		Wholesale	4970	26275	59345	90590	
8	CA Total		11122	31504	69759	112385	
9	ID	Retail	193	493	1174	1860	
10	ID Total		193	493	1174	1860	
11	NV	Retail	13419	8785	15305	37509	
12		Wholesale	4440	4540	5145	14125	
13	NV Total		17859	13325	20450	51634	

When you add a new row field, it always appears to the right of all existing row fields. The Position property allows you to "drag" the field to the left.

5   Type **myPivot.PivotFields("Channel").Position = 1** and press ENTER.

	A	B	C	D	E	F	G
1	Sum of UNITS		PRICE				
2	CHANNEL	STATE	High	Low	Mid	Grand Total	
3	Retail	AZ	783	2869	3789	7441	
4		CA	6152	5229	10414	21795	
5		ID	193	493	1174	1860	
6		NV	13419	8785	15305	37509	
7		OR	6336	22291	30094	58721	
8		UT	380	1376	1867	3623	
9		WA	3341	12489	17072	32902	
10	Retail Total		30604	53532	79715	163851	
11	Wholesale	AZ	2940	6140	8820	17900	
12		CA	4970	26275	59345	90590	
13		NV	4440	4540	5145	14125	
14		OR	26530	51230	43035	120795	

Row and column fields group the data in the PivotTable. In the same way that you change pages in a magazine to select which part you wish to see, you can filter the data in a PivotTable by using a page field. In this case you'll filter by date.

6 Type **myPivot.PivotFields("Date").Orientation = xlPageField** and press ENTER.

	A	B	C	D	E
1	DATE	(All) ▾			
2					
3	Sum of UNITS		PRICE		
4	CHANNEL	STATE	High	Low	Mid
5	Retail	AZ	783	2869	3789

The CurrentPage property works only with page fields.

To actually filter the data, assign a date value to the CurrentPage property of the Datepage field.

7 Type **myPivot.PivotFields("Date").CurrentPage = "1/1/96"** and press ENTER.

	A	B	C	D	E
1	DATE	1/1/96 ▾			
2					
3	Sum of UNITS		PRICE		
4	CHANNEL	STATE	High	Low	Mid
5	Retail	AZ	97	233	391
6		CA	180	372	478
7		ID	93	256	594
8		NV	1257	556	1701

To remove a field from one of the areas of the PivotTable, assign it to the secret, *hidden*, orientation.

8 Type **myPivot.PivotFields("Price").Orientation = xlHiddenField** and press ENTER.

	A	B	C	D	E
1	DATE	1/1/96 ▾			
2					
3	Sum of UNITS				
4	CHANNEL	STATE	Total		
5	Retail	AZ	721		
6		CA	1030		
7		ID	943		
8		NV	3514		

The Orientation, Position, and CurrentPage properties of PivotFields are what make the PivotTable pivot.

The PivotTable object also has a shortcut method that can assign several fields, all at once, to the different PivotTable areas.

9   Type **myPivot.AddFields "Category", "State", "Channel"** and press ENTER.

	A	B	C	D	E	F	G	H	I	J
1	CHANNEL	(All)								
2										
3	Sum of UNITS	STATE								
4	CATEGORY	AZ	CA	ID	NV	OR	UT	WA	Grand Total	
5	Art	5292	28787	295	14275	53185	6080	26263	134177	
6	Dinosaurs	8192	16575	250	6160	10950	5990	27207	75324	
7	Environment	3356	14685	170	5070	35965	5345	22500	87091	
8	Humorous	1577	6970	290	1784	7466	8140	1423	27650	

The Category field becomes the row field, the State field becomes the column field, and the Channel field becomes the page field. The arguments to the AddFields method always appear in Row, Column, Page order.

To add more than one field to one of the orientations, you need to use multiple field names as a single argument. The Array function allows you to treat multiple field names as a single argument.

10   Type **myPivot.AddFields Array("Channel","State"), "Price", "Date"** and press ENTER.

Both Channel and State become row fields, Price becomes the column field, and Date becomes the page field. This one statement accomplishes everything you did in steps 2 through 8.

Use the AddFields method of the PivotTable object to make major changes to a PivotTable; use the Orientation, Position, and CurrentPage properties of the PivotField objects to fine-tune the table.

NOTE   In addition to the PivotFields collection, the PivotTable object has sub-collections that contain only PivotFields of a particular orientation. For example, the RowFields collection contains only the fields whose Orientation property is set to xlRowField. The sub-collections are RowFields, ColumnFields, PageFields, DataFields, and HiddenFields. These collections do not have corresponding object classes. A member of the RowFields collection is still a PivotField object, not a RowField object.

Refining PivotTables

Manipulate pivot items

The unique values that appear in a PivotField are called *items*. You can manipulate individual items within a PivotField.

1   Click the Microsoft Excel Help button on the Windows taskbar to return to the Orientation Property topic. Then click the Back button to return to the PivotField topic.

2   Click the PivotItem box in the diagram to show the PivotItem object topic.

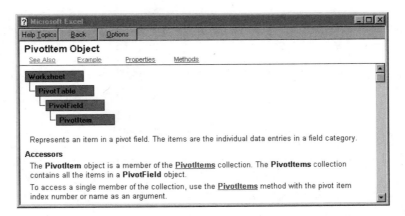

A PivotItem object has a list of properties similar to the list of properties for the PivotField object. In this lesson, you will learn some of the most useful pivot item properties. As you need to learn about other properties, this PivotItem Help topic is where you can find them.

3   Click the Microsoft Excel button on the Windows taskbar to switch back to Excel.

PivotItems is a collection, so you can find out how many items are in the State PivotField.

4   Type **?myPivot.PivotFields("State").PivotItems.Count** and press ENTER.

The number 7 appears, indicating that there are seven different states in the State field. Save a pointer to one of the pivot items in a variable.

5   Type **Set myWA = myPivot.PivotFields("State").PivotItems("WA")** and press ENTER to assign the pivot item for Washington state to a variable.

Now that myWA refers to an individual pivot item, you can manipulate that item using its properties.

6   Type **myWA.Position = 1** and press ENTER.

	A	B	C	D	E	F	G
1	DATE	(All)					
2							
3	Sum of UNITS		PRICE				
4	CHANNEL	STATE	High	Low	Mid	Grand Total	
5	Retail	WA	3341	12489	17072	32902	
6		AZ	783	2869	3789	7441	
7		CA	6152	5229	10414	21795	

A pivot item has a Position property, just as a PivotField does.

7 Type **myWA.Name = "Washington"** and press ENTER.

	A	B	C	D	E	F	G
1	DATE	(All)					
2							
3	Sum of UNITS		PRICE				
4	CHANNEL	STATE	High	Low	Mid	Grand Total	
5	Retail	Washington	3341	12489	17072	32902	
6		AZ	783	2869	3789	7441	
7		CA	6152	5229	10414	21795	

The name of the pivot item is what displays in the PivotTable. If you don't like the way the database designer abbreviated state names, you can fix the problem in the PivotTable. Of course, sometimes it's better to leave conventions alone. Fortunately, the PivotItem object remembers for you what the original name was.

8 Type myWA.Name = myWA.SourceName and press ENTER.

The name changes back to the original. For obvious reasons, the SourceName property is read-only.

Perhaps changing the spelling of the state name is not enough. Perhaps you don't like Washington state (I really do feel sorry for you), and want to eliminate it entirely.

9 Type **myWA.Visible = False** and press ENTER.

	A	B	C	D	E	F	G	H
1	DATE	(All)						
2								
3	Sum of UNITS		PRICE					
4	CHANNEL	STATE	High	Low	Mid	Grand Total		
5	Retail	AZ	783	2869	3789	7441		
6		CA	6152	5229	10414	21795		
7		ID	193	493	1174	1860		

Perhaps, however, you suddenly realized how foolish you were not to like Washington. Fortunately, you can put it back, the same way you got rid of it.

10 Type **myWA.Visible = True** and press ENTER.

Another useful thing you can do with a pivot item is hide or show the detail to the right of a field. Try hiding the detail for the Retail channel.

11 Type **myPivot.PivotFields("Channel").PivotItems("Retail").ShowDetail = False** and press ENTER.

	A	B	C	D	E	F	G
1	DATE	(All)					
2							
3	Sum of UNITS		PRICE				
4	CHANNEL	STATE	High	Low	Mid	Grand Total	
5	Retail		30604	53532	79715	163851	
6	Wholesale	WA	26430	60255	34430	121115	
7		AZ	2940	6140	8820	17900	
8		CA	4970	26275	59345	90590	

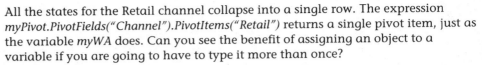

All the states for the Retail channel collapse into a single row. The expression *myPivot.PivotFields("Channel").PivotItems("Retail")* returns a single pivot item, just as the variable *myWA* does. Can you see the benefit of assigning an object to a variable if you are going to have to type it more than once?

12 Type **myPivot.PivotFields("Price").Orientation = xlHiddenField**

Manipulating pivot items is not generally as dramatic as manipulating PivotFields, but you can use the Position, Name, SourceName, Visible, and ShowDetail properties to refine the effect of the PivotTable.

Manipulate data fields

Data fields do the real dirty work of the PivotTable. This is where the numbers get worked over. Data fields are like other PivotFields in many ways, but they do have a few unique twists of their own. You can see how data fields are unique when you add a second data field.

1 Type **myPivot.PivotFields("Net").Orientation = xlDataField** and press ENTER to add a second data field.

	A	B	C	D	E
1	DATE	(All) ▼			
2					
3	CHANNEL	STATE	Data	Total	
4	Retail		Sum of UNITS	163851	
5			Sum of NET	569673.61	
6	Wholesale	WA	Sum of UNITS	121115	
7			Sum of NET	237721.05	

As soon as you have two data fields in the PivotTable, you get a new field tile, labeled *Data*. The Data field is not a field from the database, but provides a way to manipulate multiple data fields. The Data field begins as a row field, but you can change it into a column field.

2 Type **myPivot.PivotFields("Data").Orientation = xlColumnField** and press ENTER.

	A	B	C	D	E
1	DATE	(All) ▼			
2					
3			Data		
4	CHANNEL	STATE	Sum of UNITS	Sum of NET	
5	Retail		163851	569673.61	
6	Wholesale	WA	121115	237721.05	
7		AZ	17900	38507.55	

When you made the State field into a row field, a tile labeled *State* appeared on the PivotTable. Likewise for the other row, column, and page fields. But when you made Units and Net into data fields, you didn't see tiles labeled *Units* and *Net*. Rather, you saw labels *Sum of Units* and *Sum of Net*. These summary fields are new, derived, fields that have been added to the PivotTable. See what happens when you try to remove Net as a data field.

155

3   Type **myPivot.PivotFields("Net").Orientation = xlHiddenField** and press ENTER.

Nothing happens. Now try again, using the name of the temporary data field.

4   Type **myPivot.PivotFields("Sum of Net").Orientation = xlHiddenField** and press ENTER.

The Sum Of Net column disappears — along with the Data tile, since there is now only one data field. To create a data field, you change the orientation of the database field. To remove a data field, you change the orientation of the derived field.

5   Type **Set myUnits = myPivot.PivotFields("Sum of Units")** and press ENTER to assign the data field to a variable.

The default calculation for a number field is to sum the values. The Function property of a data field allows you to change the way the PivotTable aggregates the data.

6   Type **myUnits.Function = xlAverage** and press ENTER.

	A	B	C	D
1	DATE	(All) ▾		
2				
3	Average of UNITS			
4	CHANNEL	STATE	Total	
5	Retail		104.2972629	
6	Wholesale	WA	258.792735	
7		AZ	72.17741935	
8		CA	306.0472973	

The values change to averages, and the label changes to *Average of Units*. If you don't want the label switching around on you, you can use the Name property to control it yourself.

7   Type **myUnits.Name = "Avg Units"** and press ENTER.

	A	B	C	D
1	DATE	(All) ▾		
2				
3	Avg Units			
4	CHANNEL	STATE	Total	
5	Retail		104.2972629	

TIP   Once you replace the default name for the derived data field, Excel will not automatically change the name, even if you change the Function property. To have Excel automatically adjust it, change the Name property to what the automatic name would be for the current function. For example, if the data field currently displays averages for the Units field, change the name to "Average of Units."

When you assign xlDataField to a field's Orientation property, you do not actually change the Orientation property for that field; rather, you create a new, derived field that does have xlDataField as its Orientation property. These derived fields allow you to create multiple data fields from a single source field. Then you can set one derived data field to show sums, another derived field to show averages, and so forth.

The umbrella Data field, which exists only when the PivotTable has more than one data field, acts like "ordinary" PivotFields, except that it can be assigned only to the row or column orientation.

Find PivotTable ranges

A PivotTable resides on a worksheet. It does not use ordinary worksheet formulas to perform its calculations, but it does take up worksheet cells. If you want to apply a special format to a specific part of a PivotTable, or if you want to add formulas to cells outside the PivotTable that align with cells in the PivotTable, you need to know which cells contain which parts of the PivotTable. Fortunately, all the objects relating to PivotTables have properties to help you find the cells that contain the various parts of the PivotTable.

1 Click the Microsoft Excel Help button on the Windows taskbar to return to the PivotItem Object topic in Help.

2 Click the PivotTable box to return to the PivotTable Object topic.

3 Click the word *Properties* at the top of the topic.

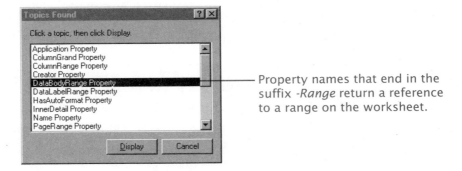

Property names that end in the suffix -*Range* return a reference to a range on the worksheet.

In the list of properties, some of the property names end with the suffix -*Range*. For example, ColumnRange, DataBodyRange, DataLabelRange, and PageRange are all immediately visible in the list of properties. Pick one, say DataBodyRange, and see how it works.

4 Press ESC to close the list of properties, and then click the Microsoft Excel button on the Windows taskbar to return to the Immediate pane.

5 Type **myPivot.DataBodyRange.Select** and press ENTER.

	A	B	C	D	E
1	DATE	(All)			
2					
3	Avg Units				
4	CHANNEL	STATE	Total		
5	Retail		104.2972629		
6	Wholesale	WA	258.792735		
7		AZ	72.17741935		
8		CA	306.0472973		
9		NV	81.17816092		
10		OR	275.7876712		
11		UT	350.4326923		
12	Wholesale Total		232.0428241		
13	Grand Total		171.2097605		
14					
15					
16					

In Lesson 8 you will work more with Range objects.

Excel selects the range containing the summarized data, the *body* of the data. If you want, you can try selecting other ranges of the PivotTable as well. Pivot fields and pivot items also have associated ranges that you can select. Just look for the suffix -*Range* on the end of a property name.

Save your work

You have done a lot of exploring in the Immediate pane. When you close Excel, everything you have done will evaporate. You can save your explorations from the Immediate pane by converting them to a macro.

1 Scan through all the statements in the Immediate pane, and delete all lines that follow statements beginning with a question mark (?). In other words, delete the values that are displayed (but not the statements that displayed them).

2 Select the entire contents of the Immediate pane. (Scroll to the top and click before the first word, then scroll to the bottom and hold down the SHIFT key as you click below the last line.)

3 Press CTRL+C to copy the contents of the Immediate pane.

4 Click in the bottom half of the Debug window, the Code pane.

5 Type **Sub ExplorePivots()** and press ENTER. Then type **End Sub** and click just before the word *End.*

You may want to indent each statement in the body of the macro to make it easier to read.

6 Press CTRL+V to paste the contents of the Immediate pane.

Each question mark from the Immediate pane changes to the word *Print* in the Code pane.

7 On the Edit menu, click Replace. Type **Print** in the Find What box, type **Debug.Print** in the Replace With box, select Procedure from the Look In list, and click Replace All.

As you run the macro, the Debug.Print statement prints values in the Immediate pane of the Debug window.

8 Close the Debug window, and close the Orders.dbf workbook without saving changes.

Step Macro button

9 Save the workbook and give it the name **Lesson 7**

10 With the insertion point anywhere in the ExplorePivots macro, click the Step Macro button to start running the macro in step mode. Click the Step Into button repeatedly to repeat (and review!) everything you did in this lesson. Watch for the values to show up in the Immediate pane as you step through.

Step Into button

This macro may not do much useful work, but now you understand how PivotTables work, and how to find out more about them using Help.

Lesson Summary

To	Do this
Create a new default PivotTable and save a pointer to it	Use the statement *Set myPivot = ActiveSheet.PivotTableWizard*.
Assign a PivotField to the row area of a PivotTable	Assign *xlRowField* to the Orientation property of the Field.

For online information about	**From the Excel Help menu, choose Contents, choose Retrieving and Analyzing Data, and then**
Working with PivotTables	Select the topic "Analyzing Data with PivotTables"

Preview of the Next Lesson

In this lesson you learned how PivotTable objects work and how to use Help to learn about objects. In the next lesson, you will learn how to use Range objects — one of the most important classes of objects in Excel — and how to use the Object Browser to quickly find information about objects.

Explore Range Objects

Estimated time

30 min.

In this lesson you will learn how to:

■ Manipulate Range objects from Visual Basic statements.

■ Use the Object Browser to learn about objects, properties, and methods.

■ Put formulas and values into cells.

The world would be much simpler if everybody were the same size. Cars would not need adjustable seats; heads would never get bumped on door frames; feet would never dangle from a chair. Of course, some new complexities would probably arise. When exchanging that ghastly outfit you received for your birthday, you would not be able to claim it was the wrong size.

If your worksheets and data files are all the same size, you don't need to worry about Range objects. If you never insert new lines into a budget, if you always put yearly totals in column M, if every month's transaction file has 5 columns and 120 rows, the macro recorder can take care of dealing with ranges for you.

In the real world of humans, people are different sizes, and clothes and cars have to adjust to fit them. In the real world of worksheets, models and data files are different sizes, and you want your macros to fit them. Excel provides many methods and properties for working with Range objects. In this lesson you will explore Range objects, and along the way you will find out how to use tools that will help you learn more about all objects, properties, and methods.

Exploring the Object Browser

The Help system is a comprehensive tool for finding names of properties, methods, and object classes. But sometimes Help can be cumbersome. Sometimes you want to browse objects quickly. For example, you may need to find out the order of arguments for a method, or you may want to confirm the spelling of a property name. Visual Basic's Object Browser allows you to find object classes, properties, and methods quickly. First take a look at how the Object Browser works with the familiar Workbook object you explored in Lesson 6, and then see how the Object Browser can help you explore one of the most important objects in Excel: the Range object.

Paste the Add method from the Object Browser

In Lesson 6, you created a new workbook by typing the *Workbooks.Add* statement. Now construct that same statement using the Object Browser to see how the Object Browser works.

1 Open Microsoft Excel with a blank workbook.

Insert Module button

2 Click the Insert Module button on the Visual Basic toolbar, click the Debug Window command on the View menu, resize the Debug window so you can see the windows behind it, and activate the Immediate pane.

Object Browser button

You can also press F2 to activate the Object Browser.

3 Click the Object Browser button on the Visual Basic toolbar.

The Object Browser dialog box appears. The name of the active workbook appears in the Libraries/Workbooks box.

4 Select Excel from the Libraries/Workbooks list.

The Objects/Modules list changes to show the names of all Excel's object classes.

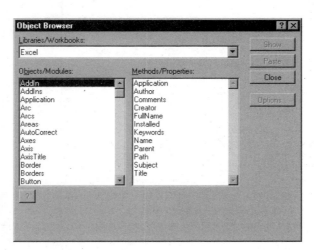

5   Select Workbooks from the list of objects.

The Methods/Properties list changes to show the methods and properties available for Workbooks. Notice that Add is at the top of the list. This is the same Add method that you used in Lesson 6 to create a new workbook.

6   Select the Add method from the Methods/Properties list.

A brief description of the Add method appears at the bottom of the dialog box, and the text on the Paste button changes from gray to black because the button is now enabled. You can paste only words that appear in the Methods/Properties list, because you never put object class names directly into your macros.

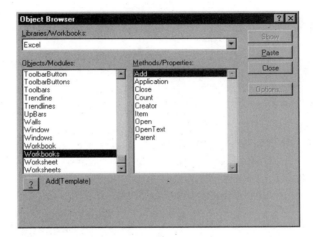

7   Click the Paste button.

The Add method of the Workbooks object allows you to specify a template for the new workbook.

If you are not familiar with workbook templates, search Help for "AutoTemplates."

8   Delete the argument (including the parentheses).

Paste the Workbooks method from the Object Browser

The Object Browser pastes the method (*Add*), along with any arguments (*Template:=*), but it does not paste the name of the object. You never enter the name of an object class directly into your code. You always establish a link to an object by using a method or a property. To put a link to the Workbooks *object* into your macro, you need to use the Workbooks *method*. Workbooks is a method of the Application object.

Object Browser button

1 Click in front of the word *Add*, click the Object Browser button, and select Application from the Objects/Modules list on the left.

2 From the Methods/Properties list on the right, select Workbooks, and click Paste.

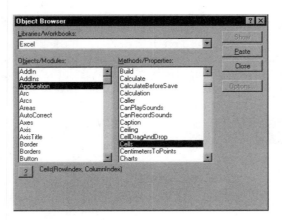

The words *Workbooks(Index:=)* appear before the word *Add*. The word *Workbooks* is the Workbooks method, which returns a Workbooks object. The word *Index* is an argument that allows you to specify a single workbook from the collection.

3 Select the argument *(Index:=)* and delete it. (Be sure to delete the parentheses along with the argument name.)

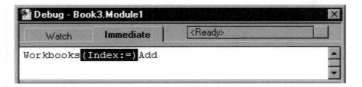

4 Type a period (.) to separate the Workbooks method (which returns a Workbooks object) from the Add method (which can be used with a Workbooks object), and press ENTER.

The new workbook appears.

Obviously, typing the statement *Workbooks.Add* directly is easier than going through the Object Browser — provided that you remember how to spell the methods or properties you need to type.

The Object Browser can help you understand the difference between the name of an object class and the process you use to refer to a specific object in your macro. In the Object Browser, the Objects/Modules list (on the left) is a list of object class names. You never put the name of an object class from this list directly into a macro statement. If you

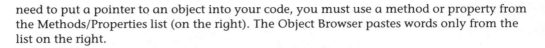

need to put a pointer to an object into your code, you must use a method or property from the Methods/Properties list (on the right). The Object Browser pastes words only from the list on the right.

Exploring Ranges Using the Object Browser

Range objects are probably the most important object class in Excel. You put values into ranges. You put formulas into ranges. You format ranges into reports. You base charts on the numbers in ranges. You put drawing objects on top of ranges. You manipulate PivotTables in ranges. The Object Browser can be a useful tool for exploring this important object.

Explore the Range method

1   Click the Object Browser button. The Application object should still be selected in the list on the left.

2   From the list on the right, select the Range method and click Paste.

The expression *Range(Cell1:=, Cell2:=)* appears in the Immediate pane.

3   Type "**A1**" as the value for the Cell1 argument, type "**B4**" as the value for the Cell2 argument, and append **.Select** to create this statement:

```
Range(Cell1:= "A1",Cell2:= "B4").Select
```

4   Press ENTER to select the rectangular range from A1 through B4.

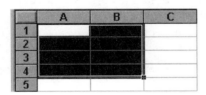

The Range method returns a Range object, which you can manipulate with any methods or properties that apply to the Range object class, such as the Select method.

You do not need to include the argument names. If you leave out the argument names, the above statement looks like *Range("A1","B4").Select.* The two arguments you give to the Range method must be the single-cell corner points of a rectangular block of cells. A rectangular block of cells, defined by opposite corner cells, is the traditional definition of a range.

A Range object, however, does not have to be a rectangular block of cells. The Range method has an alternate form that allows for a more flexible definition of a range.

5   Click the Object Browser button. The Range method should still be selected in the list on the right.

6 Click the ? button to jump to the Range Method topic in Help.

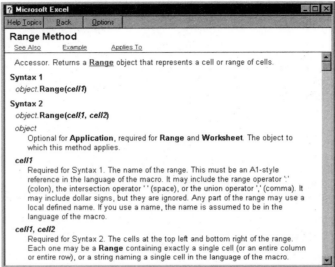

The Range Method topic describes two forms of the Range method, one with a single argument and another with two arguments. As you have already seen, the two-argument form returns a rectangular range based on corner cells. The one-argument form returns whatever Range object you describe using "an A1-style reference." Go back to the Immediate pane and see what this means.

7 Switch back to Excel, to the Object Browser, and click Paste to paste the Range method into the Immediate pane.

8 Replace everything inside the parentheses with "**B4**" and append **.Select** to create this statement:

```
Range("B4").Select
```

9 Press ENTER to select the single cell B4.

To select a specific cell address, use the cell address (in quotation marks) as the argument to the Range method.

10 Type **Range("B3:C8").Select** and press ENTER to select the range B3:C8.

You can use any valid Excel reference (in quotation marks) as the single argument to the Range method.

11 Type **Range("B2,C7,D3,A5").Select** and press ENTER to create a single Range object consisting of four separate cells.

The commas between the cell addresses do not mean separate arguments. All four cell addresses are part of a single text string, and that one text string is a single argument.

12 Type **Range("B2:C4").Name = "TestRange"** and press ENTER to give a name to the Excel range.

13 Type **Range("TestRange").Select** and press ENTER to select the range B2:C4.

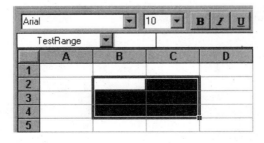

You should see the word *TestRange* in the Reference area to the left of the formula bar, showing the name of the selected range. You can use a defined Excel range name as the argument to the Range method.

The Range method is a flexible way of establishing a link to an arbitrary Range object. As arguments to the Range method, you can either use a text string that contains any valid reference, or you can use two cells to define a rectangular range.

Explore the Cells method

1   Click the Object Browser button. The Application object should still be selected in the list on the left. From the list on the right, select the Cells method and click Paste.

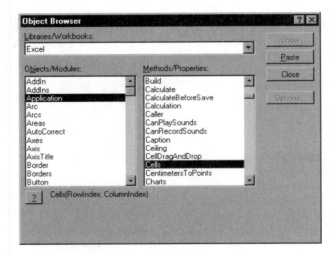

The expression *Cells(RowIndex:=,ColumnIndex:=)* appears in the Immediate pane.

2   Type **2** as the value of the RowIndex argument, type **3** as the value of the ColumnIndex argument, and append **.Select** to create this statement:

```
Cells(RowIndex:=2,ColumnIndex:=3).Select
```

3   Press ENTER to select cell C2, which is row 2, column 3.

You can leave out the argument names as long as you always remember to put the row number first and the column number second. The statement *Cells(2,3).Select* is equivalent to the statement you just executed.

NOTE   For Excel developers familiar with the R1C1 notation used by Excel 4 macros, the Cells method with two arguments provides the same benefits as R1C1 notation, without the requirement of combining the row and column numbers into a single text string.

The Cells method treats the cells on the worksheet as a collection, much like the other collections you have seen. You can refer to a single item in the collection, as you just did, or you can work with the collection as a whole.

4   Type **Cells.Select** and press ENTER.

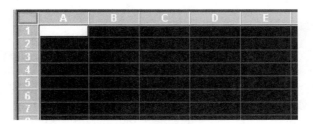

All the cells on the worksheet are selected.

5   Type **?Cells.Count** and press ENTER.

The number 4194304 appears. That's how many cells are in the worksheet.

You may wonder what kind of object the Cells method returns.

6   Type **?TypeName(Cells)** and press ENTER.

The word *Range* appears. The Cells method returns a pointer to an object from the Range object class.

NOTE   The word *Range* is both the name of the method that returns a Range object and the name of the Range object class itself. In the Object Browser, you will find the word *Range* as an object name (on the left) and also as a method name for a Worksheet object (on the right).

The word *Cells*, however, is only the name of a method. The Cells method returns a Range object. In the Object Browser, you will *not* find the word *Cells* in the list of object names, but you will find it as a method name for a Worksheet object.

Most collections in Excel contain only one or two dozen items at most, so you use only one number to point to an item in the collection. An Excel worksheet, however, has millions of cells, and cells in a worksheet have a natural row and column orientation. Accordingly, the Cells method allows you to use two numbers to point to an individual cell. The Cells method, however, also allows you to use a single number to point to a cell within the collection.

7   Type **Cells(5).Select** and press ENTER to select cell E1.

8 Type **Cells(257).Select** and press ENTER to select cell A2.

	A	B	C
1			
2			
3			
4			

When you use a single number to point to an item with the Cells method, the number wraps at the end of each row. Each row of the worksheet contains 256 cells, so cell 257 is the first cell on the second row.

Rather than selecting the range, you may want to see its address. You can use the Address method of the Range object to display the cell address.

9 Type **?Cells(260).Address** and press ENTER.

The address *D2* appears. Cells(260) is equivalent to Range("D2"). (You can ignore the dollar signs unless you are putting the cell address into a formula.)

The Cells method is very effective when you need to work with a range as a collection of cells. Sometimes, however, you want to think of a range as a collection of columns or of rows.

Explore the Columns method

The Cells method returns a Range object as a collection of cells. Since rows and columns are so important in a worksheet, they have their own collections, too.

1 Click the Object Browser button. The Application object should still be selected in the list on the left. Select Columns from the list on the right and click Paste.

The words *Columns(Index:=)* appear in the Immediate pane.

2 Replace the contents of the parentheses with the number **3** and append **.Select** to the end to create this statement:

```
Columns(3).Select
```

3 Press ENTER to select all of column C.

	A	B	C	D
1				
2				
3				
4				
5				
6				
7				

The expression *Columns(3)* returns a range consisting of a single column, just as the expression *Cells(3)* returns a range consisting of a single cell.

4 Type **?Cells.Count** and press ENTER.

The number 4194304 appears. That's how many cells are in the worksheet.

5 Type **?Columns.Count** and press ENTER.

The number 256 appears. That's how many columns are in the worksheet.

As you might expect, the Rows method works like a transposed Columns method. The two most likely reasons for using the Rows method or the Columns method instead of the Cells method are to count the number of rows or columns and to select an entire row or column.

Exploring Derived Range Objects

So far in this lesson, all the methods you have used have belonged to the Application object. They have all operated on the entire worksheet. When you use the Range, Cells, Columns, and Rows methods of the Application object, you select ranges relative to cell A1. You select entire columns and entire rows. Often, however, you will need to select a range relative to a smaller range within the worksheet. For example, you may want to select whatever cell happens to be one cell below the active cell. Or you may want to put a row of headings on top of a named range.

Explore the Range method of a range

1 Open the Object Browser. The Application object should still be selected in the list on the left. The methods you have used so far have belonged to the Application object. Similar methods exist for the Range object.

2 Select the Range object from the list on the left. Then select the Range method from the list on the right. The Range method is a method of the Range object. It works the same as the Range method of the Application object, except that you must put another Range object in front of it.

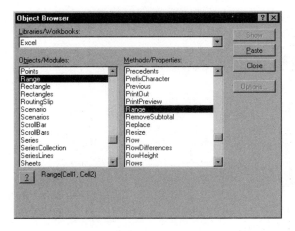

Go back to the Immediate pane and compare the two Range methods.

3   Press ESC to close the Object Browser, and then in the Immediate pane, type **Range("A2").Select** and press ENTER.

As you might have guessed, Excel selects cell A2. The Range method in this example belongs to the Application object. The address A2 refers to "the second cell down in the first column," and the Application object uses cell A1 of the worksheet as the starting point.

4   Type **ActiveCell.Range("A2").Select** and press ENTER.

As you might *not* have guessed, Excel selects cell A3. The Range method in this example belongs to the Range object. The address A2 still refers to "the second cell down in the first column," but this statement uses cell A2, the Range object returned by the ActiveCell property, as the starting point.

5   Reexecute the *ActiveCell.Range("A2").Select* statement two or three times.

Each time, Excel selects the cell A2 — as long as you think of the active cell as the top left cell of a virtual worksheet.

The range B2:C4 on the active worksheet is named TestRange. Select cells relative to that.

6   Type **Range("TestRange").Range("C1").Select** and press ENTER.

Excel selects cell D2, because that's the third cell to the right, starting from the top left cell of TestRange.

Explore collection methods of a range

Just as you can use the Cells, Columns, and Rows methods on an entire worksheet, you can also use these collection methods with ranges. If you change the color of the TestRange range, you will be able to see where it is as you change the selection.

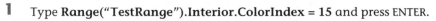

1 Type **Range("TestRange").Interior.ColorIndex = 15** and press ENTER.

The cells in TestRange change to a light gray. Assigning a value to the ColorIndex property of the interior of a Range object changes the fill color of the range. The number 15 corresponds to light gray on the default color palette.

Compare the Columns method of the Range object with the Columns method of the Application object.

2 Type **Columns(2).Select** and press ENTER.

Excel selects all of column B, because the second column on the worksheet is column B.

3 Type **Range("TestRange").Columns(2).Select** and press ENTER.

Excel selects the range C2:C4, because now the Columns collection is relative to the TestRange range. The second column of TestRange is column C and TestRange extends only from row 2 to row 4.

4 Type **Cells(4,2).Select** and press ENTER.

	A	B	C	D
1				
2				
3				
4				
5				
6				

Excel selects cell B4, because that's the fourth cell down in the second column over.

5 Type **Range("TestRange").Cells(4,2).Select** and press ENTER.

	A	B	C	D
1				
2				
3				
4				
5				
6				

Excel selects cell C5. The Cells method is not restricted to the original range. It treats the top left cell of TestRange as if it were cell A1 of the worksheet.

6 Type **?Rows.Count** and press ENTER.

The number *16384* appears because that's how many rows are on the entire worksheet.

7 Type **?Range("TestRange").Rows.Count** and press ENTER.

The number 3 appears because that's how many rows are in TestRange.

The Cells, Columns, and Rows methods are useful when you want to think of a range — either the complete range of cells on the worksheet, or a specified range — as a collection. You can count the items, or select a specific item, from any of those collections.

Calculate flexible ranges

Excel has other methods that can calculate a new range based on an existing range. One particularly useful method is the Offset method. The Offset method takes one Range object and calculates a new Range object from it.

1 Type **Range("TestRange").** (do type the period), and then click the Object Browser button. With the Range object selected in the list of objects, select the Offset method from the list on the right. Then click Paste to paste the Offset method, along with its arguments, into the Immediate pane.

2 Type **1** as the value of the RowOffset argument, type **0** as the value of the ColumnOffset argument, and append **.Select** to create this statement:

```
Range("TestRange").Offset(RowOffset:=1,ColumnOffset:=0).Select
```

This statement consists of three methods: Range, Offset, and Select.

- The Range method returns a Range object consisting of the starting range, B2:C4.

- The Offset method operates on that range and calculates a new Range object, shifted one row down and zero columns to the right of the original range, B3:C5.

- The Select method operates on that range and makes it the new selection.

3 Press ENTER to select the range B3:C5.

As long as you first type the number of rows to shift down, and then type the number of columns to shift right, you can leave out the argument names of the Offset method.

4 Type **Range("TestRange").Offset(-1,2).Select** and press ENTER to select a new range (D1:E3), one row up and two columns to the right of the TestRange range.

The Offset method is a powerful tool for calculating a new range from a starting range. You give the Offset method two arguments: the number of rows to shift the selection down, and the number of columns to shift the selection to the right. To shift the selection up or to the left, use negative numbers for the arguments. The expression *Selection.Offset(0, 0)* returns the same range as the expression *Selection* all by itself.

Another method, the Resize method, allows you to change the number of rows and columns in a range. Like the Offset method, the Resize method takes one Range object and calculates another Range object from it. Combining the Resize method with the Offset method gives you almost unlimited control over a range.

5 Type **Range("TestRange").** (do type the period), and then open the Object Browser. From the list on the right, select Resize method, and click Paste.

6 Type **1** as the value of the RowSize argument, type **5** as the value of the ColumnSize argument, and append **.Select** to create this statement:

```
Range("TestRange").Resize(RowSize:=1,ColumnSize:=5).Select
```

In this statement, the Range method finds the range with the given name. Then the Resize method calculates a second new range, changing the number of rows and columns. Finally, the Select method selects the range returned by the Resize method.

7 Press ENTER to select a new range (B2:F2) one row tall and five columns wide, starting from the top left cell of the TestRange range.

Rather than thinking of a range as a rectangle defined by a top left cell and a bottom right cell, think of it as a rectangle defined by a starting position (the top left cell) and a size (the width and height). The Offset method calculates a new starting position for a range, and the Resize method calculates a new size.

The Resize method takes two arguments: the number of rows (the "row size") and the number of columns (the "column size"). If you omit an argument, the Resize method retains the same size for that dimension as the one you defined for the original range.

You can get very elaborate when calculating range sizes. Here's how to select a range that extends one cell further on all sides than the original selection:

8 Type **Range("TestRange").Offset(-1,-1).Resize(Range("TestRange") .Rows.Count+2,Range("TestRange").Columns.Count+2).Select** (all on one line) and press ENTER.

NOTE The combined functionality of the Offset and Resize methods is equivalent to that of the OFFSET function available on worksheets and in Excel 4 macros.

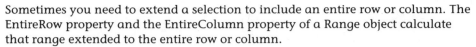

Sometimes you need to extend a selection to include an entire row or column. The EntireRow property and the EntireColumn property of a Range object calculate that range extended to the entire row or column.

9 Type **Range("TestRange").EntireRow.Select** and press ENTER.

Excel selects all of rows 2 through 4, the rows included in the original TestRange range.

	A	B	C	D	E	F
1						
2						
3						
4						
5						

The Offset and Resize methods, along with the EntireRow and EntireColumn properties, provide you with flexible tools for calculating new Range objects based on an original starting range.

Exploring the Contents of Ranges

Selecting ranges helps you understand how to manipulate Range objects, but to get real work done, you must format cells, put values and formulas into cells, retrieve values from cells, retrieve formulas from cells, and retrieve formatted values from cells. This section will show you how.

Put values and formulas into a range

1 Type **Worksheets(2).Select** and press ENTER to get a fresh worksheet.

2 Type **Range("B2:B6").Select** and press ENTER to select a starting range of cells.

3 Type **Selection.Formula = 100** and press ENTER.

	A	B	C
1			
2		100	
3		100	
4		100	
5		100	
6		100	
7			

The number 100 fills all the cells of the selection. Formula is a property of the range. When you set the Formula property for the selection, you change the formula for all the cells in the selection.

177

The number 100 is not actually a formula; it is a constant. But the Formula property is equivalent to whatever you see in the formula bar when the cell is selected. The formula bar can contain constants as well as formulas, and so can the Formula property.

4 Type **ActiveCell.Formula = 0** and press ENTER.

	A	B	C
1			
2		0	
3		100	
4		100	
5		100	
6		100	
7			

Only cell B2 changes to zero, because you changed the formula of only the active cell.

Suppose you want to enter a value in the first cell above the active cell and you don't want to assume that the active cell is cell B2.

5 Type **ActiveCell.Offset(-1, 0).Formula = 1** and press ENTER.

	A	B	C
1		1	
2		0	
3		100	
4		100	
5		100	
6		100	
7			

The cell B1 changes to the number 1.

This statement starts with the active cell, uses the Offset method to calculate a new cell one up from that starting cell, and then sets the Formula property for the resulting cell.

This formula is very similar to the one you created with the macro recorder in Lesson 2.

6 Type **Selection.Formula = "=B1*5"** and press ENTER.

	A	B	C
1		1	
2		5	
3		25	
4		125	
5		625	
6		3125	
7			

The value in each cell of the selection changes to five times that of the cell above it.

Now the selected cells each contain a real formula, not a constant. When you entered the formula, the active cell was B2. From the point of view of cell B2, the reference B1 means "one cell above." As Excel enters the formula into all the cells of the range, it adjusts the reference as needed to always mean "one cell above." Excel has an additional way of referring to "one cell above" that does not require you to know where you are putting the formula: R1C1 notation.

Range objects in Excel have one property for entering and reading the formula in A1 notation and another property for entering and reading the formula in R1C1 notation. R1C1 notation allows you to specify a relative cell reference in a way that is independent of the current location of the formula.

For more information about R1C1 notation, select Answer Wizard from the Help menu, search for "Reference Style" and select the topic "How Microsoft Excel Identifies Cells"

7 Type **?ActiveCell.FormulaR1C1** and press ENTER.

The formula *=R[-1]C*5* appears. This is the same formula as *=B1*5*, except that it is displayed using R1C1 notation. This formula means "multiply the value of the cell one row above me by 5." When you use R1C1 notation for relative references in a formula, you don't have to worry about the actual location of the cell that contains the formula.

All cells have both a Formula property and a FormulaR1C1 property. You can assign a formula to either one, and you can read the formula from a cell with either one. If you are assigning a constant or a formula that doesn't include cell addresses, the Formula and FormulaR1C1 properties are identical.

Format the contents of a range

Excel ranges offer a wide variety of formatting options. You can use the Object Browser and the Help system together to help you learn how to format cells.

Object Browser button

1 Click the Object Browser button, and select Range from the list of object names.

2 From the Methods/Properties list, select the NumberFormat property.

The Object Browser does not tell you what kind of value to assign to the NumberFormat property.

3 Click the ? (question mark) button at the bottom of the Object Browser.

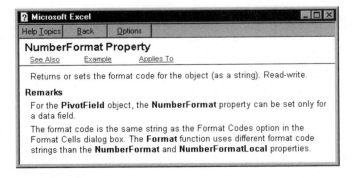

179

The NumberFormat Property topic appears in Help. According to the Help topic, the value you assign to the NumberFormat property is the same string that Excel uses in the Format Cells dialog box.

4 Close Help and close the Object Browser.

For more information about formatting, search Help for "NumberFormat."

5 In the Immediate pane, type **Selection.NumberFormat = "$#,##0"** and press ENTER.

	A	B	C
1		1	
2		$5	
3		$25	
4		$125	
5		$625	
6		$3,125	
7			

The cells within the selection change to the new format, but the cell above the selection does not change.

6 Immediately after the word *Selection*, type **.EntireColumn** to create this statement:

```
Selection.EntireColumn.NumberFormat = "$#,##0"
```

7 Press ENTER to format all the cells in the column as currency.

	A	B	C
1		$1	
2		$5	
3		$25	
4		$125	
5		$625	
6		$3,125	
7			

By looking around in the Object Browser and switching to Help for more information and examples you can copy and use, you can quickly learn how to manipulate Excel objects.

Retrieve the contents of a cell

In addition to putting values and formulas into cells, sometimes you will want to retrieve the contents of cells. The contents of a cell, however, can be more than just its value.

1 Type **?Range("B2").Formula** and press ENTER.

The formula for the cell, *=B1*5*, appears. (If you want to retrieve the formula with references displayed in R1C1 notation, use the FormulaR1C1 property.)

2 Type **?Range("B2").Value** and press ENTER.

The value of the cell, *5,* appears. The value is the result of the formula's calculation. If the cell contains a constant, the value and the formula are the same.

3   Type **?Range("B2").Text** and press ENTER.

The formatted contents of the cell, *$5*, appears.

The Text property is read-only. To change the contents of the cell, you must use the Value property or the Formula property. To change the number formatting of the cell, you must use the NumberFormat property.

4   Type **?Range("B2")** and press ENTER.

The unformatted value of the cell, 5, appears, the same as it did when you used the Value property. If you do not specify a property for a Range object, you get the Value property as a default.

5   Type **Range("B1") = 10** and press ENTER.

	A	B	C
1		$10	
2		$50	
3		$250	
4		$1,250	
5		$6,250	
6		$31,250	
7			

Since Value is the default property for a Range object, you can assign a new value to a range simply by assigning the value to the Range object. You don't need to specify the Value property explicitly.

6   Type **Selection.Formula = Selection.Value** and press ENTER.

This statement does not change the appearance of the worksheet, but it converts all the formulas in the selection to the values from those cells. This statement has the same effect as copying the cells and then using the PasteSpecial method to paste just the values.

See Lesson 2 for a macro that uses the PasteSpecial method.

The Range object is probably the most important single object in Excel. Ranges—with formulas, values, and formats—are what define a spreadsheet program. Excel's Range object has many properties and methods for you to utilize, and the Object Browser can help you learn how to use them.

Quit Excel

➤   In the Immediate pane, type **Application.Quit** and click No when asked to save changes.

Lesson Summary

To	Do this
Select the fifth cell in the third row of the active worksheet	Use the statement *Cells(3,5).Select*.
Select the range B2:C5 on the active worksheet	Use the statement *Range("B2:C5").Select*.
Count the columns in the current selection	Use the expression *Selection.Columns.Count*.
Select a new range one row down from the selection	Use the statement *Selection.Offset(1,0).Select*.
Fill the cells in the selection with the value 100	Use the statement *Selection.Formula = 100*.
Enter into the active cell a formula that calculates the value of the cell above	Use the statement *ActiveCell.FormulaR1C1="=R[-1]C"*.
Retrieve a value from the active cell	Use the expression *ActiveCell.Value*.
Retrieve a formula from the active cell	Use the expression *ActiveCell.Formula* or the expression *ActiveCell.FormulaR1C1*.
Retrieve the formatted value from the active cell	Use the expression *ActiveCell.Text*.
Go to Help for a method or property from the Object Browser	With the method or property selected in the Object Browser, click the ? (question mark) button.
Go to Help for a method or property from a module or the Immediate pane	Select the method or property name and press F1.

For online information about	From the Excel Help menu, choose Contents, choose Getting Started with Visual Basic, and then
Working with Range Objects	Select the topic "Referencing and Selecting Cells and Ranges"

Preview of the Next Lesson

Excel is well-known for exceptional graphical output. In the next lesson you will explore graphical objects. Graphical objects include not only circles and rectangles on the worksheet, but also text boxes and charts. Even dialog box controls are graphical objects in Excel. As you learn to work with graphical objects, you will see how to use the macro recorder in an entirely new way: as a reference tool for learning about objects.

Explore Graphical Objects

Estimated time
35 min.

In this lesson you will learn how to:

■ Manipulate drawing objects on a worksheet.

■ Manipulate chart objects.

■ Use the macro recorder as a reference tool.

On a warm summer day, nothing is grander than to lie on your back in a grassy field and watch clouds float across the sky. Trees and mountains and buildings just sit there; they are attached firmly to the ground. But clouds move. Clouds change shape. They change color. Clouds can come in layers, too, with closer clouds drifting in front of the clouds in back.

On a worksheet, ranges with their formulas and formats are attached firmly to the worksheet just as buildings are attached to the ground. Cell A1 will always be in the top left corner of the worksheet. Drawing objects, however, are like clouds. They float freely above the worksheet. They can disappear and reappear. They can change color and shape.

Drawing objects — including not only shapes such as rectangles, ovals, and lines, but also charts, and even list box controls and spinner controls — add interest, information, and functionality to a worksheet. In this lesson, you will learn how to work with drawing objects from within a Visual Basic macro, and along the way you will find out more about how to use Microsoft Excel's reference tools to learn more about all objects, properties, and methods.

Exploring Graphics Using the Macro Recorder

The Object Browser and the Help system are like a spelling dictionary: in the same way that you practically have to know how to spell a word before you can find it in the dictionary, you practically have to know the property or method before you can find it in the Object Browser or in Help. One of the most useful reference tools for learning how to use Excel objects may not seem to be a reference tool at all: the macro recorder.

Some people think of the macro recorder as a tool for beginners — and it is. In Part 1 of this book, you did use the macro recorder to build finished macros without having to understand very much about how Excel objects really work. But the macro recorder is also a powerful reference tool for advanced developers. In this lesson you will see how you can use the macro recorder as one more reference tool for learning how to work with Excel objects.

Record creating a rectangle

Graphical objects—such as rectangles, ovals, text boxes, and charts — can make your worksheets appealing and understandable. The macro recorder is a very good tool for learning how to work with graphical objects. Record creating a rectangle, and see how much you can learn from a simple recorded macro.

Drawing button

1 Open Excel with a blank workbook, and click the Drawing button on the Standard toolbar to display the Drawing toolbar.

Record Macro button

2 Click the Record Macro button on the Visual Basic toolbar, replace the default macro name with **MakeRectangle**, and click OK.

Rectangle button

3 Click the Rectangle button on the Drawing toolbar (not the Filled Rectangle button), and then click the top left corner of cell B2 and drag to the bottom right corner of cell B3.

Color button

4 Click the arrow next to the Color button on the Formatting toolbar, and then click the third box in the top row of the color palette: the color red.

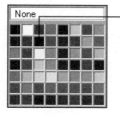

None

Click here to change the color of the selection to red.

The rectangle changes to red.

Stop Macro button

5 Click the Stop Macro button and activate the Module1 sheet to look at the resulting macro.

```
Sub MakeRectangle()
    ActiveSheet.Rectangles.Add(48, 13, 48, 25.5).Select
    Selection.Interior.ColorIndex = xlNone
    Selection.Interior.ColorIndex = 3
End Sub
```

This macro is very short, but a lot happens in those three statements. Look at the second statement:

```
ActiveSheet.Rectangles.Add(48, 13, 48, 25.5).Select
```

It starts by pointing at the active sheet and ends by selecting something. The word *Rectangles* is a plural noun, and it's followed by the word *Add*, so it looks like Rectangles is a collection. The word *Add* is followed by a list of numbers in parentheses. (Your numbers may differ somewhat.) You can probably guess that the numbers have something to do with the location and size of the rectangle since nothing else in the macro sets the location.

These recorded statements give you several clues about how to create a new rectangle. Now you can use Excel's other reference tools—the Object Browser, the Help system, and the Immediate pane—to fill in the details.

Create a rectangle

1   On the View menu, click the Debug Window command, and resize the Debug window as needed so that you can see the workbook behind it.

2   With the Debug window still open, activate the Workbook window, click the Sheet1 tab so that you can see the rectangle, and then reactivate the Debug window.

   Your macro appears in the Code pane, the bottom half of the Debug window.

3   Select the words *ActiveSheet.Rectangles.* (including both periods) in the Code pane, and click Copy on the Edit menu.

   You can copy code from the Code pane and paste it into the Immediate pane to test specific statements. (As long as you are not stepping through a macro, you can also copy code from the Immediate pane and paste it into the macro in the Code pane.)

4   Click the Immediate pane, and click Paste on the Edit menu.

5   Click the Object Browser button on the Visual Basic toolbar, select Excel from the Libraries/Workbooks list, select Rectangles from the Objects/Modules list, and select Add from the Methods/Properties list.

Object Browser button

185

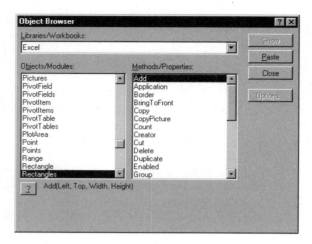

At the bottom of the Object Browser dialog box is a list of the arguments used by the Add method. However, the name of an argument does not let you know whether to enter values for the arguments using inches or centimeters or something else. You can find more detailed information in Help.

? button

6 Click the ? (question mark) button at the bottom of the dialog box.

The Help system opens and the Add Method topic appears. Several different object classes have an Add method, and it works differently depending on the object class, so the main Add Method topic has pointers to other Help topics.

7 Click the underlined word Rectangles to jump to the Add Method topic for drawing objects.

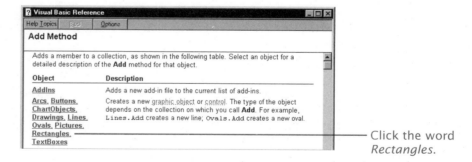

Click the word *Rectangles.*

The Add Method (Graphic Objects And Controls) topic appears.

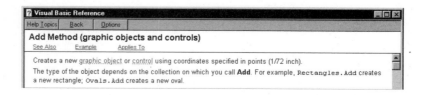

A point is the unit of measurement traditionally used to lay out text for publishing.

In the first line of the description you see that the unit of measurement used with graphic objects is a *point*, equal to ¹/₇₂ inch. That is what you needed to know.

8 Switch back to Excel (you should still be in the Object Browser dialog box with the Add method selected) and click Paste to paste the Add method and its arguments into the Immediate pane.

9 For the arguments, type **72** for Left, **36** for Top, **72** for Width, and **36** for Height.

10 Move the insertion point to the end of the statement. Type **.Select** and press ENTER.

A new rectangle appears on the worksheet, about ¹/₂ inch from the top and 1 inch from the left. The rectangle is ¹/₂ inch high and 1 inch wide. The rectangle also has selection handles around its border to show that it is the current selection. You can't see the gridlines through the rectangle, because the default rectangle is not transparent—it is filled with white.

In this example, you were able to create a rectangle by following the pattern given by the recorder, but you also used the Object Browser and Help to find out how to modify and control the recorded statement.

Set the color of the rectangle

The next two statements in the recorded macro set the color of the rectangle:

```
Selection.Interior.ColorIndex = xlNone
```

```
Selection.Interior.ColorIndex = 3
```

The first statement changes the color of the selection from the default white color to transparent, and the second statement changes the color from transparent to that of the third color in the palette. You can execute similar statements in the Immediate pane.

1 Copy the statement *Selection.Interior.ColorIndex = xlNone* from the Code pane to the Immediate pane, and press ENTER.

The new rectangle you created now becomes transparent.

If you want to use a color that is not in the palette, search Help for the topic "RGB function".

2 Replace the word *xlNone* with the number **1** and reexecute the statement.

The rectangle changes to black. In Excel's default color palette, black is the first color. The color palette holds 56 different colors, so you can use any number from 1 through 56 for the ColorIndex property.

The macro's recorded statement did not set the color of the rectangle directly but rather changed the color of the interior of the rectangle. That might make you curious about the ColorIndex property.

3 Double-click the word *ColorIndex* to select the entire word, and press F1 to display the Help topic for the ColorIndex property.

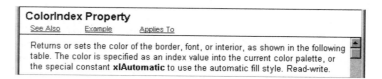

> **ColorIndex Property**
> See Also   Example   Applies To
>
> Returns or sets the color of the border, font, or interior, as shown in the following table. The color is specified as an index value into the current color palette, or the special constant **xlAutomatic** to use the automatic fill style. Read-write.

As the Help description shows, the ColorIndex property controls the color of the border, borders, and font as well as the color of the interior. To find the border of a Rectangle object, should you use the word *Border* or the word *Borders*?

4 Switch back to Excel. Double-click the word *Interior* and click the Object Browser button. Select Rectangle from the list of object names.

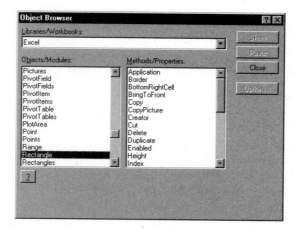

The word *Border* appears in the list of methods and properties, but the word *Borders* does not. So you should use the word *Border* to refer to the border of a rectangle.

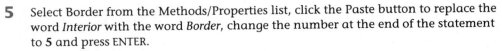

5 Select Border from the Methods/Properties list, click the Paste button to replace the word *Interior* with the word *Border*, change the number at the end of the statement to **5** and press ENTER.

A thin blue border appears around the rectangle.

Because a rectangle has a border, perhaps a border has other attributes you can set.

6 Type **Selection.Border.** (with both periods), click the Object Browser button, select Border from the list of object names, and look at the list of methods and properties.

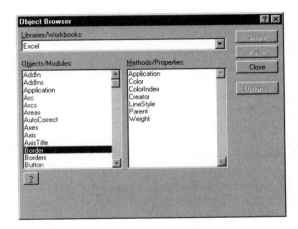

Aside from the standard properties and methods, the Border object lists only Color, ColorIndex, LineStyle, and Weight.

7 Select Weight from the list of methods and properties, click Paste to paste it into the Immediate pane, type **= 4** and press ENTER.

The thin blue border around the rectangle changes to a thick blue border.

You can find valid settings for the border's Weight property either by reading the Weight property topic in Help or by trial and error.

Once you have recorded a statement, you can use the Help system and the Object Browser to help you find related properties and methods that might be useful.

Create a rectangle without selecting it

The statement you used to add a new rectangle has the word *Select* at the end of it. After the Add method creates the rectangle, it returns a link to the newly created object. The Select method uses that link to select the object. All Add methods return a link to the objects they create. If you don't need to select the new drawing object, you can leave off the Select method.

NOTE When you use the Add method of the Workbooks object to create a new workbook, you usually just discard the link that the Add method returns. Because the new workbook becomes the active workbook, you can establish a link with it at any time using the ActiveWorkbook property.

1 In the Immediate pane, type **ActiveSheet.Rectangles.Add Left:=144, Top:=36, Width:=72, Height:=36** and press ENTER. This is the same as the Add statement you used before, except that the value of the Left argument is 144, the *.Select* is missing from the end, and the parentheses are gone.

 NOTE If a method takes arguments and you use the return value of the method, you must include parentheses around the arguments; if you do not use the return value of the method, you must *not* include the parentheses. Adding the Select method to the end of the statement does use the object returned by the Add method.

A new rectangle appears on the worksheet, next to the rectangle you created earlier. The selection handles are still on the previous rectangle.

2 Type **Selection.Interior.ColorIndex = 6** and press ENTER.

The interior of the selected rectangle changes to yellow. The new rectangle is unchanged.

If you don't select the new object as you create it, you may wonder how to change its interior color now. The Rectangles object is a collection, and you can work with rectangles using the same techniques you use with other collections.

190

3   Type **?ActiveSheet.Rectangles.Count** and press ENTER.

The number of rectangles, probably 3, appears. You want the most recently created rectangle, so that is rectangle number 3.

4   Type **ActiveSheet.Rectangles(3).Interior.ColorIndex = 4** and press ENTER.

The interior of the newest rectangle changes to green, but the selection handles indicate that the other rectangle is still the current selection.

Sometimes you want to create and manipulate objects without changing the selection. You can do that, but if you discard the link to the object that the Add method offers you, be sure you can establish a link some other way. In Lesson 11, you will learn how to save the link to the object so that you can use it later.

5   Close the Debug window.

Excel has several classes of Drawing objects: rectangles, ovals, arcs, and so forth. All these Drawing objects work in much the same way that rectangles do. Even dialog controls such as check boxes, option buttons, and scroll bars are drawing objects, and they are very similar to rectangles. Embedded charts are also Drawing objects in Excel. You add, manipulate, and delete Chart objects in the same way you do Rectangle objects. Chart objects, of course, have additional properties that are unique to charts; the macro recorder is an effective tool for finding out what they are.

Exploring Chart Objects

Charts and Chart objects have hundreds of properties and methods. Many of the attributes of a chart are themselves separate objects. Learning how to create and manipulate charts by reading a reference manual is very difficult because charts have so many objects and properties. But creating and manipulating a chart is easy to record, and even though you may see many new methods, properties, and objects, the new objects work according to the same principles as other objects do in Excel.

Record creating a Chart object

1 Click the Sheet2 tab to activate a new worksheet, enter the sample values for the chart into the range A1:C4 as shown here, and select the range A1:C4.

	A	B	C	D
1	Price	Units	Net	
2	High	6,443	17,594	
3	Mid	12,599	33,817	
4	Low	8,670	19,401	
5				

Record Macro button

2 Click the Record Macro button on the Visual Basic toolbar, type **MakeChart** as the name for the macro, and click OK.

3 Click the ChartWizard button on the Standard toolbar, and then, while holding down the ALT key, drag a rectangle from the top left corner of cell B7 through the bottom right corner of cell F13.

Chart Wizard button

Step 1 of the ChartWizard appears. Notice that the selected cells have a moving border around them. The ChartWizard temporarily copies the selected range to the Clipboard while it creates the chart.

To see the list of Gallery settings in Help, select the word "ChartWizard" and press F1.

4 Click the Finish button to create the default chart.

	A	B	C	D	E	F	G
1	Price	Units	Net				
2	High	6,443	17,594				
3	Mid	12,599	33,817				
4	Low	8,670	19,401				
5							
6							
7							
8							
9							
10							
11							
12							
13							
14							

When you use the ChartWizard method on an existing chart, omit the arguments for any attributes you don't want to change.

Stop Macro button

5 Click the Stop Macro button and activate the module sheet to look at the recorded macro:

```
Sub MakeChart()
    ActiveSheet.ChartObjects.Add(48, 76.5, 240, 89.25).Select
    Application.CutCopyMode = False
    ActiveChart.ChartWizard Source:=Range("A1:C4"), Gallery:=xlColumn, _
        Format:=6, PlotBy:=xlColumns, CategoryLabels:=1, SeriesLabels _
        :=1, HasLegend:=1
End Sub
```

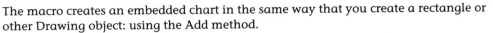

The macro creates an embedded chart in the same way that you create a rectangle or other Drawing object: using the Add method.

The statement with the Add method produces an empty box — a container for the chart.

The statement that sets the CutCopyMode property to False is in the macro because the ChartWizard temporarily copies the selection. You can delete this statement without changing the result, because the ChartWizard method in the next statement turns off copy mode anyway.

The statement with the ChartWizard method is what really defines the chart that goes inside the box. The ChartWizard method has several arguments; these arguments correspond to various possible settings for the chart.

Now see how you can control the chart yourself from the Immediate pane.

Modify a Chart object

1 On the View menu, click Debug Window, and activate the Immediate pane.

2 Activate the Workbook window, and click the Sheet2 tab. If the chart container does not have selection handles on the edges, click it. Then reactivate the Debug window.

3 Type **ActiveChart.ChartWizard Gallery:=xlBar** and press ENTER.

The chart becomes a horizontal bar chart.

	A	B	C	D	E	F	G
1	Price	Units	Net				
2	High	6,443	17,594				
3	Mid	12,599	33,817				
4	Low	8,670	19,401				
5							
6							
7							
8							
9							
10							
11							
12							
13							
14							

This statement is the same as the recorded ChartWizard statement from the Code pane, except that you kept only the Gallery argument and you changed its value to *xlBar*.

Because the chart's container is a Drawing object—just like a rectangle—you can set its properties, and the properties of its interior and border, in the same way that you do with a rectangle.

4 Type **Selection.Interior.ColorIndex = 6** and press ENTER.

The color of the chart's container box changes to yellow.

193

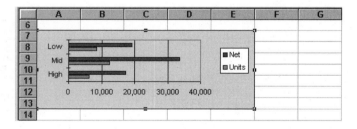

Notice that here you use the word *Selection* with the ColorIndex property, and in step 3 you used the word *ActiveChart* with the ChartWizard method.

Selection refers to the container box for the chart. It is a Drawing object on the worksheet, similar to a rectangle, with its own properties, such as its size and position. You set the ColorIndex property of the interior of the container box. The word *ActiveChart* refers to the chart inside the box. You use the ChartWizard method to modify the chart inside the box.

The container box is a ChartObject object. The chart inside the box is a Chart object. Never confuse a ChartObject object with a Chart object. A ChartObject object can exist only on a worksheet, and is a Drawing object. A Chart object can exist either inside a ChartObject container box or on its own separate sheet in the workbook.

5   Type **Selection.Left = 0** and press ENTER to shift the chart to the left side of the worksheet.

6   Type **Selection.Width = Columns("A:D").Width** and press ENTER to make the width of the chart the same as the width of columns A through D.

7   Close the Debug window.

You change the properties of a chart's container box by using the ChartObject object, which you refer to by using the word *Selection*. You can also change some of the properties of the chart itself using the ChartWizard method on the Chart object, which you refer to by using the word *ActiveChart*. But to change many of the properties of a Chart object, you need to get down inside the Chart object itself.

Record modifying a chart

Interactively, if you want to change elements of a chart, you activate the chart by double-clicking it. Activating a chart is different from merely selecting it. When you select a chart, you select the chart's container box: the ChartObject object. When you activate a chart, you activate the chart inside the box: the Chart object. When you activate it, the border of the chart becomes thick and gray, and the menu bar changes to include commands specifically designed for working with charts.

Once you activate a Chart object, you can select and modify all the objects inside the chart. You can use the macro recorder to see how to do this.

Record Macro button

1 With the chart selected, click the Record Macro button, type **EditChart** as the name for the macro, and click OK.

2 Double-click the chart to activate the Chart object.

3 Click the legend box, and press DELETE to remove it.

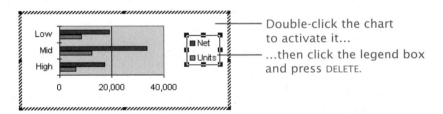

Double-click the chart to activate it...

...then click the legend box and press DELETE.

4 To enlarge the plot area, click the plot area to select it, and drag one of the sizing handles on the right side further to the right to fill the space left by the legend.

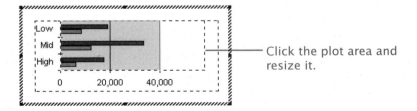

Click the plot area and resize it.

5 On the Format menu, click AutoFormat, select Combination from the Galleries list, select number 3 from the set of formats, and click OK.

The chart becomes a line chart with a separate vertical axis for each of the two chart series, Net and Units.

6 Double-click one of the number labels on the left value axis (the vertical axis on the left side of the chart) to display the Format Axis dialog box, and click the Scale tab. Replace the default Maximum value with **30000**, replace the default Major Unit value with **10000**, and click OK.

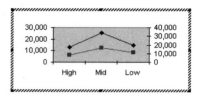

7 Press ESC once to deselect the left axis, and press ESC a second time to deactivate the Chart object. Now the ChartObject container object is the selection again.

8 Click the Stop Macro button and activate the Module1 sheet to look at the recorded macro:

Stop Macro button

```
Sub EditChart()
    ActiveSheet.DrawingObjects("Chart 1").Select
    ActiveSheet.ChartObjects("Chart 1").Activate
    With ActiveWindow
        .Top = 43
        .Left = 40
    End With
    With ActiveWindow
        .Width = 197.25
        .Height = 94.5
    End With
    ActiveChart.Legend.Select
    Selection.Delete
    ActiveChart.PlotArea.Select
    Selection.Width = 210
    ActiveChart.AutoFormat Gallery:=xlCombination, Format:=3
    ActiveChart.Axes(xlValue).Select
    With ActiveChart.Axes(xlValue)
        .MinimumScaleIsAuto = True
        .MaximumScale = 30000
        .MinorUnitIsAuto = True
        .MajorUnit = 10000
        .Crosses = xlAutomatic
        .ReversePlotOrder = False
        .ScaleType = False
    End With
    ActiveChart.Deselect
    ActiveWindow.Visible = False
End Sub
```

196

In brief, this macro activates the embedded chart, superfluously notices the size of the activated window, deletes the legend, changes the width of the plot area, formats the chart as a combination chart, selects the left value axis, changes the axis settings, deselects the axis, and deactivates the chart.

The macro recorder does not always record the simplest way of accomplishing a task, but it does show you the names of the object classes, properties, and methods you will need to work with. Now you can go into the Immediate pane and see how to really control the chart.

Modify the chart

1 On the View menu, click Debug Window, and activate the Immediate pane.

2 Activate the Workbook window and click the Sheet2 tab. If the chart's container object is not selected, click it once to select it. Then reactivate the Debug window.

The statement *ActiveSheet.ChartObjects("Chart 1").Activate* is what the recorder produced when you activated the chart in step 2 of the previous procedure. But specifying the chart by name may make the macro difficult to use with a different chart. Because the chart container is already the current selection, you can use the more general word *Selection* to refer to it.

3 In the Immediate pane, type **Selection.Activate** and press ENTER to activate the chart.

In the workbook window, the chart becomes activated.

With the chart activated, you can select various objects inside the chart.

4 Type **ActiveChart.PlotArea.Select** and press ENTER to select the plot area.

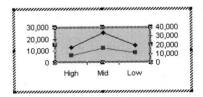

5 Type **Selection.Width = 100** and press ENTER to make the plot area narrower.

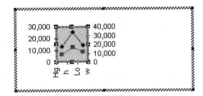

197

To make the plot
area as wide as
possible, assign
a value greater
than the width
of the chart.

6 Type **Selection.Width = 500** and press ENTER to make the plot area as wide as possible.

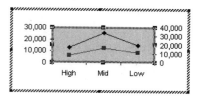

7 Type **ActiveChart.Axes(xlValue,xlSecondary).Select** and press ENTER to select the value axis on the right side of the chart (the secondary value axis).

8 Type **Selection.Minimumscale = 10000** and press ENTER to change the range of the secondary value axis.

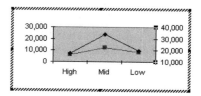

In the recorded EditChart macro that you created in the previous section, there is a With structure beginning at the line *With ActiveChart.Axes(xlValue)* that sets the axis properties. The recorder did not know you changed only two of the settings. You don't need to add statements for the settings you did not change.

9 Type **ActiveWindow.Visible = False** and press ENTER to deactivate the chart.

The thick gray border around the chart disappears and the selection changes from the secondary value axis back to the chart container.

The recorded EditChart macro treats the activated chart as a separate window, even though it does not look like a typical window. (If you want, you can enter the statement *?Windows.Count* in the Immediate pane while the chart is active, to see that the chart is in a separate window.) Normally, to close a window you use the Close method, but you close the special chart-editing window by setting its Visible property to False.

The macro recorder included the statement *Windows("Workbook1").Activate* at the end of the macro. You do not need this statement, because by hiding the chart's editing window the macro has already activated the original workbook window. You should eliminate this statement from all the macros you create, because it will cause the macro to fail if you save the workbook with a new name.

If you now return to the recorded EditChart macro and simplify it based on the exploring you've done in the Immediate pane—but without changing the functionality of the macro at all—this is what you get:

```
Sub EditChart()
    Selection.Activate
    ActiveChart.Legend.Select
    Selection.Delete
    ActiveChart.PlotArea.Select
    Selection.Width = 176
    ActiveChart.AutoFormat Gallery:=xlCombination, Format:=3
    ActiveChart.Axes(xlValue).Select
    With Selection
        .MaximumScale = 30000
        .MajorUnit = 10000
    End With
    ActiveWindow.Visible = False
End Sub
```

Modify the chart remotely

When you modify a chart interactively, you must activate the chart in order to select or modify any of the objects inside the chart. From a macro, you can manipulate a chart's objects even if they are not selected, as long as you refer to the correct object.

1 In the Immediate pane, type **Range("A1").Select** and press ENTER to make cell A1 the selection. Now not even the chart container is selected.

2 Type **ActiveSheet.ChartObjects(1).Chart.PlotArea.Width = 50** and press ENTER to make the plot area narrow.

Even though this is the current selection...

...you can still modify objects inside the chart.

This means, "Start with the active sheet. Find its collection of chart container boxes. Find the first container box in the collection. Find the actual chart inside the container box. Find the plot area of that chart. Set the width of that plot area to 50."

The entire statement may look long and intimidating, but if you break it into separate pieces, each piece simply returns the next object down the chain until you finally get to the object that has a property you want to change.

3 Type **ActiveSheet.ChartObjects(1).Chart.PlotArea.Left = 100** and press ENTER to shift the plot area to the right.

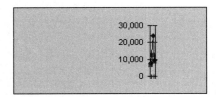

In the Immediate pane, each command must be on a single line, so you can't use With structures.

In a macro, when you use the same long chain of objects more than once, you can put the entire chain of objects into a With structure to make the macro easier to read and faster to run. Using a With structure, the two statements that change the plot area could be written like this:

```
With ActiveSheet.ChartObjects(1).Chart.PlotArea
    .Width = 50
    .Left = 100
End With
```

Using a With structure is similar in some ways to selecting an object interactively. When you include an object in a With statement, you can think of the object as "virtually selected" until you use End With to deselect it. The object is not really selected, but any properties or methods that begin with a period apply to the object.

When you record actions, the resulting macro always selects each object before it changes the object. That's because you must select an object before you can change it when you work interactively. You can use the macro recorder to help you find out the names of the object classes, properties, and methods you need to work with, and then you can change the recorded macro to manipulate objects without selecting them. Manipulating objects without selecting them makes a macro run much faster.

Exploring the Application Object

You have seen references to the Application object in passing a few times. For example, to find the Workbooks method in the Object Browser, you select Application from the list of object names. Also, every object class name listed on the left side of the Object Browser includes the Application property in the list on the right.

The Application object is Excel itself. It is the ultimate parent object for every object in Excel. The Application object is also the repository for all the workspace-wide settings, and for all the actions that just don't fit anywhere else.

The Application object's properties and methods

If you select the Application object from the list of object names in the Object Browser, you will find about 400 entries in the list of properties and methods on the right. Don't panic, however; you don't have to learn very many of those 400 properties and methods to function effectively in Excel. The Application object's properties and methods fall into a few broad groups:

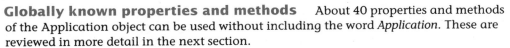

Globally known properties and methods   About 40 properties and methods of the Application object can be used without including the word *Application*. These are reviewed in more detail in the next section.

Worksheet functions   Excel has more than 200 worksheet functions—functions like SUM and PMT. You can access any of these functions from a macro as methods of the Application object.

Recordable workspace settings   Excel has about 60 properties and methods that you can set or run using standard commands, keyboard actions, and mouse move-ments. For example, you can use the mouse to set the size and location of Excel's window. You can use the Formula Bar command on the View menu to hide or display the formula bar. Or you can recalculate the current workbook by pressing F9. These attributes and actions are all properties and methods of the Application object. The easiest way to learn these is to use the macro recorder.

Workspace information   Excel has about 30 properties that tell you about the working environment, such as whether you are operating on a Macintosh or in Windows, and how much memory is available.

Macro settings   About a dozen of the Application object's properties are properties that you can set to control Excel as your macros work. For example, you can keep Excel from updating the screen while your macro runs, or you can add a message to the status bar.

Miscellaneous methods   The remaining approximately 30 methods cover a wide range of uses, from converting centimeter measurements to points, to managing mail, to starting the Help system.

Most of the Application object's properties and methods are easily recorded or else apply to advanced macro applications. When you are ready to learn more about the Applica-tion object, look in the Object Browser and the Help system.

Global properties and methods

When you refer to the first cell on the active worksheet, you use the expression *Cells(1)*. But when you refer to the first rectangle on that same worksheet, you must include a reference to the worksheet—for example, *ActiveSheet.Rectangles(1)*. Similarly, the word *Workbooks* can stand alone, but the word *ChartObjects* must be preceded by the parent worksheet object—for example, *Worksheets(1).ChartObjects*. Likewise, the words *Selection* and *ActiveCell* can stand alone, but the words *Interior* and *Border* must be preceded by a parent object.

Why can some objects stand alone, while others must be preceded by a parent object?

When you address a letter, you always need to include the recipient's name, street address, city, state, and ZIP code. If you are sending the letter to another country, you must also include the name of the country. If you were sending the letter to London, however, or to New York City, you could probably leave off the country name, and the letter would still arrive at its destination. Some cities are big enough to be globally known.

About 40 of the Application object's properties and methods are important enough to be globally known in Excel, and you don't need to specify an object for them. For example, the Workbooks method is globally known. Technically, you should use the expression *Application.Workbooks* instead of just *Workbooks,* but Excel "knows" what Workbooks is, just as most post offices "know" where Tokyo is.

For a property or method to be globally known, it must belong to the Application object. In Help, if a method or property does not need the object specified, the Help topic for the method or property includes the word *Optional* after the description of the object.

The globally known properties and methods fall into a few groups:

The ThisWorkbook property points to the workbook containing the macro, in case that workbook is different from the active workbook.

Pointer properties   The Selection property, the ThisWorkbook property, and all the "Active" properties: ActiveCell, ActiveChart, ActiveDialog, ActiveMenuBar, ActivePrinter, ActiveSheet, ActiveWindow, and ActiveWorkbook.

Range object methods   The most common methods that return range objects: Range, Union, Intersect, Cells, Columns, and Rows.

Sheet collections   Methods that return the various sheet collections that can occur in a workbook: Sheets, Worksheets, Charts, DialogSheets, Modules, Excel4MacroSheets, and Excel4IntlMacroSheets.

Other collections   Methods that return other common collections: AddIns, MenuBars, Names, ShortcutMenus, Toolbars, Windows, and Workbooks.

Commands   Methods that perform common tasks: Calculate, Evaluate, Run, and SendKeys, along with six commands for Dynamic Data Exchange (DDE), which is used in certain advanced applications.

Lesson Summary

To	Do this
Create a 1-inch rectangle in the top left corner of the active sheet	Use the statement *ActiveSheet.Rectangles.Add(0,0,72,72).Select.*
Change the color of the selected object to red	Use the statement *Selection.Interior.ColorIndex = 3.*
Create a chart	Use the ChartWizard method.
Modify specific items on an existing chart	Use the ChartWizard method, deleting all arguments except the ones you need to change.
Activate a chart so you can select objects inside the chart	Select the chart and use the statement *Selection.Activate.*
Deactivate a chart	Use the statement *ActiveWindow.Visible = False* while the chart is active.
Select the second chart on the active sheet	Use the statement *ActiveSheet.ChartObjects(2).Select.*

For online information about	**From the Excel Help menu, choose Contents, choose Getting Started with Visual Basic, and then**
Using charts	Select the topic "Manipulating Charts and Graphic Objects"

Preview of the Next Lesson

In Part 3, you have worked intensively with Excel objects. You have learned to control those objects, largely by executing single statements in the Immediate pane. To build applications that control Excel objects, you need to execute more than a single statement. Visual Basic is the tool that manages large numbers of statements. You have already worked with Visual Basic code as produced by the macro recorder. In Lesson 10 and Lesson 11, you will explore how to develop Visual Basic code to achieve results that cannot be done with the macro recorder alone.

Exploring
Visual Basic

Explore Visual Basic Procedures

In this lesson you will learn how to:

Estimated time
35 min.

- ■ Use various conditional expressions in your procedures.
- ■ Create subroutine procedures.
- ■ Create function procedures.
- ■ Create custom worksheet functions.
- ■ Use named constants in your procedures.

Have you ever driven a radio remote controlled car? On the remote control, you use one lever to make the car go forward or reverse, another lever to make it turn left or right, and another lever to control the speed. You can stand on a table in your dining room and make that little car crash its way all around the room. Now imagine that, instead of a table, you're standing on an apartment building; instead of a miniature car, you're controlling a full-size sedan; and instead of being empty, the car has a real driver inside. Both you and the driver can control the car. You have levers on the remote control; the driver has a stick shift, a steering wheel, and a gas pedal. Inside the car, the driver uses one set of controls, and outside the car, you use a different set of controls.

Microsoft Excel is like a car that has two sets of controls. Excel has certain inherent capabilities which it *exposes* to the interactive user using one set of controls — menus, toolbar buttons, keyboard keys, and mouse clicks — and which it *exposes* to a Visual Basic program using a different set of controls. The controls that Excel exposes to Visual Basic are the objects you learned about in Part 3 of this book.

In this part, you will learn more about working with Visual Basic. Everything you learn about Visual Basic in Excel will apply to writing a stand-alone Visual Basic program, and to writing macros in Excel, Microsoft Project, or other Microsoft applications that include Visual Basic for Applications.

You will start with a very small, simple macro—a *seed* macro—and then gradually modify and enhance the macro to make it more sophisticated, powerful, and error-resistant. Along the way, you will learn much about how to organize and control macros using Visual Basic.

Start the lesson

> Start Excel with a new workbook. Delete all but one of the worksheets in the workbook, and save the file as **Lesson 10** in the folder containing the practice files for this book.

Creating a Seed Macro

In this lesson you will practice Visual Basic skills by constructing a macro to format selected cells in a block of data. The example is similar to the formatting task in Lesson 3, and the first few steps in building this macro are similar to the first few steps in that lesson. This time, however, you will format random numbers, and you will learn more powerful techniques for controlling Visual Basic programs.

Create sample data

1 Double-click the tab for the current worksheet, and rename the worksheet **SampleData**

2 Select the range A1:D8.

3 Type **=RAND()** and then hold down the CTRL key and press ENTER.

Random numbers ranging from 0 to 1 fill all the selected cells.

	A	B	C	D	E
1	0.119294	0.79386	0.7103	0.07198	
2	0.125907	0.747114	0.62061	0.22305	
3	0.781277	0.13391	0.343258	0.344568	
4	0.218	0.190483	0.94162	0.858311	
5	0.6846	0.670039	0.668322	0.803163	
6	0.073373	0.808609	0.560891	0.723504	
7	0.7459	0.691508	0.506672	0.234038	
8	0.700699	0.772516	0.09208	0.531071	
9					

Percent Style button

4 Click the Percent Style button on the Formatting toolbar to make the random numbers more readable.

5 On the Tools menu, click Options, and click the Calculation tab. Select the Manual option button, and click OK.

These numbers will now change to new random numbers whenever you press F9.

Your first task is to format all the cells that have values greater than 50%. Start by recording a macro to format a single cell, much as you did in Lesson 3.

Format a single cell

Record Macro button

Color button

Stop Macro button

Create Button button

1 In the SampleData worksheet, select any cell within the block of random numbers whose value is greater than 50%.

2 Click the Record Macro button on the Visual Basic toolbar, type **FormatExceptions** as the name for the macro, type **Format a single cell** as the description, and click OK.

Using the macro recorder is an easy way to create the shell for a new macro.

3 Click the arrow next to the Color button on the Formatting toolbar, click the red box in the color palette (third from the left in the top row), and then click the Stop Macro button.

4 Create a button that extends from the top left corner of cell F2 to the bottom right corner of cell H3, and assign the FormatExceptions macro to it. (Use the Create Button button on the Drawing toolbar.)

5 Type **Format Exceptions** as the label for the button, and press ESC twice to deselect the button.

6 Select another cell that's greater than 50%, and click the Format Exceptions button to turn the cell red.

7 Activate the new Module1 sheet, rename the sheet **FormatModule**, and look at the FormatExceptions macro:

```
Sub FormatExceptions
    With Selection.Interior
        .ColorIndex = 3
        .Pattern = xlSolid
    End With
End Sub
```

This macro changes the interior color of the selected cell. (It also changes the pattern—more on this in "Make constants easier to read" later in this lesson). This macro will be the seed for developing more sophisticated procedures for formatting the exception cells.

NOTE The terms *macro* and *procedure* are often used interchangeably. In the Visual Basic environment, the word *procedure* has historically been used to refer to the code you write, whereas in the Excel environment, the word *macro* has historically been used. In general, I will use the word *procedure* to refer to an individual Visual Basic routine, and *macro* to refer to code as it is run from Excel, whether that code consists of one or multiple procedures.

Making Decisions

FormatExceptions is a perfectly fine simple procedure. It makes the current selection red. But you want a procedure that will format the active cell only if its value is greater than 50%, and will then move down to the next cell. Rather than add the new statements to your current perfectly fine procedure as you did in Lesson 3, make a separate master procedure that uses the current FormatExceptions procedure when necessary. Treat the procedure you have now as a subordinate, or servant, procedure. When a master wants a servant to do something, the master *calls* the servant. When a Visual Basic procedure wants a subroutine to do something, it *calls* the subroutine.

Add a master procedure

1   Change the name of the FormatExceptions procedure to **FormatColor**. You will reserve the name FormatExceptions for the master procedure since that is the name linked to the button on the worksheet.

2   Move the insertion point above the FormatColor procedure, and type the following:

```
Sub FormatExceptions()
    If ActiveCell > .5 Then FormatColor
    ActiveCell.Offset(1,0).Select
End Sub
```

You can put the master procedure above or below the subordinate procedure, but if you always put subordinates below master procedures, you will be able to find them easily, even as your projects get larger and you have more layers of master and subordinate procedures.

NOTE   A subordinate procedure is typically called a *subroutine*, which accounts for the word *Sub* used to define the name of a procedure. Since master procedures can also be subordinate to other, higher masters, you use the word *Sub* when defining both master and subordinate procedures.

3   Switch back to the SampleData worksheet, select the top cell in one of the columns, and click the Format Exceptions button several times.

A master procedure can delegate a task to a subordinate procedure, or subroutine. Using a subroutine has several advantages over putting all the statements into the master procedure: the master procedure usually becomes simpler and easier to read, and you often find that other procedures can utilize the subroutine. The subroutine becomes a specialist at a single task, serving many masters.

Watch the procedures work

The macro formats the cells nicely, but you may want to watch the macro at work. In Lesson 2 you learned how to use the Step button in the Macro dialog box to step through a macro. Using the Macro dialog box to run the macro, however, is less convenient than using this very nice Format Exceptions button. You can tell the macro to proceed one statement at a time, starting with any statement in the macro you want.

1 Activate the FormatModule sheet and put the insertion point anywhere on the *Sub FormatExceptions()* statement.

2 Click the Toggle Breakpoint button on the Visual Basic toolbar.

Toggle Breakpoint button

You can also press F9 to toggle a breakpoint.

The background color of the statement changes. This statement is now a *breakpoint* because every time the macro gets to this point, it breaks into a walk, stepping through all subsequent statements.

3 Activate the SampleData worksheet, select a cell whose value is less than 50%, and click the Format Exceptions button.

The Debug window appears, showing the FormatExceptions procedure in the Code pane. The breakpoint statement is highlighted with a box around it, indicating that this is the next statement that will run.

4 Resize the Debug window so that you can see the worksheet behind it, and keep clicking the Step Into button to step through the procedure as you watch it work.

Step Into button

The statement

```
If ActiveCell > 0.5 Then FormatColor
```

calls the FormatColor subroutine if the value of the active cell is greater than .5. The whole If statement fits on a single line, so you don't need to put the words *End If* at the end. An If statement that fits on a single line is sometimes called an *inline* or *single-line* If. You could also write this statement as

```
If ActiveCell > 0.5 Then
    FormatColor
End If
```

which you may find easier to recognize as an If structure. An If structure that is made up of several statements and ends with End If is called a *block* If.

The statement

```
ActiveCell.Offset(1,0).Select
```

starts with the active cell, calculates a new cell reference one cell down, and selects the new cell. You can record moving the active cell down with the macro recorder, but once you are comfortable with manipulating a Range object, you may prefer to type the statement directly into the procedure.

5 After the macro finishes, select a cell with a large value and click the Format Exceptions button again. The macro starts stepping in the same place.

6 Click the Step Into button repeatedly to step through the rest of the macro. Observe how the FormatExceptions procedure calls the FormatColor subroutine.

7 To turn off the breakpoint, activate the FormatModule sheet, position the insertion point in the breakpoint statement, and click the Toggle Breakpoint button.

Add an argument to the subroutine

What if you want to change the new color for the cells from red to yellow? Rather than create one subroutine that makes a cell red and a second subroutine that makes a cell yellow, the master procedure should be able to give the subroutine instructions on how to do its job. When you use an Excel method, you give it instructions on how to do its job by giving it arguments. You can make the FormatColor subroutine capable of accepting arguments when it is called.

Imagine a human master who needs to give secret instructions to a servant. The master calls the servant, writes the instructions on a note, puts a code on the outside of the note so that the servant can identify the instructions, and *passes* the note to the servant. Compare the human situation to that of a Visual Basic procedure that needs to give an instruction to a subroutine. The master procedure calls the subroutine and *passes* an argument to the subroutine, using an argument name as a code to clarify the type of instruction.

1   In the FormatColor line of the subroutine, position the insertion point between the open and close parentheses and type **NewColor**

Type **NewColor** between the parentheses.

When you put a word inside the parentheses after a procedure name, you add that word as an argument name for the procedure. The argument name is the subroutine's way of letting any procedures that want to call it know what argument it will accept. You can invent whatever name you wish for an argument, but avoid any names that are already used by Excel or Visual Basic. When a master procedure calls the FormatColor subroutine, it passes a number as the value of the NewColor argument.

2   Replace the number 3 after the word *ColorIndex* with the word **NewColor**

The subroutine uses the argument name in the same way it uses any other variable. (A *variable* is simply a word to which you assign a value.)

3   In the FormatExceptions procedure, change the word *FormatColor* to **FormatColor NewColor:=6**

The number 6 is the color index number of the color yellow in Excel's default color palette.

To have a statement in a master procedure call a subroutine with an argument, you type the argument name, then a colon and an equal sign (:=), and then the value of the argument. Calling a subroutine using an argument is exactly the same as calling an object method with an argument.

Here's what the resulting macro looks like. You can now easily switch the formatting color without having to modify the FormatColor procedure at all.

```
Sub FormatExceptions()
    If ActiveCell > 0.5 Then FormatColor NewColor:=6
    ActiveCell.Offset(1, 0).Select
End Sub

Sub FormatColor(NewColor)
    With Selection.Interior
        .ColorIndex = NewColor
        .Pattern = xlSolid
    End With
End Sub
```

4 Activate the SampleData worksheet, select the top cell in one of the columns, and try the macro.

Color button

5 To clear all the color formatting for the random number cells, select the range of random numbers, click the arrow next to the Color button on the Formatting toolbar, and click the word *None* in the color palette.

6 To change to a new set of sample random numbers, press F9.

Using arguments makes a subroutine flexible and easy to use more than once. Instead of having four different subroutines to format cells with four different colors, you can use a single subroutine and pass it an argument for the color.

Add more conditions

Suppose you don't want to format just the cells whose values are greater than 50%. Suppose you want to make cells greater than 80% green, cells greater than 50% yellow, cells greater than 30% red, and all other cells white. Now that the FormatColor procedure can handle any color, enhancing the macro will be simple.

1 Select the FormatModule sheet. In the FormatExceptions macro, replace the statement beginning with the word *If* with these lines:

```
If ActiveCell > 0.8 Then
    FormatColor NewColor:=4
ElseIf ActiveCell > 0.5 Then
    FormatColor NewColor:=6
ElseIf ActiveCell > 0.3 Then
    FormatColor NewColor:=3
Else
    FormatColor NewColor:=2
End If
```

Because you pass the color as an argument to FormatColor, you can handle multiple colors without making any changes at all to the FormatColor subroutine.

2 Switch back to the SampleData worksheet, select the top cell in a column of random numbers, and try out the macro a few times.

213

When you use the block form of the If structure, you can add new conditions with new results by preceding each condition with the word *ElseIf*. Notice that *ElseIf* is all one word, with no space. When you have one or more statements you want to run if none of the preceding conditions is true, put them after the word *Else*.

Watch the value of the argument change

An expression is any combination of words and symbols that returns a value.

Sometimes while you are developing procedures, you need to know the value of a variable or argument. Visual Basic provides a tool that allows you to *watch* the value of an expression in your procedures.

1 Activate the FormatModule sheet, put the insertion point anywhere on the Sub FormatColor(NewColor) statement, and click the Toggle Breakpoint button.

Toggle Breakpoint button

2 Activate the SampleData worksheet, select a cell that contains a number, and click the Format Exceptions button.

When the FormatColor procedure starts to run, the Debug window appears for you to start stepping through the statements.

Instant Watch button

3 Select the word *NewColor* inside the parentheses and click the Instant Watch button on the Visual Basic toolbar.

The Instant Watch dialog box appears, showing you the current value of the expression *NewColor*. Depending on the value in the active cell, the number is 2, 3, 4, or 6.

4 Click the Add button.

The Instant Watch dialog box disappears, but nothing else seems to happen.

5 Click the Watch tab in the Debug window.

The Watch pane appears, replacing the Immediate pane. The NewColor expression appears in the left column, with its current value next to it.

 NOTE The Instant Watch button shows you the value of an expression *instantly*, but only for as long as the dialog box is displayed. Adding an expression to the Watch pane allows you to watch the value of the expression over time.

Resume Macro button

6 Click the Resume Macro button to let the macro finish, and then click the Format Exceptions button again. When the Debug window appears, look to see whether NewColor has a new value.

7 In the Code pane, select the breakpoint statement and click the Toggle Breakpoint button. Then click the Resume Macro button to let the macro finish.

Make constants easier to read

When you recorded setting the color of a cell, the macro recorder set both the color and the pattern of the cell. This is the statement the macro recorder generated to give the cell a solid pattern: *.Pattern = xlSolid*.

The word *xlSolid* represents the number 1. You could give a cell a solid pattern with the statement *.Pattern = 1*. But the word *xlSolid* is easier to interpret than the number 1. Excel supplies a long list of constants you can use when setting Excel object properties. (To see the list of constants you can use in Excel, open the Object Browser, select Excel from the Libraries/Workbooks list, select Constants from the Objects/Modules list, and look at the entries in the Methods/Properties list.)

When the FormatExceptions procedure calls FormatColor, it passes the new color as a number. You may forget that the number 3 corresponds to the color red. Excel does not have built-in constants for the color index numbers. But you can make your color index numbers readable the same way that Excel made the pattern number readable.

1 Activate the FormatModule sheet, and position the insertion point at the end of the *Sub FormatExceptions()* statement.

2 Press ENTER and then TAB.

3 Enter these new lines:

```
Const myWhite = 2
Const myRed = 3
Const myGreen = 4
Const myYellow = 6
```

To define a constant in Visual Basic, you use the word *Const* followed by the name you want to use for the constant, an equal sign, and the value for the constant. A constant is like a variable, except that you cannot change it later in the procedure. The only time you can assign a value to a constant is when you first define it. The difference between a constant and a variable is that a variable can change values, and a constant cannot.

NOTE You can use any name you want for the constant, but as with argument names, you should avoid names already used by Excel or Visual Basic. Visual Basic constants all have the prefix *vb* (in lowercase). Excel constants all have the prefix *xl*. You might want to decide upon a similar prefix for constants you define.

Once you have defined constants equal to the color index numbers you want to use, you can replace the numbers in the FormatExceptions procedure with constants that are easier to interpret.

4 In the statements that call FormatColor, change the constant 4 to **myGreen**, 6 to **myYellow**, 3 to **myRed**, and 2 to **myWhite**

When you're finished, FormatExceptions should look like this:

```
Sub FormatExceptions()
    Const myWhite = 2
    Const myRed = 3
    Const myGreen = 4
    Const myYellow = 6
    If ActiveCell > 0.8 Then
        FormatColor myGreen
    ElseIf ActiveCell > 0.5 Then
        FormatColor myYellow
    ElseIf ActiveCell > 0.3 Then
        FormatColor myRed
    Else
        FormatColor myWhite
    End If
    ActiveCell.Offset(1, 0).Select
End Sub
```

5 Activate the SampleData worksheet and try the revised macro. It should work exactly the same as before.

Clarify lists of conditions

The FormatExceptions macro distinguishes four conditions for formatting a cell. The conditions are all parallel—they all compare ActiveCell to various values.

When you have several ElseIf conditions in a row, it's hard to tell whether they contain unrelated tests or, as in this case, whether they compare different values to a single expression. When each comparison is a single expression, you can use a special *Select Case* structure to clarify the nature of the test.

1 Select the FormatModule sheet. In the FormatExceptions macro, select the If structure (the lines from the If statement through the End If statement):

```
Sub FormatExceptions()
    Const myWhite = 2
    Const myRed = 3
    Const myGreen = 4
    Const myYellow = 6
    If ActiveCell > 0.8 Then
        FormatColor myGreen
    ElseIf ActiveCell > 0.5 Then
        FormatColor myYellow
    ElseIf ActiveCell > 0.3 Then
        FormatColor myRed
    Else
        FormatColor myWhite
    End If
    ActiveCell.Offset(1, 0).Select
End Sub
```

—— Select these lines...

2 Type the following new lines:

```
Select Case ActiveCell
Case Is > 0.8
    FormatColor NewColor:=myGreen
Case Is > 0.5
    FormatColor NewColor:=myYellow
Case Is > 0.3
    FormatColor NewColor:=myRed
Case Else
    FormatColor NewColor:=myWhite
End Select
```

—— ...and replace them with these lines.

The Select Case structure begins with the words *Select Case* followed by the expression you are comparing. You can use Select Case only when you are comparing a single base expression (such as ActiveCell) against multiple possible values (such as the various percentages). Each part of the structure compares the base expression to a new value. You could read the first comparison section in this example as "In case the active cell is greater than 80%...." As with an If structure, you can use the word *Else* to catch all the other options: "In case the active cell is anything else..."

3 Activate the SampleData sheet and try out the macro.

It should work the same way it did before, and you might find the Select Case structure easier to understand.

Making decisions is an important task in almost all macro applications. In Visual Basic you can choose between an inline If statement, a block If structure—possibly with several ElseIf clauses — and a Select Case structure.

217

Returning Values from Procedures

A master procedure delegates tasks to subordinate procedures. Often the master procedure wants to get a job done: "Take care of formatting that cell." Sometimes the master procedure wants some research done: "Please figure out what the formatting of that cell should be." When the subordinate procedure carries out an action, you call the procedure a subroutine, and you use the word *Sub* to define it. When the subordinate procedure does research to return a value, you call the procedure a function, and you use the word *Function* to define it.

Create a research assistant

Creating a function is like creating a research assistant. The assistant does a lot of work and returns information to the supervisor.

1   Select the FormatModule sheet. Between the end of the FormatExceptions macro and the beginning of the FormatColor macro, enter these two statements:

```
Function ChooseColor()
End Function
```

You use the word *Function* along with the name of the function to begin a function, and you use the words *End Function* to end it.

2   In the FormatExceptions procedure, select all the lines from the first Const line through the End Select line, and click Cut on the Edit menu.

3   Paste the lines into the ChooseColor function, in front of the End Function statement.

The ChooseColor function should now look like this:

```
Function ChooseColor()
    Const myWhite = 2
    Const myRed = 3
    Const myGreen = 4
    Const myYellow = 6
    Select Case ActiveCell
    Case Is > 0.8
        FormatColor NewColor:=myGreen
    Case Is > 0.5
        FormatColor NewColor:=myYellow
    Case Is > 0.3
        FormatColor NewColor:=myRed
    Case Else
        FormatColor NewColor:=myWhite
    End Select
End Function
```

The ChooseColor function calculates the color for the active cell, but it should not call the FormatColor subroutine directly. Keep the subprocedures independent, to make them easy for other procedures to call.

NOTE The word *procedure* applies to both subroutines and functions. I will use the term *procedure* when the distinction between a subroutine and a function is not important. A procedure can be a subordinate procedure, a master procedure, or both at the same time. I will use the term *subprocedure* to refer to a procedure that is being called by another procedure.

In a function, you pass a value back to the calling procedure by assigning the value to the name of the function. In the new ChooseColor function, you need to replace the phrase *FormatColor NewColor:=* with *ChooseColor =*

4 Select any occurrence of the phrase *FormatColor NewColor:=* in the ChooseColor function, and then click Replace on the Edit menu.

The Replace dialog box appears, with the phrase *FormatColor NewColor:=* already entered in the Find What box. (If you have one or more words selected when you click Replace, the selected words become the default find value.)

To undo the changes made by Replace All, press CTRL+Z.

5 Type **ChooseColor =** in the Replace With box, select Procedure from the Look In list, and click Replace All. (If you are cautious, you can click the Replace button four times and then close the dialog box.)

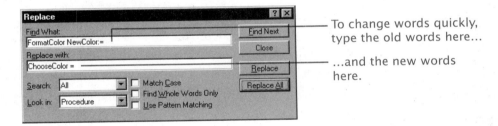

To change words quickly, type the old words here...

...and the new words here.

The ChooseColor function is now finished. It should look like this:

```
Function ChooseColor()
    Const myWhite = 2
    Const myRed = 3
    Const myGreen = 4
    Const myYellow = 6
    Select Case ActiveCell
    Case Is > 0.8
        ChooseColor = myGreen
    Case Is > 0.5
        ChooseColor = myYellow
    Case Is > 0.3
        ChooseColor = myRed
    Case Else
        ChooseColor = myWhite
    End Select
End Function
```

The ChooseColor function looks at the value in the active cell and calculates which color that cell should be.

The ChooseColor function should return the value to the FormatExceptions procedure. In a function, you return a value for the function by assigning the value to the name of the function. For example, the following function returns the value 5.

```
Function ThisFunction()
    ThisFunction = 5
End Function
```

The function uses the name of the function as if it were a variable.

Use the research assistant

The FormatExceptions procedure can now delegate the task of finding out the correct color to the ChooseColor function. FormatExceptions can then turn around and give that value to the FormatColor subroutine to implement.

1   In the FormatExceptions procedure, insert a new line right before the *ActiveCell.Offset(1, 0).Select* statement.

2   On the new line, type **FormatColor NewColor:=**

At this point, you would normally type 4, or myGreen, or some other color number. Instead, you want to use the value returned by the ChooseColor function.

3   Type **ChooseColor.**

The finished statement should be *FormatColor NewColor:=ChooseColor*

The finished FormatExceptions macro should look like this:

```
Sub FormatExceptions()
    FormatColor NewColor:=ChooseColor
    ActiveCell.Offset(1, 0).Select
End Sub
```

4   Activate the SampleData worksheet and test the macro. It should work the same way it did before.

Save the result from the function

When you click the Format Exceptions button, the FormatExceptions procedure delegates the task of calculating the appropriate color for the active cell to the ChooseColor function. It then turns around and delegates the task of formatting the cell to the FormatColor subroutine in the same statement. You might find delegating to only one subprocedure per statement less confusing. You can save the value returned by the ChooseColor function until you are ready to use it.

1   Select the FormatModule sheet. Insert a new line before the *FormatColor* statement in the Format Exceptions procedure.

2   In the new line, type **Let myColor = ChooseColor**

The Let statement accepts the result of the ChooseColor function and assigns that value to a name, myColor. In the statement on the previous page, the variable is myColor. You can use any name you want for the variable, but as with argument names and constants, you should avoid names already used by Excel or Visual Basic.

3 In the statement *FormatColor NewColor:=ChooseColor* (the next line down), replace the word *ChooseColor* with **myColor**

When you assign a value to a variable, you can then use the value later in the macro. Once you assign a value to myColor, you can use myColor as the argument value for the FormatColor subroutine.

The revised FormatExceptions procedure should look like this:

```
Sub FormatExceptions()
    Let myColor = ChooseColor
    FormatColor NewColor:=myColor
    ActiveCell.Offset(1, 0).Select
End Sub
```

4 Activate the SampleData worksheet and test the macro. It should work the same way it did before.

Make the subprocedures independent

All three procedures in the macro know that you are working with the active cell. The FormatExceptions procedure moves down one cell from the active cell to define a new active cell. The ChooseColor function analyzes the value of the active cell. The FormatColor subroutine formats the active cell. You can make subprocedures much more flexible and reusable if you make them get all the information they need from the master procedure. You use arguments to communicate from the master procedure to the subprocedures.

1 Select the FormatModule sheet. Between the parentheses in the *Function ChooseColor()* statement, type **TestValue**

The word *TestValue* is the name of an argument. This is what the ChooseColor function will call the test value it receives from the master procedure.

2 In the statement *Select Case ActiveCell* of the same procedure, replace the word *ActiveCell* with the word **TestValue**

Once you change the word *ActiveCell* to *TestValue*, the ChooseColor function no longer knows anything about how the test value was obtained.

3 In the FormatExceptions procedure, after the word *ChooseColor* type **(TestValue:=ActiveCell)**

When you pass arguments to the ChooseColor function, you must put parentheses around the arguments, because you will be assigning the value returned by the function to the variable myColor.

221

4 In the statement *Sub FormatColor(NewColor)*, immediately before the word *NewColor* type **NewCell,** (with the comma).

The word *NewCell* is the name that the FormatColor subroutine will use for the cell address that the master procedure will pass it. You don't need to use the same name for FormatColor's argument as for ChooseColor's argument because these two subprocedures are completely independent of each other.

5 In the statement *With Selection.Interior* in the same procedure, change the word *Selection* to **NewCell**

6 In the FormatExceptions procedure, after the statement *FormatColor NewColor:=myColor* type **,NewCell:=ActiveCell**

When you pass one or more arguments to a subroutine, you must *not* put parentheses around the arguments, because you do not use a return value from the subroutine. (A subroutine does not return a value.)

When you include the names of the arguments in the master procedure, you can put the arguments in any order you like. If you put the arguments in the order that they are defined in the subprocedure, you can leave out the names.

7 Activate the SampleData worksheet and test the macro. It should work the same way it did before.

The revised macro should look like this:

```
Sub FormatExceptions()
    myColor = ChooseColor(TestValue:=ActiveCell)
    FormatColor NewColor:=myColor, NewCell:=ActiveCell
    ActiveCell.Offset(1, 0).Select
End Sub

Function ChooseColor(TestValue)
    Const myWhite = 2
    Const myRed = 3
    Const myGreen = 4
    Const myYellow = 6
    Select Case TestValue
    Case Is > 0.8
        ChooseColor = myGreen
    Case Is > 0.5
        ChooseColor = myYellow
    Case Is > 0.3
        ChooseColor = myRed
    Case Else
        ChooseColor = myWhite
    End Select
End Function
```

```
Sub FormatColor(NewCell, NewColor)
    With NewCell.Interior
        .ColorIndex = NewColor
        .Pattern = xlSolid
    End With
End Sub
```

Use a function from a worksheet

One of the benefits of making a subprocedure work completely through the master procedure is that the subprocedure then becomes usable in a wide variety of contexts. Suppose, for example, that you want to call the ChooseColor function from a cell on the worksheet. Because the ChooseColor function gets information only from the procedure that calls it, and passes information back only as a return value, you can put the ChooseColor function directly into a worksheet cell, just as you do with Excel's standard functions such as SUM and PMT. For example, below the random cells you can create a block of cells that contains the appropriate color numbers for the random cells.

Excel's Function Wizard helps you enter built-in functions into cells on the worksheet. You can use the Function Wizard with the ChooseColor function as well.

1   Select cell A11 on the SampleData worksheet.

    You will enter a formula here to calculate the color for cell A1, and then you can fill that formula into a rectangle of cells.

2   Click the Function Wizard button on the Standard toolbar.

3   In Step 1, select User Defined from the Function Category list.

Function Wizard button

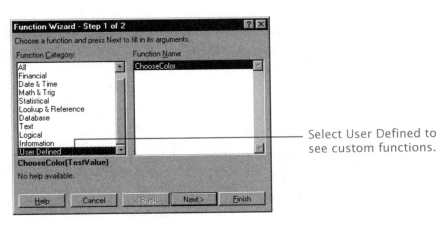

Select User Defined to see custom functions.

4   Select ChooseColor from the Function Name list, and click Next.

5   In Step 2, type **A1** in the box labeled TestValue, and click Finish.

223

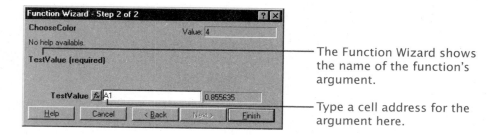

The Function Wizard shows the name of the function's argument.

Type a cell address for the argument here.

The color index number appropriate for the value in cell A1 appears in cell A11. The worksheet cell is taking the place of the master procedure and is calling the ChooseColor function.

6 Select the range A11:D18 on the SampleData worksheet. This is a range the same size and shape as the range of random numbers. This is where you want the color numbers for the sample values.

7 Press F2 to edit the cell with the formula, and then press CTRL+ENTER to fill the formula into the entire range.

8 Press F9 to calculate new random numbers.

As Excel recalculates the worksheet and creates new random numbers, it calls your function for each cell that changes. The color numbers change to match the values of the new random numbers.

When you have long, complex formulas on a worksheet, you can create custom functions so that you don't have to squeeze all the computations into a single worksheet cell.

Creating a function that you can use from a worksheet is exactly the same as creating a function that you can use from a master procedure in a macro. As long as you ensure that the function gets all the information it needs through arguments, and does nothing but return a result value, you can call the function from a worksheet cell.

Prevent spelling errors

When you need to use a name in Visual Basic—whether as a variable, an argument, or a constant—you just start using the name and Visual Basic takes care of all the housekeeping involved with setting up a storage location for the value in the variable and so forth. Because Visual Basic allows you to use new names at any time, starting to use names is easy. But creating new names any time you like is also dangerous—if you're the kind of person who has ever misspelled a name. See what happens when you do misspell a name, and also see how to fix it.

1 Select the FormatModule sheet. In the FormatExceptions procedure, in the statement *FormatColor NewColor:=myColor, NewCell:=ActiveCell* change the word *myColor* to **myColorr**, a simple enough typographical error.

2 Activate the SampleData worksheet, select the range containing the random numbers, click the arrow next to the Color button, and click None as the fill color.

3 Click cell A1, and try out the Format Exceptions button on several sample cells.

The macro turns every cell white.

The macro turns the cells white because Visual Basic assumed you meant to use a new variable when you used the word *myColorr*, and it put the initial value zero into the variable for you. Every time the FormatExceptions procedure calls the FormatColor subroutine, it passes the value zero as the color.

In this case, Visual Basic assumed you wanted to create a new variable. As far as Visual Basic was concerned, the procedure performed exactly as you intended.

4   Select the FormatModule sheet. At the very top of the module, enter the statement **Option Explicit** on a line all by itself.

The Option Explicit statement tells Visual Basic that you want to explicitly tell it the name of every variable you will use so that it can warn you if you misspell one of them. The Option Explicit statement applies only to the current module sheet.

5   Insert a new line below the Sub FormatExceptions() statement, and enter the statement **Dim myColor**

The word *Dim* tells Visual Basic that you want to *dimension* a word as a variable. When you put a word after the keyword *Dim*, you *declare* to Visual Basic that you intend to use that word as a variable. This is called *declaring a variable*, and the Dim statement is sometimes called a *variable declaration*.

The variable *myColor* is the only variable you need to declare. Both NewColor and NewCell are variables also, but since you used them as argument names for a function or subroutine, Visual Basic counts that as a declaration.

6   Activate the SampleData worksheet and try running the macro.

An error message appears informing you that there is a variable that is not defined. The word *myColorr* is not defined, and the Option Explicit statement requires you to explicitly declare all variables.

7   Click the OK button to go to the offending line in the procedure, correct the spelling, switch back to the worksheet, and try the macro again.

Spelling and typographical errors are so dangerous that you may want to consider always putting Option Explicit at the top of every module you create. You can tell Visual Basic to do that for you.

8   On the Tools menu, click Options, and click the Module General tab. Select the Require Variable Declaration check box, and click OK.

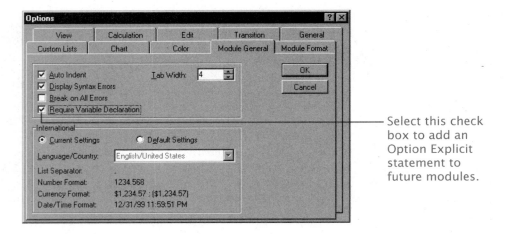

Select this check box to add an Option Explicit statement to future modules.

Setting the Require Variable Declaration check box does not put the Option Explicit statement into any existing modules, but it adds the statement to any modules you create in the future.

The top part of the module now looks like this:

```
Option Explicit
Sub FormatExceptions()
    Dim myColor
    Let myColor = ChooseColor(TestValue:=ActiveCell)
    FormatColor NewColor:=myColor, NewCell:=ActiveCell
    ActiveCell.Offset(1, 0).Select
End Sub
```

You have now learned how to delegate tasks from a master procedure to both functions and subroutines. Functions are very similar to subroutines. The only difference is that a function can return a value. The only real advantage to creating subroutines instead of functions is that the word *Sub* is shorter than the word *Function*, so you have fewer characters to type.

Lesson Summary

To	Do this	Button
Execute statements only if a condition is true	Insert the statements between If and End If statements.	
Test for different values of a single variable	Use a Select Case structure.	
Create a custom worksheet function	Create a function procedure that gets information from arguments and returns a value.	
Set a breakpoint	Select a statement and click the Toggle Breakpoint button.	

For online information about	From the Excel Help menu, choose Contents, choose Getting Started with Visual Basic, and then	
Creating procedures	Select the topic "Writing Procedures"	
Making decisions	Select the topic "Using Loops and Conditional Statements"	
Stepping through code and watching expressions	Select the topic "Debugging"	

Preview of the Next Lesson

This lesson was the first part of your exploration of Visual Basic tools. In the next lesson you will explore additional capabilities of Visual Basic, including creating different kinds of loops and watching for errors.

Explore Visual Basic Control Structures

Estimated time
40 min.

In this lesson you will learn how to:

- Use various loops in your procedures.
- Assign objects to variables.
- Handle run-time errors.
- Communicate with Microsoft Excel 4 macros.

Single-cell organisms are all small. Bacteria, amoebas, paramecia—none are even large enough to see with the naked eye. Large, sophisticated organisms require multiple cells. Cells give structure and add specialization to living things.

Recorded macros are like single-cell organisms. The macro recorder puts everything you do into a single procedure. Like single-cell organisms, single-procedure macros should be small. Large, sophisticated applications, however, require multiple procedures and control structures such as conditional statements and loops. Large, sophisticated applications require mechanisms for dealing with error conditions. In this lesson, you will learn more about Visual Basic control structures, the tools you need to make more sophisticated applications.

Start the lesson

> Start Microsoft Excel, open the workbook Lesson 10 that you created in Lesson 10, and save a new copy of it as **Lesson 11**.

Repeating Tasks

In Lesson 10, you learned how to have a master procedure delegate tasks to a subprocedure. To format all the cells in a block, however, you still needed to click the Format Exceptions button once for each cell.

In Lesson 3, you learned how to format exception cells for an entire range. In that lesson, you used a Do Loop structure to repeat statements in the macro until the macro reached a blank active cell. Visual Basic has tools specially designed for repeating statements in a loop. These tools are particularly useful when you repeat an action for each item in a collection, such as a range of cells.

Process all the cells in a range

When you instruct another human to format cells in a rectangular range, you don't say, "Look at the first cell in the first column, look at the second cell in the first column, look at the first cell in the second column," and so forth. You just say, "Look at each cell in the range." You can also tell Visual Basic to look at each cell in a range.

1   Activate the FormatModule sheet, which contains the FormatExceptions macro.

2   Create a new line after the *Dim myColor* statement, and type **Dim myCell**

   This declares the word *myCell* as a variable. You will use myCell to store the address of the current cell as you work through the range.

3   Create another new line, and enter the statement **For Each myCell in Selection**

You can use For Each with any collection, not just ranges.

   The For Each statement tells Visual Basic to put the first item in the collection into the variable myCell. In this case, the collection is the selected range. After the For Each statement runs, the variable myCell contains a single-cell Range object.

4   Change the word *ActiveCell* to **myCell** in the statements that call ChooseColor and FormatColor.

   Instead of using the ActiveCell property to refer to the active cell, the statements will now use the myCell variable, which contains a link to the first cell in the selected range as provided by the For Each statement.

5   Replace ActiveCell.Offset(1, 0).Select with **Next myCell**

   This statement tells Visual Basic to go back to the For Each statement, assign the next item (the next cell) from the collection (the selected range) to the variable myCell, and reexecute the statements inside the loop.

6   Indent the two statements between the For Each statement and the Next statement so that you can tell they are controlled by the loop.

7   Activate the SampleData worksheet, select the entire range of random numbers, and click the Format Exceptions button to test the macro.

The revised FormatExceptions procedure should look like this:

```
Sub FormatExceptions()
    Dim myColor
    Dim myCell
```

```
    For Each myCell in Selection
        myColor = ChooseColor(TestValue:=myCell)
        FormatColor NewColor:=myColor, NewCell:=myCell
    Next myCell
End Sub
```

Process the cells in a named range

Formatting all the exceptions in the range at once is much more convenient than formatting one cell at a time. But for the Format Exceptions button to work, you have to preselect the range of cells. If you give a name to the range you want to test, you can make the macro work even if you don't remember to preselect the range.

If you do not press ENTER after typing the name, Excel will not name the range.

1 On the SampleData worksheet, select the range of random numbers, type **NewValues** in the Reference area, and press ENTER to name the range.

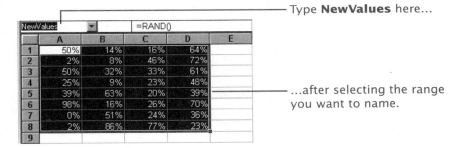

Type **NewValues** here...

...after selecting the range you want to name.

2 Activate the FormatModule sheet, and replace the word *Selection* with **Range("NewValues")**

You can use a named range as the argument to the Range method.

3 Activate the SampleData worksheet, and press F9 to calculate new random numbers.

4 Select any cell (do not select the range of random numbers) and click the Format Exceptions button to watch the macro format the numbers in the NewValues range.

When you create a macro using the macro recorder, the resulting code makes extensive use of the current selection. When you write procedures directly in Visual Basic, you can make the macro work independently of the current selection. The revised FormatExceptions procedure should now look like this:

```
Sub FormatExceptions()
    Dim myColor
    Dim myCell
    For Each myCell In Range("NewValues")
        myColor = ChooseColor(TestValue:=myCell)
        FormatColor NewColor:=myColor, NewCell:=myCell
    Next myCell
End Sub
```

Compare cells from two ranges

A For Each loop is perfect for working through all the cells in a range. Sometimes, however, you need to work through two parallel ranges. For example, suppose you have an old copy of the range of values and you want to compare the old values with the new ones. You need to work through both ranges simultaneously. A For Each loop cannot do that.

Visual Basic has another kind of loop, a For loop, that uses a counter to work through the loop. The loop counter allows you to look at the corresponding values of two ranges.

1 On the Insert menu, click Worksheet, and rename the new worksheet **Archive**

2 Activate the SampleData worksheet, select the NewValues range, and press CTRL+C to copy the range.

Percent Style button

3 Activate the Archive worksheet, click Paste Special on the Edit menu, select the Values option, and click OK. Then click the Percent Style button on the Formatting toolbar to format the numbers.

4 Give the name **OldValues** to the current selected range and press ENTER.

   The OldValues range is a frozen copy of the NewValues range.

5 Activate the SampleData worksheet, and press F9 to calculate new random numbers.

   After you recalculate, the numbers in the NewValues range are different from the numbers in the OldValues range. You can write a macro to highlight any new values that are greater than the corresponding old values.

Create a macro to compare two ranges

1 On the FormatModule sheet, insert a couple of blank lines above the FormatExceptions procedure, and then type in this new procedure:

```
Sub FormatDifferences()
    Dim myCellPtr
    For myCellPtr = 1 To Range("NewValues").Count
        If Range("NewValues").Cells(myCellPtr) _
                > Range("OldValues").Cells(myCellPtr) Then
            FormatColor _
                NewCell:=Range("NewValues").Cells(myCellPtr) _
                , NewColor:=3
        Else
            FormatColor _
                NewCell:=Range("NewValues").Cells(myCellPtr) _
                , NewColor:=2
        End If
    Next myCellPtr
End Sub
```

Here is an explanation of each line in the macro:

```
Sub FormatDifferences()
```

defines the new procedure.

```
Dim myCellPtr
```

tells Visual Basic that you will be using a variable named *myCellPtr* ("my cell pointer"). This variable will act as a loop counter.

The next line begins the For loop:

```
For myCellPtr = 1 To Range("NewValues").Count
```

You give the For loop the name of a variable (myCellPtr), a number to store in the variable as the initial value (1), and the highest value you ever want in the variable (the number of cells in the NewValues range). Each time this line runs, it increases the value of the variable by one, until the value of the variable is greater than the limit.

```
If Range("NewValues").Cells(myCellPtr) _
```

is the first part of the If statement. This statement is too long to print on a single line. The underscore at the end of the line tells Visual Basic to treat this line and the next as a single statement, as if the statement were typed on a single line.

```
> Range("OldValues").Cells(myCellPtr) Then
```

is the second statement of the If structure. This statement compares a single cell in the NewValues range with the corresponding cell in the OldValues range. When the value of myCellPtr is 5, for example, this statement compares the fifth item from the first collection with the fifth item from the second collection.

```
FormatColor _
    NewCell:=Range("NewValues").Cells(myCellPtr) _
        ,NewColor:= 3
```

is the statement you want to execute if the new value is greater than the old value. You want to tell the FormatColor subroutine to format the current cell in the NewValues range with a red color (color index number 3). Even though you originally wrote FormatColor as a subroutine for the FormatExceptions macro, you can call it from FormatDifferences as well because you made it able to run independently.

```
Else
```

means that any statements that follow should be executed only if the new value is *not* greater than the old value.

```
FormatColor _
  NewCell:=Range("NewValues").Cells(myCellPtr) _
        ,NewColor:=2
```

tells FormatColor to format the cell as white (color index number 2).

```
End If
```

closes the If structure; any statements that follow will execute, regardless of which cell value is greater.

```
Next myCellPtr
```

adds one to the loop counter variable (myCellPtr) and then tells Visual Basic to go back up to the For statement. The For statement then compares the variable to the limit (the count of cells in the range). As soon as the variable is greater than the limit, the procedure continues with the statement following the Next statement.

```
End Sub
```

ends the procedure.

Run Macro button

2   With the insertion point anywhere within the FormatDifferences procedure, click the Run Macro button on the Visual Basic toolbar.

Nothing in the macro assumes that any particular cell is selected, so you can run the macro from anywhere.

When the insertion point is *not* in a procedure, clicking the Run Macro button displays a list of macros. When the insertion point *is* in a procedure, clicking the Run Macro button runs the current procedure.

3   Activate the SampleData worksheet.

The numbers are formatted according to whether they are greater than the original values. (Deselect the range if necessary to see the new formatting.)

4   Hold down the CTRL key and click the Format Exceptions button to select it. While holding down the CTRL key, drag the button down a little to make a copy.

5   On the Tools menu, click Assign Macro, select FormatDifferences from the list of macro names, and click OK.

6   Type **Format Differences** as the label for the new button, and click a cell to deselect the button.

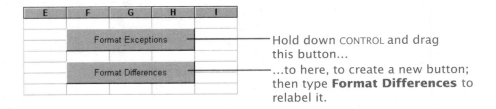

7   Press F9 to calculate new random numbers, and then click the Format Differences button so that you can watch the macro work.

Remember cell ranges

The FormatDifferences procedure accomplishes the desired task of comparing the old and new ranges, but it is more complicated than it needs to be. You use the expression *Range("NewValues")* four times. Each time you use *Range("NewValues")*, Excel has to go find the name *NewValues*, figure out which range it refers to, and establish a link to that Range object. Since the expression is inside a loop, Excel ends up establishing a new link to the Range object dozens of times. You can let the FormatDifferences procedure establish the link to the Range object once, and then have the procedure store that link in a variable to use for the rest of the procedure.

1 Activate the FormatModule sheet.

2 After the statement *Dim myCellPtr*, enter the statement **Dim myNew** and press ENTER. Then enter the statement **Dim myOld**

These statements declare these two names as variables.

3 Press ENTER to get a new line, and type **Set myNew = Range("NewValues")**

This statement assigns the Range object for the range named *NewValues* to the variable *myNew*. The word *Set* tells Visual Basic to assign the link to the object (not just the current value of the object) to the variable.

 NOTE In early versions of Basic, when assigning an ordinary value, such as a text string or a number, to a variable, you had to use the keyword *Let*. For example, *Let myValue = 5*. In Visual Basic, because assigning a value is so common, you do not need to use the keyword Let. When you assign an object (that is, a link to an object) to a variable, however, you do use the keyword *Set*. Whenever you see a value assigned to a variable, imagine that the keyword *Let* is at the beginning of the statement. When you assign an object to a variable don't just imagine that the keyword *Set* is at the beginning.

---

4 Press ENTER to get a new line, and type **Set myOld = Range("OldValues")**

5 Without moving the insertion point, click Replace on the Edit menu.

6 Type **Range("NewValues")** in the Find What box, type **myNew** in the Replace With box, select the word *Down* from the Search list, select the word *Procedure* from the Look In list, and click Replace All. This replaces the four subsequent occurrences of the expression *Range("NewValues")* in the procedure with the new variable name.

Click No when asked if you want to start searching from the beginning.

7 In the line > *Range("OldValues").Cells(myCellPtr)* select the expression *Range("OldValues")* and replace it with **myOld**

A Range object can be a collection of cells, of columns, or of rows. If you don't use the Columns method or the Rows method to specify which type of collection, a Range object behaves like a collection of cells. This means that you can also eliminate the use of the Cells method after the Range objects.

235

8   On the Edit menu, click Replace. Type **.Cells** in the Find What box, clear the Replace With box, select All from the Search list, select Procedure from the Look In list, and click Replace All.

The comparison statement and the two FormatColor statements are now short enough to fit on a single line.

9   Position the insertion point immediately before the underscore character in the comparison statement, hold down the SHIFT key, click immediately before the first character in the next line, and press DELETE to join the lines. Repeat for the two FormatColor statements.

10   Activate the SampleData worksheet, recalculate the random numbers, and test the revised macro.

The simplified macro should look like this:

```
Sub FormatDifferences()
    Dim myCellPtr
    Dim myNew
    Dim myOld
    Set myNew = Range("NewValues")
    Set myOld = Range("OldValues")
    For myCellPtr = 1 To myNew.Count
        If myNew(myCellPtr) > myOld(myCellPtr) Then
            FormatColor NewCell:=myNew(myCellPtr), NewColor:=3
        Else
            FormatColor NewCell:=myNew(myCellPtr), NewColor:=2
        End If
    Next myCellPtr
End Sub
```

Share the constants

The FormatDifferences procedure uses the number constants 3 and 2 to tell FormatColor which colors to use. The ChooseColor function has constants named for these colors, but FormatDifferences cannot use them because those constants apply only within the ChooseColor procedure. You can make the constants available to all the procedures in the current module.

1   Activate the FormatModule sheet.

2   In the ChooseColor function, select the block of Const lines, and press CTRL+X to cut them.

3   Move the insertion point to the beginning of the line following *Option Explicit*, and press CTRL+V to paste the constants.

4   Change the numbers in the FormatDifferences procedure to the color constant names, and test the macro.

When you use Const or Dim inside a procedure—that is, after the procedure's name—the constants or variables you declare are valid only within that one procedure. When you put declarations outside of any procedures, the constants and variables become available to every procedure in the module.

Handling Errors

Believe it or not, computer programs do not always work perfectly. Every now and then you may actually write a macro that doesn't do quite exactly what you want. Errors come in several different types:

Syntax errors   These are mistakes such as using an opening quotation mark and leaving off the closing quotation mark. When you type a statement into a procedure, the Visual Basic editor checks the statement for syntax errors as soon as you leave the statement.

Compiler errors   Some mistakes cannot be detected on a single-line basis. For example, you might start a For Each loop but forget to put a Next statement at the end. The first time you try to run a procedure, Visual Basic translates that procedure (along with all the other procedures in the module) into internal computer language. Translating to computer language is called *compiling*, and errors that Visual Basic detects while translating are called *compiler errors*. Syntax errors and compiler errors are usually easy to find and fix.

Logic errors   The computer can never detect some mistakes. For example, if you mean to change a workbook caption to "My Workbook", and you accidentally spell the caption "My Werkbook", the computer will never complain. Or if you compare the new values with the wrong copy of the old values, the computer won't find the error for you. You can toggle breakpoints, step through the procedures, and watch values, but you still have to find the problem.

Run-time errors   Sometimes a statement in a procedure works most of the time but fails under certain conditions. For example, you might refer to a named range on a worksheet. As long as the name exists, the statement works. If, however, you delete the range name, Visual Basic doesn't know what else to do but quit with an error message. These errors cannot be detected until you run the procedure, so they are called *run-time* errors. This section will show you how to handle run-time errors gracefully.

Cause an error

1   On the FormatModule sheet, in the statement *Set myNew = Range("NewValues")*, change *"NewValues"* to **"NweValues"**, which is an error.

Run Macro button

2   Click the Run Macro button to run the macro.

An error message appears, informing you that the Range method did not work. You would prefer to have the macro give you a descriptive warning and quit without offering potentially confusing options.

3   Click the End button to dismiss the error message.

Respond to the error

You can tell Visual Basic not to halt when it discovers a run-time error. Instead, when an error occurs, Visual Basic can set a special variable, named Err, to a nonzero number. Your procedure can then check to see if Err contains a nonzero number.

1   Insert a line after the statement *Dim myOld*, and enter the statement **On Error Resume Next** Put a blank line above and below the new statement so that you can see it better.

This statement tells Visual Basic that if it encounters a run-time error, it should just assign an Error value to the variable Err and continue with the next statement.

2   Insert a new line after the *Set myNew = Range("NweValues")* statement, and enter these four new lines:

```
If Err <> 0 Then
    MsgBox Prompt:="Undefined range name"
    End
End If
```

If no error has occurred, the built-in Err variable is equal to zero. If an error has occurred, Err will be a nonzero value. MsgBox is a built-in Visual Basic function that displays a message; you use the Prompt argument to tell MsgBox what to display. The keyword End means to stop the macro.

3   Copy the four new lines and insert them below the statement *Set myOld = Range("OldValues")* because this statement could fail as well if someone deleted the OldValues range name.

4   Click the Run Macro button.

The macro still quits, but this time it displays your descriptive message rather than the standard error message.

Run Macro button

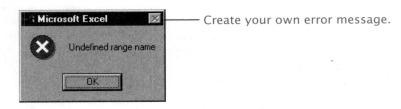
Create your own error message.

5   Click OK.

The FormatDifferences procedure should now look like this:

```
Sub FormatDifferences()
    Dim myCellPtr
    Dim myNew
    Dim myOld

    On Error Resume Next

    Set myNew = Range("NweValues")
    If Err <> 0 Then
        MsgBox Prompt:="Undefined range name"
        End
    End If
```

```
        Set myOld = Range("OldValues")
        If Err <> 0 Then
            MsgBox Prompt:="Undefined range name"
            End
        End If
        For myCellPtr = 1 To myNew.Count
            If myNew(myCellPtr) > myOld(myCellPtr) Then
                FormatColor NewCell:=myNew(myCellPtr), NewColor:=myRed
            Else
                FormatColor NewCell:=myNew(myCellPtr), NewColor:=myWhite
            End If
        Next myCellPtr
End Sub
```

 WARNING   If you don't check the Err value after a statement, the procedure continues with the next statement. Sometimes you don't care whether a statement had an error. For example, your procedure may delete a file from the hard disk to make sure the file is not there. You don't care if the delete fails. The Err variable, however, remembers the error. The next time you check for an error, you may think an error has occurred because of the previous statement. If you intentionally ignore a possible error, reset the Err variable to zero by adding the statement *Err = 0* immediately after the statement where the error might have occurred.

Trap an error

You can usually create more meaningful error messages than the standard ones Visual Basic displays. And if you need to put in only a few checks for common problems, adding a few error-checking statements here and there is not a bad solution. But you may not be happy with the prospect of adding four or more error-checking statements after every working statement in a procedure.

One solution would be to write a subroutine named *CheckError* that checks the Err value and, if it is not zero, displays a message along with the error value, and then quits. In this scenario you would need to enter CheckError only after each statement you want to check. Visual Basic gives you an even better solution, however. You can tell Visual Basic just once to check the error value after each statement and go to your display error message procedure only if the error value is not zero.

1   Replace the statement *On Error Resume Next* with **On Error Goto HandleError**

This tells Visual Basic to check the Err value after each statement and to go to a special place in the procedure that you will name *HandleError*. (You can use any name you want for the name of the error handler.)

2   Immediately above the *End Sub* statement at the bottom of the FormatDifferences procedure, insert a new line and type **Exit Sub**

239

You have to put the instructions for handling errors inside the same procedure as the On Error Goto statement, but you must also stop the regular procedure before it gets to those instructions. The statement *Exit Sub* is the way to quit a subroutine before reaching the End Sub statement.

3 On the next line, type **HandleError:**

This must be the same name you used in the On Error Goto statement above, and it must be followed by a colon (:). This name is called a *label*. The only time you should ever need to use a label in a procedure is when creating error-handling instructions.

4 On the next line, press TAB, and then type **Dim Msg** to let Visual Basic know you intend to use a variable named *Msg*.

5 On the next line, type **Msg = "Error: " & Err**

This puts the text string *Error:* into the variable Msg and then tacks the error number that Visual Basic will supply to the variable Err onto the end.

6 On the next line, type **Msg = Msg & " - " & Error()**

This takes the current value of the variable Msg, adds a hyphen, and then adds a descriptive message for the most recent error, which is supplied by the Visual Basic function named *Error*. The variable Msg is then redefined using this new composite text string.

7 On the next line, type **MsgBox Prompt:=Msg**

This displays the message you pieced together. If you want, you can also add other information to the message, such as "Please contact Tex Miller for assistance," by using the ampersand (&) again.

8 On the next line, type **End** This quits the macro, which is what you want to do in case of a run-time error.

9 Remove the error-checking lines you inserted earlier after assigning the two ranges to variables.

10 Click the Run Macro button to see if the error handler takes care of the error properly.

Run Macro button

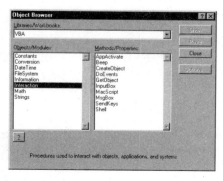

11 Click OK. Then change the misspelled *"NweValues"* to the correct **"NewValues"** and click the Run Macro button again.

The macro should run without a complaint.

The revised FormatDifferences procedure should now look like this:

```
Sub FormatDifferences()
    Dim myCellPtr
    Dim myNew
    Dim myOld

    On Error Goto HandleError

    Set myNew = Range("NewValues")
    Set myOld = Range("OldValues")
    For myCellPtr = 1 To myNew.Count
        If myNew(myCellPtr) > myOld(myCellPtr) Then
            FormatColor NewCell:=myNew(myCellPtr), NewColor:=myRed
        Else
            FormatColor NewCell:=myNew(myCellPtr), NewColor:=myWhite
        End If
    Next myCellPtr
Exit Sub
HandleError:
    Dim Msg
    Msg = "Error: " & Err
    Msg = Msg & " - " & Error()
    MsgBox Prompt:=Msg
    End
End Sub
```

Dealing with run-time errors is always a difficult part of a programming task. The error-trapping facilities of Visual Basic are a little tricky to set up, but having Visual Basic watch for errors for you is much better than adding a block of error-checking code after each statement.

Exploring Visual Basic Reference Tools

The word *MsgBox* is a Visual Basic function. The word *Error()* is a Visual Basic function. What are Visual Basic functions? In addition to the methods and properties that are available for Excel objects, Visual Basic has its own set of procedures that you can utilize in your macros. How can you learn about them? How can you use them?

In Part 3 of this book, you learned how to use the Object Browser and online Help to find out about Excel objects. You can also use these reference tools to find out about built-in Visual Basic procedures you can call from your macros.

Find Visual Basic procedures in the Object Browser

Object Browser button

1 Activate the FormatModule sheet and click the Object Browser button.

2 Select VBA from the Libraries/Workbooks list.

The Objects/Modules list changes to show categories of common tasks. These are categories of tasks for which Visual Basic has built-in procedures you can use.

The first category in the list is Constants. When you select the Constants category, the list on the right does not actually include procedures. Rather, this is a list of names you can use as arguments with Visual Basic procedures to make your code easier to read. The list of Visual Basic constants is included in the Object Browser for your convenience, just as the list of Excel constants is.

At the bottom of the Object Browser dialog box is a brief description of the selected item.

3 Select the Interaction category from the Objects/Modules list.

The selections in the Methods/Properties list change, and the text at the bottom of the dialog box describes the type of procedures in this category.

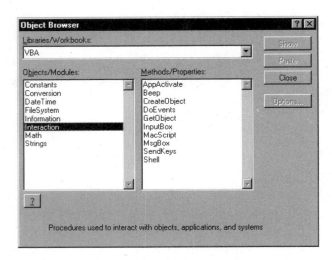

The MsgBox function you used in this lesson and the InputBox function you used in Lesson 2 are in the list of procedures for the Interaction category.

4 Select MsgBox from the Methods/Properties list.

The description at the bottom of the dialog box explains what the MsgBox function does, and above that is a list of the arguments you may want to use with the MsgBox function. Once you find the Visual Basic procedure you want in the Methods/Properties list, you can click the Paste button to insert the procedure name into your module in the same way that you can paste an Excel method or property.

Find Visual Basic procedures in Help

The Object Browser gives only a brief description of each Visual Basic procedure, along with a list of the procedure's arguments. You can get more detailed information about the procedure in online Help.

1 With the MsgBox function selected in the Object Browser, click the ? (question mark) button at the bottom of the dialog box.

The MS Excel Visual Basic Help window appears, displaying the MsgBox Function topic.

The topics for Visual Basic procedures in Help are very similar to the topics for Excel methods and properties.

2   Click the Help Topics button, click the Contents tab if necessary, scroll to the bottom of the list, and double-click the Microsoft Excel Visual Basic Reference heading.

Under the Microsoft Excel Visual Basic Reference heading are five subheadings. Three of the subheadings—Methods, Objects, and Properties—pertain to Excel objects and their methods and properties. The remaining two subheadings—Functions and Statements—pertain to Visual Basic.

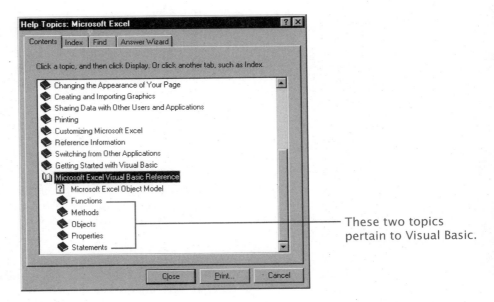

These two topics pertain to Visual Basic.

3   Double-click the Functions heading to display a list of the letters in the alphabet, then double-click the heading for the letter *M* to see a list that includes the MsgBox function.

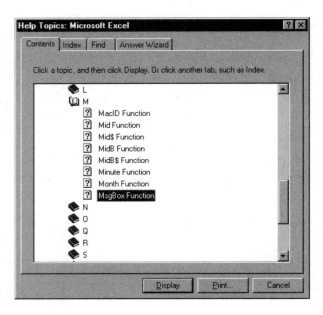

The lists of functions and statements are very similar to the lists of topics for Excel objects, methods, and properties.

NOTE When you create a Visual Basic procedure, you make it either a subroutine or a function. A subroutine is like a function except that it never returns a value. In the Visual Basic Help system, the word *Statement* essentially refers to what you would write as a subroutine: a procedure that never returns a value.

All the keywords in Visual Basic appear in Help as either functions or statements. The keywords MsgBox, InputBox, and Error are functions. The keywords Sub, If, End If, Do, Loop, and For Each are all listed as statements.

Visual Basic also includes some tools you can utilize that are neither statements nor functions. For example, the ampersand (&) that joins two text strings is neither a statement nor a function; it is an operator. You can find information about operators in Help also.

4 Click the Index tab in the Help Topics dialog box, and type **Operators** in the top box to display a list of the operators available in Excel and Visual Basic.

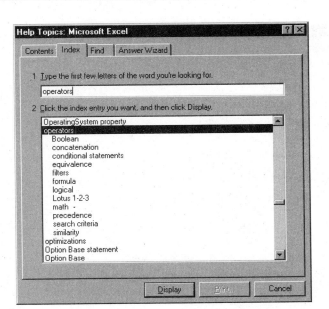

5 Double-click the word *Concatenation* to display the two concatenation operators.

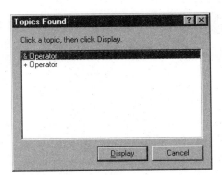

NOTE In earlier versions of Basic, the + operator was used for both addition and concatenation. The + operator topic includes this suggestion: "Although you can also use the + operator to concatenate two character strings, you should use the & operator for concatenation."

6 Select the *& Operator* topic and click Display to see the full Help topic.

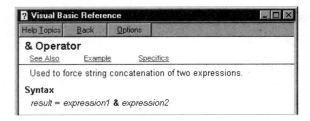

7 Close the Help window to return to the Object Browser.

8 Click the Close button to close the Object Browser.

In Lesson 13 you will learn how to control Microsoft Word from Visual Basic.

Excel and Visual Basic are two separate tools. Excel is like a home entertainment system. You can operate the system interactively or with remote controls. Visual Basic procedures are like the guy on the couch, running the remote controls that operate Excel. You can use Visual Basic to control Excel or to control other applications that can respond to the kinds of commands Visual Basic can give.

Excel exposes its capabilities to Visual Basic through objects, with their methods and properties. Visual Basic also has its own collection of procedures—statements, functions, and other keywords. You can use the Object Browser and the Help system to learn about objects, properties, and methods for Excel, and to learn about statements, functions, and other keywords for Visual Basic.

Communicating with Old-Style Macros

If you have existing applications written in Microsoft Excel 4 macros, you may need to integrate the Excel 4 macros with Visual Basic procedures.

Call an old-style command macro

The sample macros in this section are in the Lesson 11 file in the Finished folder on the disk that comes with this book.

Here is a simple Excel 4 command macro. It takes an argument and displays the value of the argument in an alert box, but it does not return a value.

Excel4Command
Call this command from Visual Basic
=ARGUMENT("Prompt")
=ALERT(Prompt)
=RETURN()

Here is a Visual Basic procedure that calls the Excel4Command macro, passing "Hello, Excel" as an argument:

```
'Call Excel4 Style Command Macro
Sub RunExcel4Command()
    Run "Excel4Command", "Hello, Excel"
End Sub
```

Use the Run method to call an Excel 4 command macro. Pass the name of the macro as the first argument, and pass any arguments for the macro as additional arguments.

Call an old-style function macro

Here is a simple Excel 4 function macro. It prompts you for your name and then returns your name to the calling procedure.

Excel4Function
Call this function from Visual Basic
=RETURN(INPUT("What is your name?",2))

Here is a Visual Basic procedure that can call the Excel4Function macro, displaying in a message box the name passed back from the function:

```
'Call Excel4 Style Function Macro
Sub RunExcel4Function()
    Dim Answer
    Answer = Run("Excel4Function")
    MsgBox Answer
End Sub
```

You use the Run method to run an Excel 4 function macro, the same way you run an Excel 4 command macro. The return value from the Excel 4 macro becomes the return value of the Run method. When you use the return value from the Run method, enclose all the arguments in parentheses.

Call a Visual Basic subroutine from an old-style macro

Here is a simple Visual Basic subroutine. Like the Excel4Command macro, it takes an argument and displays that argument in a message box:

```
'Call this Command from Excel4 Style Macro
Sub BasicCommand(Prompt)
    MsgBox Prompt
End Sub
```

Here is an Excel 4 macro that can run the BasicCommand subroutine, passing "Hello, Visual Basic" as an argument:

RunBasicCommand
This calls Visual Basic Command
=BasicCommand("Hello, Visual Basic")
=RETURN()

To call a Visual Basic subroutine from an Excel 4 macro, you enter the name of the subroutine as a function, and you include any arguments in parentheses.

247

Call a Visual Basic function from an old-style macro

Here is a simple Visual Basic function. Like the Excel4Function macro, it prompts you for your name and then returns that name as its return value.

```
'Call this Function from Excel4 Style Macro
Function BasicFunction()
    BasicFunction = InputBox("What is your name?")
End Function
```

Here is an Excel 4 macro that can run the BasicFunction function, displaying the result of the function in an alert box:

RunBasicFunction
This calls Visual Basic Function
=ALERT(BasicFunction())
=RETURN()

To call a Visual Basic function from an Excel 4 macro, you enter the name of the function as a function. The Visual Basic function is indistinguishable from a built-in function.

The fact that Excel 4 macros and Visual Basic procedures can communicate directly with each other makes it possible for you to gradually transition old applications to Visual Basic. If you are already comfortable writing Excel 4 macros, you can continue to be productive developing and supporting Excel 4 macros as you build expertise with Visual Basic.

Lesson Summary

To	Do this
Execute statements for each item in a collection	Insert the statements between a For Each statement and a Next statement.
Create a loop that uses a counter variable to keep track of the position in the loop	Use a For statement with a Next statement.
Assign an object to a variable	Use the Set keyword to make the assignment.
Cause Visual Basic to ignore errors so that you can check for an error after each statement	Use the statement *On Error Resume Next*.
Cause Visual Basic to run the statements starting on a line labeled ErrorHandler	Use the statement *On Error Goto ErrorHandler*.
Call an Excel 4 macro from a Visual Basic procedure	Use the Run statement.
Call a Visual Basic procedure from an Excel 4 macro	Use the procedure name as if it were a built-in function.

For online information about	From the Excel Help menu, choose Contents, choose Getting Started with Visual Basic, and then
Using loops	Select the topic "Using Loops and Conditional Statements"
Handling errors	Select the topic "Debugging"

Preview of the Next Lesson

You now have had a broad overview of Excel objects and Visual Basic procedures. In the next three lessons, you will put these skills to work building an application that solves a practical business problem, using the skills you have learned in Parts 3 and 4. In Lesson 12, you will write procedures that automate the production of some standard reports.

Building an Application

Part

5

Build a Report Generator

Estimated time

40 min.

In this lesson you will learn how to:

■ Use variables to store objects.

■ Control PivotTables and charts from procedures.

It's spring cleaning time. The shelves in your bedroom closet have been accumulating various treasures for some time now. You just hope you never have to find anything. Or remove anything.

But now it's time to clean it up. At first, as you remove item after item, placing them all in various piles on the floor and on the bed, the mess just gets worse. Occasionally you find a delightful surprise, such as the wide angle lens for your camera that you needed last month at the reunion, or the letter from your sister that has her new address so that you can return the book you borrowed last year. Finally, as you find boxes and files and new shelves for all the piles, the room returns to normal.

Everything is much as it was before you started. The room is clean and the treasures are in the closet. But now you are not afraid to open the closet door.

When you first create macros using the macro recorder, as you did in Parts 1 and 2 of this book, you may look at the recorded macro as you would a cluttered closet: you don't dare touch anything inside. When you first explore Microsoft Excel objects and Visual Basic structures, as you did in Parts 3 and 4 of this book, you may feel as if you are in the middle of spring cleaning: you find occasional treasures, but the piles around the room are unusable. Now you're ready to organize the closet, to put the concepts to work, to solve real-world problems, to modify recorded macros and write new procedures with confidence.

In this lesson you will create a macro that automates creating reports, in Lesson 13 you will add macros to communicate with Microsoft Word and a database, and in Lesson 14 you will package the macros into an easy-to-use application.

Start the lesson

▶ Start Microsoft Excel and open the Lists workbook. Save the workbook as **Lesson 12**.

Creating Reports from a Database

Miller Textiles has a planning meeting at the beginning of every month to discuss the previous month's orders. You are responsible for bringing order information for key market segments to the meeting. After the meeting, your manager usually asks you to put together a document with tables and charts, along with comments and explanations of unusual order activity.

You want to build a macro that will allow you to select the order information you want easily. You also want the macro to put selected charts and tables directly into a word processing file so that you can easily add explanatory text. Eventually, you want to refine the macro so that others in the company can use it even if you are not around.

Creating the Report by Hand

The reports you create for the planning meeting all look basically the same: order units and dollars summarized in a table illustrated with a chart. If you create the report once, by hand, you can then create a macro to modify the report for the different market segments you need to analyze. For the first report, you will extract the most recent month's orders from the database, create a PivotTable, and then create a chart.

Create a database extract

1 Insert a new worksheet and rename it **Extract**

If the Get External Data command is not on the Data menu, rerun the Excel Setup program and select the External Data option.

2 Select cell A1, and on the Data menu, click Get External Data.

The Microsoft Query application opens, displaying the Select Data Source dialog box.

Query is a separate application that comes bundled with Excel. Query can retrieve data from any external database that has an Open Database Connectivity (ODBC) driver available. In Lesson 5, you accessed the Query application directly from the PivotTable Wizard. In this lesson, you use Query to retrieve selected records from the database.

3 Double-click Miller Textiles in the Select Data Sources dialog box and then double-click the Orders.dbf table in the Add Tables dialog box and click Close.

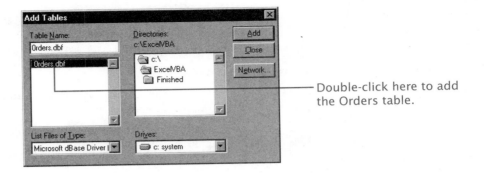

Double-click here to add
the Orders table.

NOTE If Miller Textiles is not listed in the Select Data Sources dialog box,
follow the instructions in the section "Set up the database as a data source"
at the beginning of Lesson 5. Then click Other to get the ODBC Data Sources
dialog box and double-click Miller Textiles in that list.

A window appears that allows you to select the data you want.

4 In the list of fields from the Orders table, double-click the asterisk (*) to add all the
fields to the query, and then delete the columns labeled List and Gross. (Click
each column heading and press DELETE.)

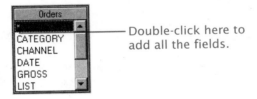

Double-click here to
add all the fields.

5 Click the heading for the Date column, and click Add Criteria on the Criteria
menu.

6 In the Add Criteria dialog box, type **2/1/96** in the Value box, click the Add
button, and then click the Close button.

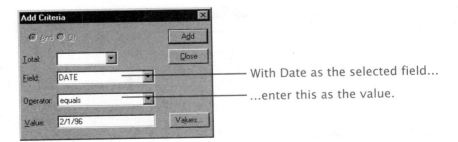

With Date as the selected field...

...enter this as the value.

255

The query now contains the Date, State, Channel, Category, Price, Units, and Net columns for the records from February 1996.

7 On the File menu, click Return Data To Microsoft Excel.

The Get External Data dialog box appears.

8 Clear the Keep Query Definition check box, select the Include Field Names check box, and click OK. Click OK again to get rid of the warning that appears.

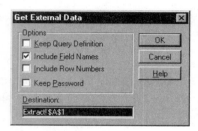

The result of the query fills into the worksheet. The dates look strange, but don't worry about it. The PivotTable will understand that these are dates. This range is an intermediate extract range from which you will supply data to a PivotTable.

9 While the retrieved range is still selected, type **Database** in the Reference area to the left of the formula bar and press ENTER to name the range. Then select cell A1.

The Database range on the Extract worksheet now contains the order information you want to analyze.

Create a tabular report

The PivotTable Wizard is the easiest way to make a summary table from the database extract.

1 On the Data menu click the PivotTable command, and in the first two steps of the PivotTable Wizard, click Next, accepting the default options.

2 In Step 3 of the PivotTable Wizard, drag the Category field tile and the Date field tile to the Page area, drag the State field tile to the Row area, and drag the Units field tile and the Net field tile to the Data area. Then click Next.

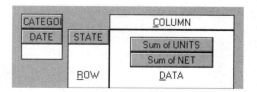

3 In Step 4, clear the PivotTable Starting Cell box, type **ReportTable** as the name for the PivotTable, clear both Grand Totals check boxes, clear the AutoFormat Table check box, and click Finish.

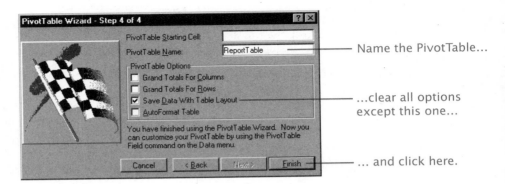

Name the PivotTable...

...clear all options except this one...

... and click here.

If you leave the AutoFormat Table check box selected, the PivotTable Wizard will adjust the column widths of the table each time you refresh or modify the PivotTable. You don't want that to happen for this report.

4 Drag the Data field tile below the word *Total* to display the unit and net dollar columns side by side.

	A	B	C	D
1	CATEGOR	(All)		
2	DATE	(All)		
3				
4	STATE	Data	Total	
5	AZ	Sum of UN	2273	
6		Sum of NE	6813.52	
7	CA	Sum of UN	2745	
8		Sum of NE	7506.84	

Drag the Data tile...

...under the Total heading to rearrange the PivotTable.

5 Change the name of the worksheet with the PivotTable to **Report**

This is essentially the tabular report you will present at the planning meeting. You can make the table easier to understand by enhancing its formatting.

Format the report table

1 Select the cell with the Data field tile, and click the Row, Hide command on the Format menu.

	A	B	C	D
1	CATEGOR	(All)		
2	DATE	(All)		
3				
4		Data		
5	STATE	Sum of UN	Sum of NET	
6	AZ	2273	6813.52	
7	CA	2745	7506.84	

Select this cell, and then hide the row.

257

*PivotTable
Wizard button*

2   Select any cell within the PivotTable, click the PivotTable Wizard button on the
Query And Pivot toolbar (or click PivotTable on the Data menu), and double-click
the field labeled Sum Of Net in the PivotTable Wizard dialog box.

3   In the PivotTable Field dialog box, replace the name *Sum of Net* with **Net $** and
click the Number button.

4   In the Format Cells dialog box, select Currency from the Category list, change the
Decimal Places value to 0, click OK to return to the PivotTable Field dialog box,
and then click OK again to return to the PivotTable Wizard.

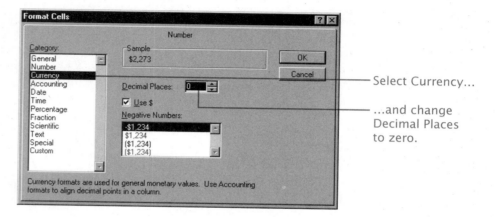

Select Currency...

...and change
Decimal Places
to zero.

You can format the cells of a PivotTable on the worksheet using standard cell
formatting tools, but if you do, the PivotTable Wizard will clear the formatting
each time you modify or refresh the PivotTable. If you define the number format
within the PivotTable Wizard, the cells will retain the correct formatting.

5   Double-click the field tile labeled Sum Of Units, and replace the name with **Units**
followed by a space. (Do not press ENTER.)

You cannot use a field name from the database as the name for a data field.
Adding a space to the end of the field name, however, satisfies the PivotTable
Wizard's requirement for a unique name.

6   Click the Number button, select Number from the Category list, change the
Decimal Places value to 0, select the Use 1000 Separator check box, click OK, and
click OK again to get back to the PivotTable Wizard. Click Finish to recalculate
the PivotTable.

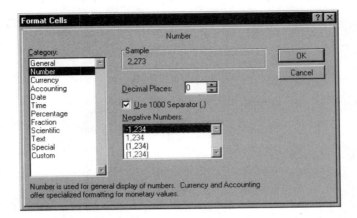

7 In the Category list, select Dinosaurs, and in the Date list, select 2/1/96.

The PivotTable is now easier to understand.

 NOTE The Date field shows the month for the current report. Since the database extract contains only values for February, the report displays the same values whether you choose 2/1/96 or (All). Explicitly showing the date, however, eliminates the need to put a separate date heading on the report.

Chart the information

Tables of numbers are almost always easier to understand if the numbers can also be seen in chart form.

ChartWizard button

3-D Column option

1 Drag from cell A12 through cell C5. This range contains the values you want to chart.

2 Click the ChartWizard button, hold down the ALT key as you drag to snap a rectangle to the corners of the range D1:H12, and click Next in the first step of the ChartWizard.

3 In Step 2 of the ChartWizard, select the 3-D Column option, and click Next.

4 In Step 3 of the ChartWizard, select option 5, and click Finish to create the chart.

	A	B	C	D	E	F	G	H	I
1	CATEGOR	Dinosau							
2	DATE	2/1/96							
3									
5	STATE	Units	Net $						
6	AZ	705	$1,918						
7	CA	420	$1,005						
8	ID	115	$443						
9	NV	525	$1,652						
10	OR	495	$1,555						
11	UT	660	$1,711						
12	WA	1,132	$2,275						
13									

5 Select from cell A12 to H1, and then type **ReportRange** in the Reference area and press ENTER to name the range.

When you view different market segments with the PivotTable, the chart will change to reflect the new table information.

Create reports for market segments

Change the definitions in the PivotTable to create reports for different market segments.

1 Click Seattle in the Category box in cell B1.

This changes the page item in the PivotTable. The values in the table and the chart change appropriately. With a PivotTable, changing from one page to another is very easy. But what if you want to change which field is in the Page area?

2 Select any cell in the PivotTable.

PivotTable Wizard button

3 Click the PivotTable Wizard button, drag the Category field tile away from the Page area, drag the State field tile from the Row area to the Page area (above the Date field tile), drag the Price field tile to the Row area, and click Finish to create the report.

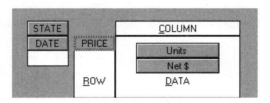

4 From the State list, select OR.

In a PivotTable, changing which field tile is in which position is not difficult, but it does entail several steps.

The basic structure of the report is in place. You have the data from the database, a PivotTable to summarize it, and a chart. You have set up all this by hand, without any macros. Now you can create a macro that changes the PivotTable for you.

Creating a Report Generating Tool

Each time you specify a market segment, you change three aspects of the PivotTable: the database field name you use as the page field (currently State), the specific item for that page field (currently OR), and the database field name you use as the row field (currently Price). You can make a macro that will switch the PivotTable for you when you specify those three items.

Create a control worksheet

1 Activate the Control worksheet.

This worksheet was provided for you in the original Lists workbook, which you renamed as Lesson 12. The Control worksheet contains a list of the key fields from the database, along with the lists of possible values for each of the key fields.

2 Enter **PageField** in cell A11, **PageItem** in cell A12, and **RowField** in cell A13.

3 Select the range A11:B13. On the Insert menu, click the Name, Create command, select the Left Column check box, and click OK.

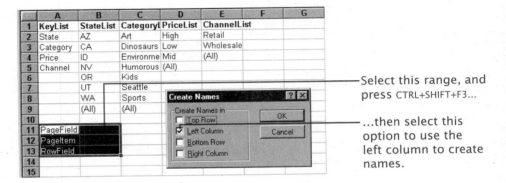

Select this range, and press CTRL+SHIFT+F3...

...then select this option to use the left column to create names.

Cells B11, B12, and B13 now have the names **PageField**, **PageItem**, and **RowField**, respectively.

4 Enter **Channel** in cell B11, **Retail** in cell B12, and **State** in cell B13.

Now if you select cell B11, the formula bar displays Channel as the cell's value, and the Reference area displays PageField as the cell's name.

You can enter any value from the list of keys in the PageField cell, and you can enter any other value from the list of keys in the RowField cell. The value of the PageItem cell must be one of the entries from the list appropriate to the current PageField name. Channel is the current value in the PageField cell, so in the PageItem cell, you can use either of the two values from the list of channels (Wholesale or Retail).

Record a macro to change the PivotTable

Now you need a macro that can put the value of the PageField cell into the Page area of the PivotTable, the value of the RowField cell into the Row area, and the value of the PageItem cell as the specific page item for the page field. Start by recording a sample macro.

1 Activate the Report worksheet.

2   Click (All) in the list of dates, so that you will be able to set the date with the macro recorder turned on. Then select any cell within the PivotTable.

3   Click the Record Macro button on the Visual Basic toolbar, type **AdjustTable** as the name for the macro, and click OK.

Record Macro button

4   Click the PivotTable Wizard button.

PivotTable Wizard button

5   Drag the State field tile from the Page area to the Row area, drag the Price field tile away from the Row area, drag the Channel field tile into the Page area (above the Date field tile), and click Finish.

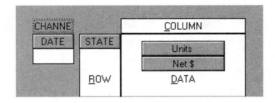

6   Click Retail in the list of channels in cell B1.

7   Click 2/1/96 in the list of dates in cell B2.

8   Click the Stop Macro button to stop the recorder.

Stop Macro button

9   Rename the Module1 sheet as **ReportModule** and look at the recorded macro:

```
Sub AdjustTable()
    ActiveSheet.PivotTables("ReportTable").AddFields _
        RowFields:="STATE", _
        ColumnFields:="Data", PageFields:=Array("DATE", "CHANNEL")
    ActiveSheet.PivotTables("ReportTable").PivotFields("CHANNEL"). _
        CurrentPage = "Retail"
    ActiveSheet.PivotTables("ReportTable").PivotFields("DATE"). _
        CurrentPage = "2/1/96"
End Sub
```

If the macro includes a statement that begins with the word "ActiveChart," then delete that statement.

The body of this macro consists of three long statements. The first statement specifies which fields to use as rows, columns, and pages. The second statement sets the item for the current Channel page field, and the third statement sets the item for the current Date page field.

Simplify the macro

The macro uses the expression *ActiveSheet.PivotTables("ReportTable")* three times. That expression establishes a link to the current PivotTable. You can establish that link once and use it over and over by assigning the PivotTable object to a variable. Rather than assume that the PivotTable is on the active sheet, set up a variable to point explicitly at the Report worksheet. Then you can run the macro regardless of which sheet in the workbook is active.

1   Insert these statements after the *Sub AdjustTable()* statement:

```
Dim myReport
Dim myPivot
Set myReport = Worksheets("Report")
Set myPivot = myReport.PivotTables("ReportTable")
```

The Dim statements tell Visual Basic that you will be using the words *myReport* and *myPivot* as variables. The first Set statement establishes a link to the worksheet named Report and assigns that link to the myReport variable. The second Set statement assigns the PivotTable named ReportTable, found on the worksheet pointed to by the myReport variable, to the myPivot variable. Now you can use the word *myPivot* in the macro instead of using the longer expression *ActiveSheet.PivotTables("ReportTable")*.

2   Insert a blank line between the Dim statements and the Set statements, and between the Set statements and the PivotTable statements, to clarify the three parts of the procedure.

3   Change all three original occurrences of *ActiveSheet.PivotTables("ReportTable")* to **myPivot** (you may want to use the Replace command on the Edit menu).

4   Delete the argument *ColumnFields:="Data",* (including the comma) from the statement with the AddFields method since you will always leave the Units and Net $ fields as the column headings in the report.

5   Delete the underscores in the last two statements and then shorten them to a single line each.

The revised macro should look like this:

```
Sub AdjustTable()
    Dim myReport
    Dim myPivot

    Set myReport = Worksheets("Report")
    Set myPivot = myReport.PivotTables("ReportTable")

    myPivot.AddFields RowFields:="STATE", _
        PageFields:=Array("DATE", "CHANNEL")
    myPivot.PivotFields("CHANNEL").CurrentPage = "Retail"
    myPivot.PivotFields("DATE").CurrentPage = "2/1/96"
End Sub
```

Link the macro to the control values

The next step is to replace the words in quotation marks—*"STATE"*, *"CHANNEL"*, and *"Retail"*—with links to the named cells on the Control worksheet. Then, by simply changing the control values and running the macro, you can change the PivotTable. First create variables inside your procedure to hold the control values, and then substitute these variable names for the constants in the statements. Since you will refer to the Control worksheet multiple times, you can create a variable to hold it.

1   After the statement *Dim myPivot*, enter these statements to let Visual Basic know the names you will use for the variables:

```
Dim myControl
Dim myRowField
Dim myPageField
Dim myPageItem
```

2   After the statement that begins with the words *Set myPivot*, enter these statements to make the variables point to the cells on the Control worksheet:

```
Set myControl = Worksheets("Control")
Set myRowField = myControl.Range("RowField")
Set myPageField = myControl.Range("PageField")
Set myPageItem = myControl.Range("PageItem")
```

   NOTE   If you use Set to assign a cell to a variable, you assign a single-cell Range object; when the value in the cell changes, the value in the variable changes as well. If you use Let to assign a cell to a variable, you assign the current value of the cell; when the value in the cell changes, the variable does not change with it.

3   Replace the word *"STATE"* (including the quotation marks) with **myRowField.Value**

State was the field tile you used for row headings. You want the macro to set the row heading field to the current value in the cell named RowField on the Control worksheet.

4   Replace both occurrences of the word *"CHANNEL"* (including the quotation marks) with **myPageField.Value**

Channel was the field tile you assigned to the Page area. You want the macro to set the page field to the current value in the cell named PageField on the Control worksheet.

5   Replace the word *"Retail"* with **myPageItem.Value**

Retail was the specific channel you assigned as the page item. You want the macro to set the page item to the current value in the cell named PageItem on the Control worksheet.

The revised procedure should look like this:

```
Sub AdjustTable()
    Dim myReport
    Dim myPivot
    Dim myControl
    Dim myRowField
    Dim myPageField
    Dim myPageItem
```

```
    Set myReport = Worksheets("Report")
    Set myPivot = myReport.PivotTables("ReportTable")
    Set myControl = Worksheets("Control")
    Set myRowField = myControl.Range("RowField")
    Set myPageField = myControl.Range("PageField")
    Set myPageItem = myControl.Range("PageItem")

    myPivot.AddFields RowFields:=myRowField.Value, _
        PageFields:=Array("DATE", myPageField.Value)
    myPivot.PivotFields(myPageField.Value).CurrentPage = myPageItem.Value
    myPivot.PivotFields("DATE").CurrentPage = "2/1/96"
End Sub
```

Change control values to change the PivotTable

Now you're ready to put the procedure to work. You need a button on the Control worksheet to make the macro easy to run. But first, if you add a second window to the workbook, you can see what is happening on the Report worksheet while you make changes on the Control worksheet.

1   Activate the Report worksheet and click New Window on the Window menu.

2   In the new window, activate the Control worksheet, and create a button to the right of the control variables. (Use the Create Button button on the Drawing toolbar.) Assign the AdjustTable macro to the button, and type **Change** as the label for the button.

3   On the Windows menu, click Arrange, and in the Arrange Windows dialog box select the Cascade option, select the Windows Of Active Workbook check box, and click OK.

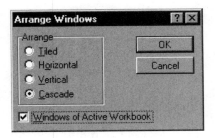

4   Reduce the size of the active window so that you can see the Report worksheet behind it.

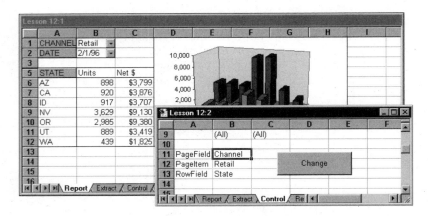

5 Enter **State** in cell B11, **OR** in cell B12, and **Price** in cell B13. Then click the Change button.

The table changes to reflect the new specifications from the Control worksheet, and the chart changes to reflect the table values.

If the macro fails, set a breakpoint and watch the values of expressions as you learned in Lesson 10.

6 Enter **Category** in cell B13, and click the Change button to change the row headings in the PivotTable.

7 Close the Control worksheet window, and save the Lesson 12 workbook.

You now have a simple macro for quickly manipulating the PivotTable. Much of the work in setting up this macro was setting up the report in the first place. The Visual Basic procedures make only relatively few changes to produce the result you want.

Exit Microsoft Excel

1 Close Excel by clicking Exit on the File menu.

2 Close Query by clicking Exit on the File menu. Do not save the query.

Lesson Summary

To	Do this
Extract data from an external database	Click Get External Data on the Data menu in Excel, specify the data you want using Microsoft Query, and then click Return Data To Microsoft Excel on the File menu in Query.
Store a pointer to a cell named ThisCell in a variable named myCell	Use the statement *Set myCell = Range("ThisCell")*.
Store the value from a cell named ThisCell in a variable named myValue	Use the statement *myCell = Range("ThisCell").Value*.

Preview of the Next Lesson

In this lesson, you built a macro for creating order status reports for various market segments. In the next lesson, you will extend the macro to work with other applications. You will learn how to send copies of the report to Microsoft Word, using Visual Basic's ability to control other applications. You will also learn how to extract information directly from the database system using powerful database connectivity tools available to Visual Basic.

Interact with the World

Estimated time
50 min.

In this lesson you will learn how to:

■ Execute commands in Microsoft Word from Excel.

■ Request data from a database directly into Excel.

In 1616, the ruler of Japan, Shogun Ieyasu, closed the doors of his country to foreign traders and missionaries. For nearly a quarter of a millennium, during which time the rest of the world was caught up in burgeoning international commerce, Japan was effectively isolated from the outside world. On July 8, 1853, Commodore Matthew C. Perry sailed with four American ships into Tokyo harbor, ending Japan's isolation.

The rest of the world was shocked by how quickly Japan imitated, assimilated, and adapted Western ideas and technology. During its years of isolation, Japan had a sophisticated and effective society, but its impact was limited. Once Japan began to interact with other nations, it became first a powerful military force and subsequently an even more powerful economic force in the world.

For years, computer applications have each functioned in isolation. Each one has been sophisticated and effective on its own, but still limited in solving complete business problems. New tools are now becoming available that allow major applications and databases to communicate freely with one another. In this lesson you will learn how to communicate directly with other applications from Microsoft Excel using Visual Basic.

Start the lesson

➤ Start Excel, open the Lesson 12 workbook, and save a copy as **Lesson 13**.

NOTE If you do not have Microsoft Word version 6 or later, you will not be able to do the exercises in the first part of this lesson. You can continue with the "Retrieving Data from a Database" section of the lesson.

Controlling Microsoft Word Immediately

In Lesson 12, you developed a macro for creating the market segment order status reports you need for your monthly review meetings at Miller Textiles. Usually, after the meeting, you are asked to prepare a document that contains discussions of the reports along with the reports themselves. You use Microsoft Word as your word processor, and you would like to enhance your macros so that they can optionally put the report directly into a Word document.

Microsoft Word for Windows 95 can receive commands directly from Visual Basic. (Before Word 6.0, you could send commands from Excel, but the procedures necessary to set up and use the connection were difficult.) Word for Windows 95 does not yet include Visual Basic for Applications, and you cannot yet work directly with objects in Word, but you can now easily control Word documents using Word's internal programming language: WordBasic.

To build a procedure that can communicate with Word, work in Excel's Debug window. First carry out the commands in the Immediate pane so that you can see the effect of each statement, and then transfer the useful statements to the Code pane.

Open communication with WordBasic

1 Make sure that the Word application is closed. Resize Excel's window to fill the right half of your monitor screen.

2 Maximize the Lesson 13 workbook window, activate the ReportModule sheet, click Debug Window on the View menu, and activate the Immediate pane.

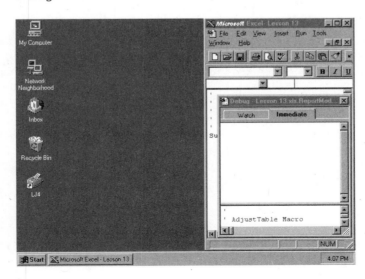

3 In the Immediate pane, type **Set myWord = CreateObject("Word.Basic")** and press ENTER.

The word *CreateObject* is a Visual Basic function that establishes a link with objects that can accept commands from Visual Basic but do not appear in the Object Browser. The WordBasic language used by Word can accept commands from Visual Basic.

To establish a connection with an object, you must find out the name that the object responds to. WordBasic responds to the name *Word.Basic*.

For a few seconds, the word "Running" appears at the top of the Debug window. During this time, the CreateObject function launches Word and returns a link to the Word.Basic object, which you assign to the variable *myWord*.

The Word application started. It really did. You just don't see it. Word starts up hidden in case you want to keep the fact that you're using it a secret. If you don't believe me, look at the object link stored in the myWord variable.

4 Type **?TypeName (myWord)** and press ENTER.

The word *wordbasic*, in all lowercase letters, appears. You successfully launched Word.

You can give commands to Word to make it reveal itself. Since version 6.0, Word has been able to accept commands from Visual Basic, but you cannot yet manipulate objects inside Word the way you can manipulate objects inside Excel. You must use WordBasic statements.

5 Type **myWord.AppMinimize True** and press ENTER.

The Microsoft Word button appears in the Windows 95 taskbar.

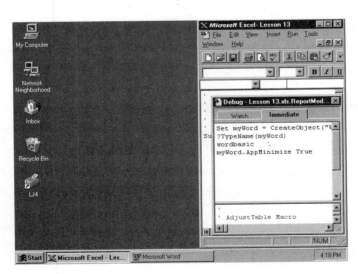

6 Type **myWord.AppRestore** and press ENTER to restore the Word window. Resize the window to fill the left half of your monitor screen.

271

7 Activate the Excel window. In the Immediate pane type **myWord.FileNew** and press ENTER.

You will be storing pictures for the February report in this file, so save it now and give it a name.

8 Type **myWord.FileSaveAs Name:="February Report"** and press ENTER.

The caption of the file changes from Document1 to February Report to show that the file has been saved.

Change the Word document so that you can see a whole page on the screen.

9 Type **myWord.ViewZoomWholePage** and press ENTER.

If the Word document page was not already completely visible, this statement changes it.

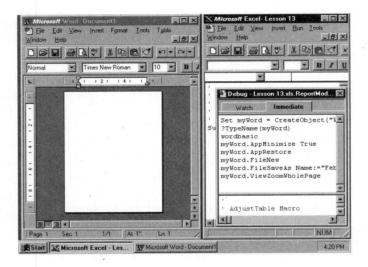

Copy the report range to Word

You want to copy the range containing the report into the Word document. The report is in the range named ReportRange.

1 Type **Range ("ReportRange").Copy** in the Immediate pane, and press ENTER.

A moving border appears around the range you copied. The range is ready to paste.

You can paste into Word using any of several formats. In this case, you want to paste the table range and the chart together, so pasting as a picture is a good choice.

2 Type **myWord.EditPasteSpecial DataType:="Pict"** and press ENTER.

Use a colon and an equal sign (:=) to separate the argument name from the argument value in WordBasic commands, the same as for Excel object methods.

A picture of the report appears in the Word document.

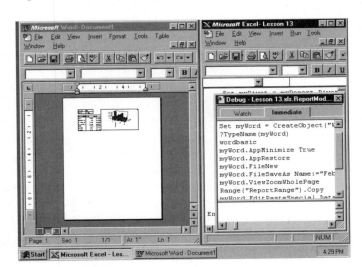

3 Type **Application.CutCopyMode = False**

The moving border disappears. You don't need to paste the report anywhere.

4 Type **myWord.InsertPara** and press ENTER to add a paragraph after the report.

Close the connection to Word

Before you close the Word document, your procedure should save any changes to the document.

1 Type **myWord.FileSave** and press ENTER.

2 Type **myWord.FileClose** and press ENTER to close the document.

When you establish a link to an object using the CreateObject function, you must always be sure to release the object when you have finished using it. Otherwise you may lose operating system resources.

3 Type **Set myWord = Nothing** and press ENTER.

The Word application closes. The word *Nothing* is a special keyword in Visual Basic that releases all the resources of an object. Notice that you do not put quotation marks around the word *Nothing*. It is a special keyword in Visual Basic.

4 Close the Debug window.

NOTE If you use the CreateObject("Word.Basic") function when Word is already running, the function returns a link to the currently running instance of the application. In that case, when you release the object, the Word application does not close. On the other hand, if Word is not running when you use CreateObject, creating the object launches the application, and releasing the object closes it.

Controlling Word from a Procedure

Now you have all the pieces necessary to create a procedure to communicate with WordBasic. You can enhance your report creation macro to optionally send the report to Word. First add new options to the Control worksheet, and then enhance the PrintReport procedure to handle the new options, create a subroutine to copy the report to Word, and create another subroutine to close the connection to Word when you finish creating reports.

Create a procedure to control WordBasic

Now you can write the actual procedure to send the report to Word. You will use many statements that you tried out in the Immediate pane. You may want to activate the Debug window and copy usable statements from the Immediate pane to the Code pane.

1   At the top of the module, insert the statement **Dim myWord**

    If you declare a variable inside a procedure, the variable and its contents are automatically discarded when the procedure ends. You want to be able to copy more than one report to Word, and you want to be able to close Word in an orderly manner. Putting the variable declaration at the top of the procedure makes it retain its value until you are through with it.

2   At the bottom of the module, insert this procedure:

```
Sub SendToWord()
    If TypeName(myWord) <> "wordbasic" Then
        Set myWord = CreateObject("Word.Basic")
        myWord.AppMinimize True
        myWord.AppRestore
        myWord.FileNew
        myWord.FileSaveAs "February Report"
    End If

    Range("ReportRange").Copy
    myWord.EditPasteSpecial DataType:="Pict"

    Application.CutCopyMode = False
    myWord.InsertPara
    myWord.FileSave
End Sub
```

You will run this procedure only on those occasions when you choose to send the report to Word. You don't want to create the WordBasic object until you actually use it for the first time, in case you never use it at all. The procedure checks to see if the WordBasic object has already been created, and if not, the procedure creates it.

Once the WordBasic object is created and the file is ready, the procedure copies the report range and pastes the picture into Word. Finally, the procedure saves the file each time you change it, so that you won't have to re-create the reports in case of a power failure, fire, or flood.

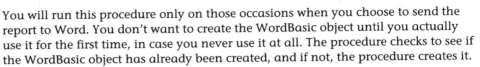

Step Into button

3 Click anywhere in the *Sub SendToWord()* statement and click the Step Into button repeatedly to step through the macro. You will have to reactivate Excel after the AppRestore statement in order to keep stepping through the macro.

4 Activate the Control worksheet, and create a new button. Assign the button to the SendToWord macro, and type **Send To Word** as the label.

5 Click the Send To Word button to run the macro.

6 Type **Price** in the RowField cell, click the Change button, and then click the Send To Word button.

7 Activate Word, and then close it by clicking Exit on the File menu.

Create a procedure to close Word

After you finish creating and copying several reports, you will need a macro to close Word and release the link stored in the myWord variable.

1 At the bottom of the ReportModule sheet, enter this procedure:

```
Sub CloseReport()
    If TypeName(myWord) = "wordbasic" Then
        myWord.FileClose
        Set myWord = Nothing
    End If
End Sub
```

Toggle Breakpoint button

2 Use the Toggle Breakpoint button to make the Sub CloseReport() statement into a breakpoint. Turn off any other breakpoints in the module.

3 Activate the Control worksheet, and create a new button. Assign the button to the CloseReport macro, and give it the label **Close Word**

	A	B	C	D	E	F
1	KeyList	StateList	CategoryI	PriceList	ChannelList	
2	State	AZ	Art	High	Retail	
3	Category	CA	Dinosaurs	Low	Wholesale	
4	Price	ID	Environme	Mid	(All)	
5	Channel	NV	Humorous	(All)		
6		OR	Kids			
7		UT	Seattle			
8		WA	Sports			
9		(All)	(All)			
10						
11	PageField	State		Change		
12	PageItem	ID				
13	RowField	Price		Send to Word		
14						
15				Close Word		
16						
17						

H ◄ ► ►H \ Report \ **Control** / Extract / F ◄ | ►

4 Save the workbook, and then send several reports to Word.

5 Click the Close Word button, and step through the CloseReport macro.

Word closes, and your document containing the various reports is saved—ready for you to add annotations.

 NOTE This is an Excel Visual Basic book, not a WordBasic book. To help you see how to use Visual Basic to control another application, you have used a few WordBasic commands in the course of this lesson. The WordBasic commands, however, are not explained in depth. To find a WordBasic command, record the action in a Word macro and see what WordBasic command was used or use Word Help.

Retrieving Data from a Database

Your report generating macro can now create any of the market segment reports you want, and it can either display the report or export it to a Word document. You can run the entire tool from the Control worksheet. So far, however, you have used your tool only with February data. In Lesson 12, you used Excel's Get External Data feature to import the February data from the database into the Extract worksheet. When March, April, and May come, you would like to be able to create reports without manually importing the new data from the database.

Excel for Windows 95 has a new feature that enables you to retrieve data quickly from a variety of data sources: dBASE files, Oracle databases, SQL Server databases, Microsoft Access databases, Paradox databases, and many others. This new feature is called Data Access Objects, or DAO for short.

DAO allows you to manipulate the external data objects in the same way that you manipulate Excel objects, eliminating the need for the Microsoft Query application.

A request for data is called a *query*. You make the request using *Structured Query Language*, or SQL (often pronounced "sequel"). SQL is an industry-standard way of making queries. SQL is a powerful query language, and some SQL queries can become very complex. You can, however, also make very simple queries using SQL. In this lesson, you will make simple SQL queries of the Miller Textiles order database.

One of the greatest benefits of Data Access Objects is that these objects are used not only by Excel, but also by Microsoft Access and the standalone version of Visual Basic. That means, for example, that anything you learn about Data Access Objects in Access can be used directly in Excel.

In this lesson, you will first ask the database for the most recent month for which data is available; then you will retrieve the order history information for that month. Start by making the queries using the Immediate pane, and then transfer the useful statements to a procedure.

Open the database

Communicating with an external data file is as simple as opening the database. First, however, you have to tell Visual Basic that you want to use the DAO.

1 Activate the ReportModule sheet, and on the Tools menu, click References.

A list labeled Available References appears, containing the names of all the object libraries that are registered with Windows. The names *Visual Basic For Applications* and *Microsoft Excel 5.0 Object Library* have check marks next to them. These two libraries are always open. They appear in the Object Browser as *VBA* and *Excel*. You add the DAO library here, and then its procedures will appear in the Object Browser.

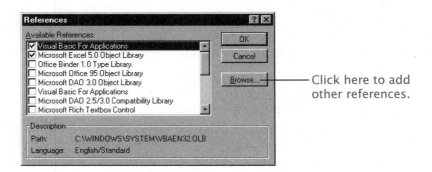

Click here to add other references.

If Microsoft DAO 3.0 Object Library *is not in the list, run Excel Setup and add the Data Access options.*

2 Scroll down the list until you find the item labeled *Microsoft DAO 3.0 Object Library*. Click it to add a check mark next to the name, and then click OK. If you have installed a recent version of Microsoft Access or the Enterprise Edition of Visual Basic, you may see a lot of items in the list.

3 In the Immediate pane, type **Set myDB =** (do not press ENTER).

The variable myDB is where you will store a pointer to the database object.

277

4   Open the Object Browser, and select DAO from the list of libraries.

The DAO library contains many objects, with many properties and methods. Fortunately, to retrieve data from a database, you need to use only a very few of them.

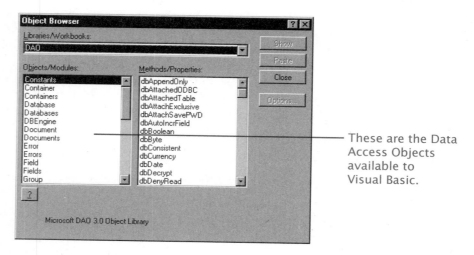

These are the Data Access Objects available to Visual Basic.

5   In the list of objects on the left, click DBEngine.

The DAO DBEngine object is analogous to the Excel Application object.

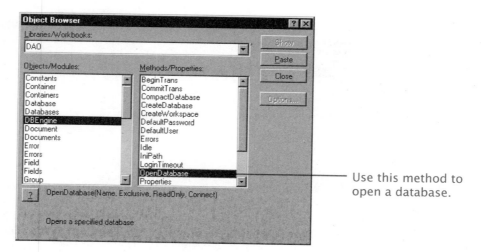

Use this method to open a database.

6   In the list of properties and methods on the right, select OpenDatabase, and then click the Paste button.

Do not use the shortcut name that appears in the Favorites list—use the actual folder name.

7 As the value of the Name argument, type the name of the folder containing the files for this book: **"C:\ExcelVBA"** (include the quotation marks). Type **False** as the value of both the Exclusive and the ReadOnly arguments, and as the value of the Connect argument, type **"dBase IV"** (include the space and quotation marks).

The final statement should be *Set myDB = OpenDatabase(Name:="C:\ExcelVBA", Exclusive:=False, ReadOnly:=False, Connect:="dBase IV")*

For a dBase database, the folder containing the tables is considered to be the database. For an Access database, you specify the database name as the Name argument, and you do not need to use the Connect argument.

8 Press ENTER.

Nothing seems to happen, so you may want to make sure that the database was properly opened.

9 Type **?TypeName(myDB)** and press ENTER.

The word *Database* should appear, because you stored a pointer to a Database object in the variable.

Retrieve a date from the database

1 In the Immediate pane, type **Set myRS = myDB.** (include the period, but do not press ENTER).

The variable *myRS* is where you will save a pointer to what the DAO library calls a *Recordset*.

2 Open the Object Browser, select Database from the list of objects on the left, select OpenRecordset from the list of methods and properties on the right, and click Paste.

3 As the value of the Name argument, type **"Select Max(Date) As MaxDate From Orders"** (include the quotation marks), and then delete the remaining arguments.

The statement should be Set myRS = myDB.OpenRecordset(Name:="Select Max(Date) As MaxDate From Orders")

The string that you used for the Name argument is a SQL statement that searches the Orders table for the largest value in the Date field, and calls that value MaxDate.

4 Press ENTER.

Once again, you can check what was assigned to the variable to see if it worked.

5 Type **?TypeName(myRS)** and press ENTER.

The word *Recordset* should appear. Now you can assign the maximum date value that you retrieved in the recordset and assign it to a variable for later use.

6 Type **myMaxDate = myRS.MaxDate** and press ENTER.

Look at the value of myMaxDate to make sure it's right.

7 Type **?myMaxDate** and press ENTER.

The date *2/1/96* should appear.

Since you requested a single value, the record set contains only a single record with a single field. You will request multiple records with multiple fields in the next section.

Retrieve one month's orders from the database

Now that you know the maximum date in the database, you can use that date to request all the order records for the most recent month. Since you will be requesting the records from the same database, you can keep using the same database variable. You won't need the recordset any more, so you can assign a new recordset to the myRS variable.

The SQL query command to retrieve all the orders for the month will require more words than the query to retrieve a single date did. If you assign the first part of the query statement to a variable and then append additional parts, the SQL query can become quite manageable. In a SQL query statement, first you specify the fields you want to *select*, then you specify the data file to get the fields *from*, and finally you specify the rule for deciding *where* to select the records.

1. Type **mySQL = "SELECT Date, State, Category, Channel, Price, Units, Net "** (include the quotation marks and leave a space after the word *Net*) and press ENTER.

   This is the list of fields you want to select from the database.

2. Type **mySQL = mySQL & "FROM Orders "** (include the quotation marks and leave a space after the word *Orders*) and press ENTER.

   This appends the data source to the list of fields.

3. Type **mySQL = mySQL & "WHERE Date = #2/1/96#"** and press ENTER.

   This appends the decision criterion for which rows to accept. Enclose dates within number signs. For now, you are using a constant for the date. Later you will replace the constant with the date you retrieved from the database.

   Before you use the SQL statement, take a look at the whole thing.

4. Type **?mySQL** and press ENTER to display the entire SQL query: *SELECT Date, State, Category, Channel, Price, Units, Net FROM Orders WHERE Date = #2/1/96#* (make sure that the query statement has spaces before the words *FROM* and *WHERE*).

 NOTE Capitalization is not important in a SQL statement, but traditionally the keywords *SELECT, FROM,* and *WHERE* are capitalized to make the SQL statement easier to read.

5. Type **Set myRS = myDB.OpenRecordSet(Name:=mySQL)** and press ENTER.

   Do not type quotation marks around the word *mySQL* because this is a variable that contains the query, not the query itself.

Create a place for the new data

The data for the month is all nicely stored away in the recordset. Now you can put it into the Extract worksheet. But first you need to prepare the location for the data. Clear the current contents of the worksheet, and add field names to the first row of the worksheet.

1   In the Immediate pane, type **Set myExtract = Worksheets("Extract")** and press ENTER to make the Extract worksheet easier to reference.

2   Type **myExtract.Select** and press ENTER to activate the Extract worksheet so that you can see what is happening.

3   Type **myExtract.Cells.Clear** and press ENTER to clear all the cells on the worksheet.

4   Type **myExtract.Cells(1).Value = myRS.Fields(0).Name** and press ENTER.

The word *Date* appears in cell A1. A Recordset object has a method named Fields that returns a collection of the fields in the recordset. Each Field object has a Name property. Just to keep life interesting, you use 0 to refer to the first item in a DAO collection, even though you use 1 to refer to the first item in an Excel object collection.

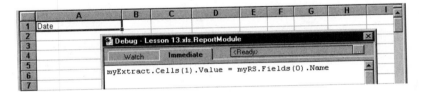

5   Type **myExtract.Cells(2).Value = myRS.Fields(1).Name** and press ENTER.

The word *State* appears in cell B1.

6   To enter the rest of the seven field names, you can either use Visual Basic statements in the Immediate pane, or you can activate the Extract sheet, type **Category**, **Channel**, **Price**, **Units**, and **Net** in the cells C1, D1, E1, F1, and G1, and wait until you can write a looping procedure to let Visual Basic fill the labels.

With the worksheet cleared and the field labels in place, you can copy the records from the recordset.

Import the new data

1   Type **myExtract.Cells(2,1).CopyFromRecordset(myRS)** and press ENTER.

The worksheet is filled with new values from the database.

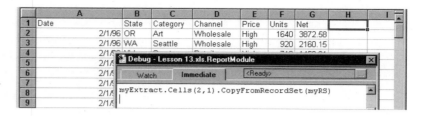

Because you specified a single cell as the destination range, the CopyFromRecordset method filled into that cell and then down and to the right. When you retrieve data, be sure cells below and to the right of the destination range are expendable.

2   Type **myExtract.Cells(1).CurrentRegion.Name = "Database"** and press ENTER to give the name *Database* to the entire retrieved region of data.

When you created the PivotTable, you told it to look for values in a range named Database. If you rename the Database range every time you retrieve the data from the database, the PivotTable will always include the correct number of records.

3   Type **Worksheets("Report").PivotTables("ReportTable").RefreshTable** and press ENTER.

The PivotTable always makes its own internal copy of the data in the table. After you retrieve new data and fill it into the Extract worksheet, you need to refresh the PivotTable so that it will use the new data. A PivotTable object has a method named RefreshTable that refreshes the data in the PivotTable.

Calculate the current date for the query

In the first query, you retrieved the date of the most recent month in the database. In the second query, you retrieved the values for that specific month. Your procedure will need to use the date retrieved by the first query in the Where clause of the second query.

1   Reexecute the statements that assign the first two parts of the SQL statement to the mySQL variable. (Perform steps 1 and 2 from the "Retrieve one month's orders from the database" procedure above.)

2   Type **mySQL = mySQL & "WHERE Date = #"** and press ENTER to add the first part of the date clause to the statement.

3   Type **mySQL = mySQL & myMaxDate** and press ENTER to add the formatted date to the statement.

4   Type **mySQL = mySQL & "#"** and press ENTER to add the closing number sign after the date.

These statements insert the date retrieved from the first query into the middle of the SQL statement.

5   Type **?mySQL** and press ENTER to see the value of the SQL query statement. It should be the same as when you entered the date directly into the statement: *SELECT Date, State, Category, Channel, Price, Units, Net FROM Orders WHERE Date = #2/1/96#*

6   Close the Debug window.

Now you have all the pieces necessary to build a procedure to retrieve the current month's orders from the database.

Write a procedure to retrieve the current orders

You will write a new procedure named *InitializeData*. Then, since you need to run this procedure only once each month, you will create a button just for this procedure. This procedure does not use any variables that need to be shared with any other procedures, so you can declare all its variables inside the procedure.

1   Add this new procedure at the bottom of the module:

```
Sub InitializeData()
    Dim myExtract
    Dim myDB
    Dim myRS
    Dim mySQL
    Dim myMaxDate
    Dim myField

    Application.StatusBar = "Retrieving data. Please wait."
    Set myDB = OpenDatabase("C:\ExcelVBA", False, False, "dBase IV")
    mySQL = "SELECT Max(Date) As MaxDate from Orders"
    Set myRS = myDB.OpenRecordset(mySQL)
    myMaxDate = myRS.MaxDate

    mySQL = "SELECT Date, State, Category, Channel, Price, Units, Net "
    mySQL = mySQL & "FROM Orders "
    mySQL = mySQL & "WHERE Date = #"
    mySQL = mySQL & myMaxDate
    mySQL = mySQL & "#"
    Set myRS = myDB.OpenRecordset(mySQL)

    Set myExtract = Worksheets("Extract")
    myExtract.Cells.Clear
    For myField = 1 To myRS.Fields.Count
        myExtract.Cells(myField).Value = _
            myRS.Fields(myField - 1).Name
    Next myField
    myExtract.Cells(2, 1).CopyFromRecordset (myRS)
    myExtract.Cells(1).CurrentRegion.Name = "Database"

    Set myRS = Nothing
    Set myDB = Nothing

    Worksheets("Report").PivotTables("ReportTable").RefreshTable
    Application.StatusBar = False
End Sub
```

You can omit argument names, as long as you keep the argument values in the proper order.

283

The procedure displays a status bar message by assigning the message to the Application object's StatusBar property. Setting the StatusBar property to False restores the default status bar message. Notice how much easier it is to copy the field names when you can use a For loop!

2 Close the Debug window if it is open, and click anywhere in the Sub InitializeData statement.

3 Click the Step Into button repeatedly to watch the macro work.

Step Into button

4 Activate the Control worksheet, create a new button, assign the InitializeData macro to it, and give it the label **Initialize**

5 Save the workbook, and click the Initialize button to test the data retrieval macro again.

Now your report generator tool can communicate with the outside world. It can retrieve the most recent orders from the database at the click of a button, and it can send the final reports to Word, ready for you to add your descriptive analysis.

Lesson Summary

To	Do this
Assign a link to WordBasic commands to the myWord variable	Use the statement *Set myWord = CreateObject("Word.Basic")*.
Find out if a link to WordBasic is in the myWord variable	Use the expression *TypeName(myWord) = "wordbasic"*.
Close the link to WordBasic	Use the statement *Set myWord = Nothing*.
Open a DAO database	Use the OpenDatabase method of the DBEngine object.
Open a DAO Recordset object.	Use the OpenRecordset method of the Database
Retrieve values from a DAO recordset	Use the CopyFromRecordset method of the Range object.
Close a DAO database	Set the database object variable to Nothing

For online information about	From the Excel Help menu, choose Contents and then
Controlling other applications	Choose Getting started with Visual Basic and then Select the topic "Accessing Data and Other Applications"
Using Data Access Objects	Choose Microsoft Data Access Objects (DAO)

Preview of the Next Lesson

The report generator macros are ready for you to use each month. Entering valid control settings, however, is still tricky. Since you created the macros, you can probably remember how to use them to produce reports. But if you make the macros easier to use, you can let others use them to create reports. If you make the macros foolproof, you can even let your boss use them. In the next lesson you will learn how to turn the report generator into a foolproof application.

Create a Packaged Application

In this lesson you will learn how to:

Estimated time
50 min.

■ Create a custom dialog box.

■ Link controls on a dialog box to cells in a worksheet.

■ Change the dialog box while it is displayed.

■ Start a macro automatically when the workbook is opened.

Take a 3-foot by 4-foot piece of plywood and cans of blue, yellow, and orange paint. Drip, dribble, splash, and spread the paint on the plywood. You now have—a mess. But put a $500 frame around the painted plywood. You now have—a work of art! Even serious art does not look serious without a good frame. The best diamond brooch does not seem to be a precious gift if given in a paper bag.

You can write macros that are practical, convenient, and useful, but until you put a frame around them, until you tighten up the edges and make them easy to use, until you *package* them, you do not have a true application.

In this lesson you will enhance the macros you built in Lessons 12 and 13. You will add a powerful and appealing dialog box interface, start and stop the application automatically, and prevent unexpected error messages. You will create a packaged application.

Start the lesson

➤ Start Microsoft Excel, and open the Lesson 13 workbook. Save a new copy of the workbook as **Lesson 14**.

Making Dynamic List Boxes

In Lessons 12 and 13, you built macros to help you create reports for different market segments. Those macros may be convenient for you, but if you type a value from the wrong list in the PageItem cell, or if you misspell the word *Portrait* in the Orientation cell, the macros will not work properly.

Your ultimate goal is to make the application simple enough and foolproof enough that others in the company could produce the charts on their own. If you create a dialog box—with list boxes, option buttons, and check boxes—you can prevent the user of the application from making invalid choices and misspelling words.

Create a dialog box sheet

On the Control worksheet, you specify three values that control the PivotTable: PageField, PageItem, and RowField. You can use list boxes to make sure the user enters only correct values into these cells. First, assume that State is the value of the PageField cell. You will create a dialog box with two list boxes: one to choose which state and another to choose the database field for row headings.

Dialog boxes in Excel have their own sheet type. To create a new dialog box, insert a *dialog sheet*.

1   On the Insert menu, click the Macro, Dialog command to create a new dialog sheet in your workbook.

2   Rename the dialog sheet as **ReportDialog** and drag it to the right of the other worksheets in the workbook.

The default dialog box includes an OK button and a Cancel button.

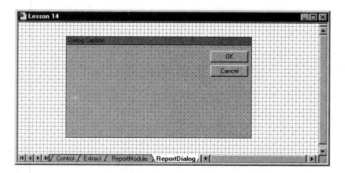

The Forms toolbar also appears when you activate a dialog sheet.

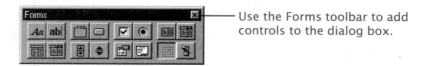

Use the Forms toolbar to add controls to the dialog box.

To add additional controls to the dialog box, use the buttons on the Forms toolbar. You want to add two list boxes: one to select the state and one to select the field for the PivotTable rows.

List Box button

3 Click the List Box button, and on the dialog box drag to create a list box. Then click the List Box button again, and drag to create another list box next to the first one.

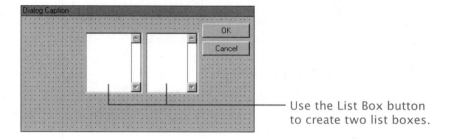

Use the List Box button to create two list boxes.

See Lesson 4 for information about using dialog box controls on a worksheet.

When you click a control button on the Forms toolbar, the mouse pointer changes to a small black cross, which you can move to the dialog box and drag to create a control of the type you chose. After you create the control, the mouse pointer changes back to an arrow, and you must click the control button again if you want to create another control of the same type. If you double-click the control button, however, you can create multiple controls of the same type.

4 Double-click the Label button, and on the dialog box drag to create two label controls, one above each list box.

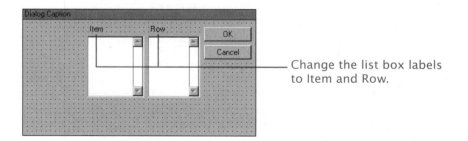

Label button

5 Click the Label button to change the mouse pointer back to an arrow.

6 Click the label above the first list box, type **Item**, click the second label, and type **Row**. Do not press ENTER or you will get a second line in the label. Instead, press ESC twice to deselect the label.

Change the list box labels to Item and Row.

The user will select a state from the Item list, and from the Row list will select a field for row headings.

Creating controls and labels on a dialog box is as easy as dragging, pointing, and typing.

Run the dialog box

On the ReportDialog sheet, you see the design view of the dialog box. To see what the dialog box really looks like, you run it.

*Run Dialog
button*

1   Click the Run Dialog button on the Forms toolbar.

The dialog box appears, looking like a real dialog box.

2   Click OK to close the dialog box.

You can also create a macro to run the dialog box.

*Record Macro
button*

3   Click the Record Macro button on the Visual Basic toolbar, type **RunDialog** as the name of the macro, and click Options.

4   Change the shortcut key to CTRL+SHIFT+D, and click OK.

5   Click the Run Dialog button, and then click OK to close the dialog box.

6   Click the Stop Macro button.

The macro recorder created a new module sheet.

*Stop Macro
button*

7   Activate the new module sheet, and rename it **DialogModule**

Macros related to the dialog box will be on the DialogModule sheet; macros related to creating the report are on the ReportModule sheet. You can use multiple modules in a workbook to keep large projects organized. Here is the macro that the recorder created:

```
Sub RunDialog()
    DialogSheets("ReportDialog").Show
End Sub
```

The word *DialogSheets* is a method that returns the collection of all dialog sheets in the active workbook. The word *Show* is a method that belongs to a DialogSheet object. It displays the dialog box.

8   Activate the ReportDialog sheet.

Link the list boxes to a worksheet

The list boxes are empty. The values you want in the list boxes are on the Control worksheet. You can connect the list boxes on the dialog box directly to the lists on the worksheet. Each of the lists at the top of the Control worksheet has already been given the name that appears at the top of its column. The range containing the list of state abbreviations, for example, is named StateList.

1   Double-click the list box labeled Item to display the Format Object dialog box, and click the Control tab.

2   In the box labeled Input Range, type **StateList** and press ENTER.

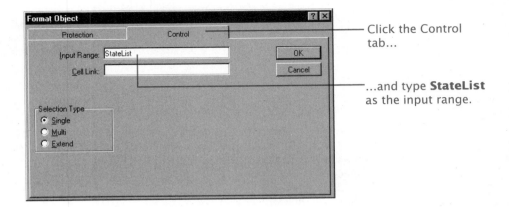

Click the Control tab...

...and type **StateList** as the input range.

The abbreviations for the states appear immediately in the list box.

3 Double-click the Row list box, type **KeyList** in the Input Range box, and press ENTER to see the list of database fields.

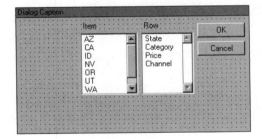

4 Press CTRL+SHIFT+D to display the dialog box.

5 Click CA in the Item list and Channel in the Row list, and then click OK to close the dialog box.

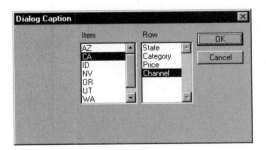

You can see the selected items in the dialog box.

The AdjustTable macro you created in Lesson 12 uses the values from cells on the Control worksheet to control a PivotTable. You need a way to get the selected item name from the dialog box back onto the Control worksheet. You can use formulas similar to those you created in Lesson 4 to link the list box value to the appropriate cell on the Control worksheet.

Link the list box results to a worksheet

When you select an entry from a list box, the list box can tell you the *position number* of the entry in the list. What you really need is the *label* for the entry. You can put the position number into a cell on the worksheet and then use an Excel formula to calculate the value of the label.

1   Activate the Control worksheet, and enter **ItemNumber** as a label in cell A15 and **RowNumber** as a label in cell A16.

2   Use the labels in cells A15 and A16 to create names for cells B15 and B16, as you did in the "Create a control worksheet" procedure in Lesson 12.

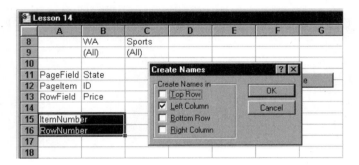

3   Activate the ReportDialog sheet, double-click the Item list box, and in the Format Object dialog box type **ItemNumber** in the Cell Link box and click OK.

4   Double-click the Row list box, type **RowNumber** in the Cell Link box, and then click OK.

5   Activate the Control worksheet. The number 2 (for CA) is in the ItemNumber cell, and the number 4 (for Channel) is in the RowNumber cell.

    You still need to convert the position numbers into readable words.

6   In cell B12, the PageItem cell, type **=INDEX(StateList,ItemNumber)** and press ENTER to change the value of the cell to CA.

7   In cell B13, the RowField cell, type **=INDEX(KeyList,RowNumber)** and press ENTER to change the value of the cell to Channel.

    The ItemNumber and RowNumber cells are linked to the list boxes on the dialog box. The PageItem and RowField cells use the INDEX function to find the corresponding descriptive words from the StateList and KeyList ranges.

8   Press CTRL+SHIFT+D to run the dialog box. Click various entries in the Item and Row list boxes and watch the values change on the Control worksheet. Then click Cancel when you are finished.

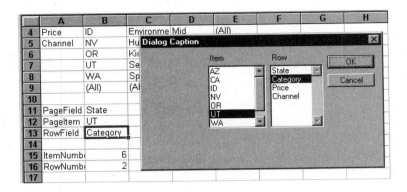

Make the dialog box change the report

Now that the dialog box changes the PageItem and RowField cells on the Control worksheet, you can use the dialog box to change the report.

1   Activate the ReportDialog sheet, click the OK button, and change the caption of the button to **Change**

You can also paste the name of the AdjustTable procedure from the Object Browser.

2   Activate the DialogModule sheet. After the statement that displays the dialog box, insert statements to activate the Report sheet and change the report. The revised procedure should look like this:

```
Sub RunDialog()
    DialogSheets("ReportDialog").Show
    Worksheets("Report").Select
    AdjustTable
End Sub
```

3   Press CTRL+SHIFT+D to run the dialog box, select any state in the Item list box, select any field (except State) in the Row list box, and click the Change button.

The dialog box closes, and the AdjustTable macro runs, changing the PivotTable. The Change button on the dialog box does not run the AdjustTable macro directly; it just closes the dialog box so that the RunDialog macro can continue. The RunDialog macro now activates the Report sheet and runs the AdjustTable macro.

The Cancel button, however, also dismisses the dialog box, so clicking the Cancel button has the same effect as clicking the Change button. You need to change the RunDialog macro so that it changes the report only if you click the Change button.

4   Activate the DialogModule sheet.

5   Change the RunDialog procedure to look like this:

```
Sub RunDialog()
    If DialogSheets("ReportDialog").Show = True Then
        Worksheets("Report").Select
        AdjustTable
    End If
End Sub
```

The Show method of a dialog box returns the value True when you click a button to dismiss the dialog box—unless the button is marked as a Cancel button, in which case the Show method returns the value False.

6 Save the Lesson 14 workbook before continuing.

Make a list box change lists

In the current dialog box, you can select orders by state, but the value of the PageField cell never changes. You want to be able to change the page field in the dialog box. If you change the page field, the list of items for that page must change as well. For example, if you choose Channel as the page field, you want the Item list to display Retail and Wholesale.

You will create a new list box for choosing the page field: First, you will make a place on the Control worksheet to put the result from the list box. Then you will create the list box on the ReportDialog sheet. Finally, you will create a macro to fill the list box with the appropriate values for the selected page field.

1 On the Control worksheet, enter **PageNumber** into cell A14, and use that label to give a name to cell B14.

2 Enter the number **4** in the PageNumber cell (B14), and enter the formula **=INDEX(KeyList,PageNumber)** in the PageField cell (B11).

The name *Channel* appears in the PageField cell, because Channel is the fourth entry in the list of keys.

List Box button

3 Activate the ReportDialog sheet, click the List Box button, and create a new list box to the left of the Item list box. If you need to make more room for the new list box, click the border of the dialog box and stretch the dialog box to the left. If you need to move controls and want to move more than one control at a time, hold down the SHIFT key as you click each control. Then you can move them as a group.

4 Double-click the new list box, type **KeyList** in the Input Range box, type **PageNumber** in the Cell Link box, and click OK.

Label button

5 Add a label control above the new list box, and change its caption to **Page**

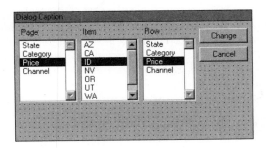

When you create a control, the control gets a name, something like *List Box 8* or *Label 9*. You can see the name of the control in the Reference area to the left of the formula bar. Give the list boxes more meaningful names that you can use when you refer to them from a procedure.

6   Click the Page list box, click the Reference area, type **lstPage**, and press ENTER. Click the Item list box, click the Reference area, type **lstItem**, and press ENTER. Then click the Row list box, click the Reference area, type **lstRow**, and press ENTER.

NOTE   When naming controls on a dialog box, many Visual Basic programmers prefix the control name with a three-letter abbreviation for the kind of control. For example, *lst* stands for list box, and *chk* and *btn* stand for check box and button.

Type a name here...

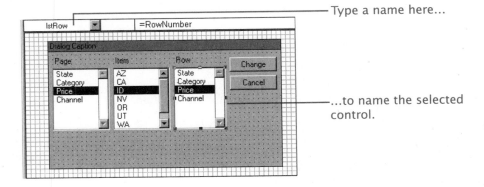

...to name the selected control.

With the list boxes named, you can now add a macro to the Page list box so that whenever you change an entry, the Item list box will point to a new list.

7   Click the Page list box, and click the Edit Code button on the Forms toolbar.

A new procedure appears on the DialogModule sheet, ready for you to enter code into. The new macro has the name *lstPage_Change*, which is obviously derived from the name of the list box.

Edit Code button

NOTE In some versions of Visual Basic, you can't change the name of a procedure that is linked to a control on a form. In Visual Basic for Applications, you *can* change the name of the procedure, but then you have to link the new procedure to the control manually. You link a procedure to a list box or some other dialog control in the same way that you link a procedure to a button on a worksheet: use the right mouse button to click the control, and click Assign To Macro on the shortcut menu.

8 Enter these two statements as the body of the lstPage_Change procedure:

```
ActiveDialog.ListBoxes("lstItem").ListFillRange = _
        Worksheets("Control").Range("PageField") & "List"
ActiveDialog.ListBoxes("lstItem").Value = 1
```

The first statement assigns the name of the appropriate range to the ListFillRange property of the lstItem list box:

ActiveDialog is a globally known property of the Application object; it returns the currently displayed dialog box. The ReportDialog dialog box is showing on the screen when the lstPage_Change procedure runs, so you can use the word *ActiveDialog* to point at it.

ListBoxes is a method of a dialog box; it returns a ListBoxes object (a collection of ListBox objects). You want the item named lstItem from the collection.

ListFillRange is a property of a ListBox object; it determines the source for the list box's list of entries. If you click Category in the Page list box, you want to change the source for the Item list box to CategoryList.

Worksheets("Control").Range("PageField") & "List" retrieves the value of the cell named PageField from the sheet named Control, and then appends the text string *List* to the end of it.

The second statement changes the Item list to select the first entry whenever the list changes.

9 Press CTRL+SHIFT+D to run the dialog box, and click various entries in the Page list box.

The entries in the Item list box change depending on which field name you select in the Page list box.

10 Select Price as the page field, select Mid as the item, and click Cancel.

Make the worksheet formula change lists

The macro changes the source list for the Item list box dynamically. You can now easily choose which page field and which page item to use. On the Control worksheet, however, the formula in the PageItem cell still returns an entry from the list of states. You need to change the PageItem formula to retrieve the item from the correct list.

1   Activate the Control worksheet, and select the cell named PageItem (B12).

Even though the list on the dialog box displays the names of Price ranges, the PageItem cell still shows the name of a state.

The INDEX function in the cell is returning a value from the StateList range. You want to calculate the name of the range for INDEX to use.

2   In the formula =INDEX(StateList,ItemNumber) replace the word *StateList* with the expression **INDIRECT(PageField&"List")**

The final formula should be =INDEX(INDIRECT(PageField&"List"),ItemNumber) When you press ENTER, the value in the cell changes to *Mid*.

The INDIRECT function allows you to calculate a range. You append the suffix *List* to the current page field name and the INDIRECT function turns that text string into a range. You can watch the INDIRECT function at work.

3   With cell B12 selected, select the expression *PageField&"List"* in the formula bar and press F9.

The text string *"PriceList"* appears in place of the expression because *Price* is the current value of the PageField cell.

4   In the formula bar, select the expression *INDIRECT("PriceList")* and press F9.

The list *{"High";"Low";"Mid";"(All)"}* appears in place of the expression. (The braces mean that this list is an array inside the formula.) The INDEX function retrieves a value from this list.

5   Press ESC to restore the formula.

6   Save the workbook.

7   Press CTRL+SHIFT+D to run the dialog box. Select various entries in the Page and Item lists and watch the cells change on the Control worksheet. Click Cancel when you are finished.

Now the dialog box and the Control worksheet display the correct values.

Make the dialog box prevent errors

When you use list boxes in a dialog box, you reduce the possibility of errors. With your dialog box, you *cannot* select an invalid page field, or select a category when you should have selected a state. This dialog box does allow one error, however, that you must still prevent: if you use State as the page field and then also use State as the row field, the PivotTable will produce an error. The entry in the Page list box and the entry in the Row list box must never be the same.

The Change button dismisses the dialog box and allows the AdjustTable procedure to run. You can make the Change button refuse to dismiss the dialog box if the selected entry in the Page list box is the same as the selected entry in the Row list box.

NOTE If you have closed and reopened the Lesson 14 workbook since you last used the Edit Code button, the Edit Code button will create a new module sheet for the new procedure. You can persuade the Edit Code button to put new procedures where you want them.

In Lesson 2 you learned how to mark the position for recording.

You mark the position for the Edit Code button to create a new procedure in the same way that you mark the position for the macro recorder to create a new procedure: Activate the DialogModule sheet, and scroll to the bottom. On the Tools menu, click the Record Macro, Mark Position For Recording command.

1 Activate the ReportDialog sheet, click the Change button to select it, and give it the name **btnChange** (don't change the name on the button face—type the name in the Reference area and press ENTER).

Edit Code button

2 With the Change button selected, click the Edit Code button on the Forms toolbar.

The DialogModule sheet appears with a new procedure: *btnChange_Click*. This procedure will now run whenever you click the Change button.

3 Enter this code as the body of the btnChange_Click procedure:

```
If ActiveDialog.ListBoxes("lstPage").Value _
        = ActiveDialog.ListBoxes("lstRow").Value Then
    MsgBox "Page field should not match Row field"
    ActiveDialog.Buttons("btnChange").DismissButton = False
Else
    ActiveDialog.Buttons("btnChange").DismissButton = True
End If
```

The first statement compares the selected value in the Page list with the selected value in the Row list. If the two values are the same, it displays an alert message.

The word *DismissButton* is a property of a Button object. If the DismissButton property of the button is True, the dialog box goes away. If the DismissButton property of the button is False, the dialog box stays. If you attach a procedure to the button, you can change the setting of the DismissButton property.

4 Run the dialog box. Select the same field in both the Page and the Row list boxes, and click Change.

The message box containing your message appears.

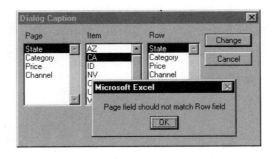

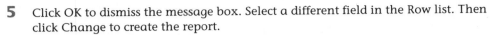

5 Click OK to dismiss the message box. Select a different field in the Row list. Then click Change to create the report.

The dialog box now allows you to enter control settings for the page field, page item, and row field, without any possibility of entering an invalid selection.

Send the report to Microsoft Word

Sometimes you want to display the report. Sometimes you want to send the report to Word. You have a procedure that will send the report to Word. You can add a check box to the dialog box to optionally send the report to Word whenever you change the report.

Check Box button

1 Activate the ReportDialog sheet, double-click the Check Box button, and create a check box control at the bottom. Change the caption of the check box to **Send to Word**

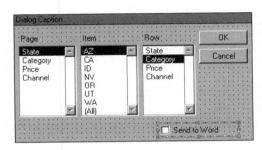

2 Name the check box **chkWord**

3 Activate the DialogModule sheet and add a statement to the RunDialog procedure, telling it to run the SendToWord procedure if the check box was selected. The procedure should look like this:

```
Sub RunDialog()
    If DialogSheets("ReportDialog").Show = True Then
        Worksheets("Report").Select
        AdjustTable
        If DialogSheets("ReportDialog").CheckBoxes("chkWord") _
            .Value = xlOn Then SendToWord
    End If
End Sub
```

You don't need to link the check box to a cell, because the procedure looks directly at the control on the dialog box. You can't use ActiveDialog to refer to the dialog box, because it is no longer active. The value remains in the control, however, even after the dialog box closes.

NOTE When you work with check boxes and option buttons, don't use the values True and False. Instead, use the built-in constants xlOn and xlOff. Excel uses xlOn and xlOff for check boxes and option buttons because a check box can also have a third value, xlMixed, which means that the check box is neither on nor off and appears gray.

4 Press CTRL+SHIFT+D to run the dialog box. Select the Send To Word check box, and click Change.

5 After sending a report to Word, activate Word and close it. Close Word each time you send a report. Later in this lesson you will change the dialog box to close Word for you.

Clean up the dialog box

When you put controls onto a dialog box, you don't have to worry too much about their exact position and size because you can easily go back and adjust their size and position later. Take a moment to get your current dialog box looking its best.

1 Activate the ReportDialog sheet, drag through the title (*Dialog Title*) at the top of the dialog box, and replace it with **Order Status Selection**

2 Select the Page list box, and change its height so that it shows only four list entries at a time. Repeat this step for the Item and Row list boxes. Adjust the widths of the boxes as needed to make them look good.

Group Box button

3 Click the Group Box button, and drag a rectangle around the Page and Item list boxes (and their labels). Then type **Select by** as the caption for the group box.

The group box does not change the functions of the list boxes, but it clarifies the fact that these two list boxes are closely related.

4 Align the controls on the dialog box to get a result similar to this one:

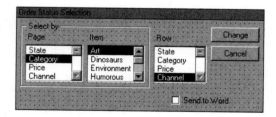

5 Save the workbook.

Taking Control of Microsoft Excel

Excel is a free-form program. Anyone who uses it can add worksheets, create charts, change formulas, and just about anything else. The fact that Excel can be used in so many ways is what makes it a very effective spreadsheet program. When you write an application designed for a specific task, however, you may not want the person using it to create charts, add worksheets, or change formulas. You may want to keep your application on track.

Excel provides various mechanisms for restricting access. You can protect a worksheet or a workbook to keep others from making changes. You can also assign a password to keep others from turning off the protection. You can change the menu bar, removing commands you don't want anyone to use.

The single most effective way to keep your application in control of Excel is never to let the person using the application out of a dialog box. When a dialog box is active on the screen, you can't select cells, scroll, or use any menu commands.

If you open your dialog box as soon as anyone opens your application workbook, and then close the workbook as soon as the dialog box closes, you can make your specialized application foolproof.

Keep the dialog box active

When you press CTRL+SHIFT+D to run the dialog box, you can click Change if you want to change the report or Cancel if you don't. In either case, the dialog box goes away, and you must press CTRL+SHIFT+D again to get it back. You can change the dialog box so that every time you click the Change button, the dialog box redisplays after changing the report.

1 Activate the DialogModule sheet, and change the RunDialog procedure to this:

```
Sub RunDialog()
    Worksheets("Report").Select
    Do While DialogSheets("ReportDialog").Show = True
        AdjustTable
        If DialogSheets("ReportDialog").CheckBoxes("chkWord") _
            .Value = xlOn Then SendToWord
    Loop
End Sub
```

The Do While statement displays the dialog box and, if the return value from the Show method is True, changes the report and optionally copies the report to Word. The Loop statement makes the procedure go back to the Do While statement to continue.

2 Press CTRL+SHIFT+D to run the dialog box. Deselect the Send To Word check box, and click Change to see the report change. Select other options and click Change again.

3 Click the Cancel button to dismiss the dialog box.

Now that the dialog box redisplays after you print a report, the label *Cancel* is not appropriate.

4 Activate the ReportDialog sheet, and change the caption of the Cancel button to **Close**

5 Save the workbook.

Initialize the application

On the Control worksheet are four buttons. The dialog box already takes care of the functions of the Change button and the Send To Word button. Typically you would use the other two buttons only once each session: Initialize Data at the beginning, and Close Word at the end. You can make the RunDialog procedure run InitializeData when it starts and run CloseReport when it finishes. While you're at it, impress your associates by changing the caption at the top of the application from Microsoft Excel to *Review Order Status*.

1 Activate the DialogModule sheet, and at the beginning of the RunDialog procedure insert these statements:

```
Application.Caption = "Review Order Status"
InitializeData
```

2 At end of the procedure, before the End Sub statement, insert these statements:

```
CloseReport
Application.Caption = Empty
```

Assigning the special keyword *Empty* to the Caption property of the application changes the caption back to the default, Microsoft Excel.

3 Save the workbook, and press CTRL+SHIFT+D to run the application.

The macro changes the application caption, reloads the data from the database, and displays the dialog box.

4 Click Close to close Word (if necessary), change Excel's caption back, and close the dialog box.

Run the dialog box when the workbook opens

If you display the dialog box as soon as the workbook opens and close the workbook as soon as the dialog box closes, you will have complete control of Excel as long as the workbook is open.

1 Activate the DialogModule sheet, and change the name of the RunDialog procedure to **Auto_Open**

The name *Auto_Open* has special meaning in Excel. When you open a workbook, Excel runs any procedure that has the name *Auto_Open*.

Name a procedure Auto_Close to run it when the workbook closes.

2 Save and close the Lesson 14 workbook.

3 Open the Lesson 14 workbook.

The macro retrieves the data, and the dialog box appears; the Auto_Open procedure ran automatically.

NOTE If you hold down the SHIFT key while you open a workbook, the Auto_Open procedure will not run. Holding down the SHIFT key allows you to test and modify the application. Users who don't hold down the SHIFT key experience the packaged application. If you need to distribute an application that is impossible to modify, you can make an add-in from your workbook. For a lead on finding information about making an add-in, search Excel Help for the phrase "creating add-in programs". Add-ins in Excel for Windows 95 are more secure than add-ins in Excel 4.

4 Click the Close button.

The dialog box closes. You want the workbook to close as soon as you click the Close button.

5 Activate the DialogModule sheet and insert the statements **ActiveWorkbook.Saved = True** and **ActiveWorkbook.Close** after the *Application.Caption = Empty* statement.

The revised procedure should look like this:

```
Sub Auto_Open()
    Application.Caption = "Review Order Status"
    InitializeData
    Worksheets("Report").Select
    Do While DialogSheets("ReportDialog").Show = True
        AdjustTable
        If DialogSheets("ReportDialog").CheckBoxes("chkWord") _
            .Value = xlOn Then SendToWord
    Loop
    CloseReport
    Application.Caption = Empty
    ActiveWorkbook.Saved = True
    ActiveWorkbook.Close
End Sub
```

6 Save the workbook and close it.

7 Open the workbook, change the report once, and then click Close.

The dialog box disappears and the workbook closes.

Prevent error messages

Even though your dialog box prevents a user of the application from making incorrect choices, errors may still occur. For example, external resources such as the database, the printer, or Microsoft Word may not be available. These are run-time errors, as discussed in Lesson 11. In case of a run-time error, Excel displays a message and halts the application without closing the workbook. You want to display your own message and close the workbook.

1   While holding down the SHIFT key, open the Lesson 14 workbook. Then activate the DialogModule sheet.

2   Change the Auto_Open procedure to look like this:

```
Sub Auto_Open()
    On Error GoTo Auto_Open_Err
    Application.EnableCancelKey = xlErrorHandler

    Application.Caption = "Review Order Status"
    InitializeData
    Worksheets("Report").Select
    Do While DialogSheets("ReportDialog").Show = True
        AdjustTable
        If DialogSheets("ReportDialog").CheckBoxes("chkWord") _
            .Value = xlOn Then SendToWord
    Loop
    GoTo Auto_Open_End

Auto_Open_Err:
    Dim myMsg
    Let myMsg = "Sorry, an error has occurred: " & Err
    Let myMsg = myMsg & " - " & Error()
    MsgBox Prompt:=myMsg

Auto_Open_End:
    CloseReport
    Application.Caption = Empty
    Application.StatusBar = False
    ActiveWorkbook.Saved = True
    ActiveWorkbook.Close
End Sub
```

The *On Error GoTo Auto_Open_Err* statement tells Visual Basic to jump to the line labeled *Auto_Open_Err* if an error should occur while the procedure runs. This is very similar to the error handler from Lesson 11.

For more information about controlling the Cancel key, search Help for the word "EnableCancelKey."

The *Application.EnableCancelKey = xlErrorHandler* statement tells Visual Basic to flag an error if the user presses the ESC key while the procedure is running.

The *GoTo Auto_Open_End* statement tells Visual Basic to jump to the line labeled *Auto_Open_End*, skipping the error handler statement if the procedure ends normally.

The statements following the Auto_Open_End label are the normal statements to end the procedure. These happen whether there is an error or not. These statements are the same ones that originally ended the procedure, plus an extra statement that clears the status bar in case the error occurs while the data is loading.

NOTE   Normally, you are better off not using GoTo statements in a proce-dure. Unfortunately, given the way error handlers work in Visual Basic, a GoTo statement is almost unavoidable in a procedure that contains an error handler.

3   Save the workbook, and press CTRL+SHIFT+D to run the application. While the *Retrieving data. Please wait.* message is in the status bar, press ESC.

The warning message appears, displaying the message *Sorry, an error has occurred: 18 - User interrupt occurred*, and then the application closes.

 NOTE   Once you know the number of an error, you may choose to add code to have the error handler respond to that specific error and then execute Resume or Resume Next to return control to the main program.

Now, your Lesson 14 workbook is a complete application. When you open the workbook, the dialog box appears, limiting access to Microsoft Excel's features. When you close the dialog box, the workbook closes with it. The application also handles any run-time errors that may occur. It is ready to give to your boss.

Lesson Summary

To	Do this
Create a new dialog box	On the Insert menu, click Macro, Dialog.
Add a control to a dialog box	Click a control button on the Forms toolbar, and then on the dialog box drag a place for the control to go.
Run a dialog sheet named *ThisDialog*	Use the statement *DialogSheets("ThisDialog").Show*.
Interpret the value of a list box	Use the INDEX worksheet function.
Prevent a button from closing a dialog box	Set the button's DismissButton property to False.
Run a procedure when a workbook opens	Give the procedure the name *Auto_Open*.

For online information about	From the Excel Help menu, choose Contents, choose Getting Started with Visual Basic, and then
Using dialog boxes	Select the topic "Creating Dialog Boxes"
Running procedures automatically	Select the topic "Writing Procedures"

Preview of the Future

Congratulations! You have now completed all the lessons in this book. You have created simple macros for everyday tasks using the macro recorder. You have made macros easy to run using controls on a worksheet. You have explored the wealth of objects available in Excel. You have learned how to use Visual Basic commands and statements to control an application. And you have built a complete application using Visual Basic in Excel.

Excel and Visual Basic are both very powerful and complex tools. You can continue learning new skills with both Excel and Visual Basic for a long time. The concepts and skills you have learned in this book will enable you to write useful and powerful applications now, and will serve as a good foundation as you continue to learn.

Special Characters

A

Index

WHO KNOWS MORE
ABOUT WINDOWS® 95
THAN
MICROSOFT® PRESS?

ISBN 1-55615-816-5
224 pages
$19.95 ($26.95 Canada)

ISBN 1-55615-683-9
320 pages
$29.95 ($39.95 Canada)

These books are essential if you are a newcomer to Microsoft® Windows® or an upgrader wanting to capitalize on your knowledge of Windows 3.1. Both are written in a straightforward, no-nonsense way, with well-illustrated step-by-step examples, and both include practice files on disk. Learn to use Microsoft's newest operating system quickly and easily with MICROSOFT WINDOWS 95 STEP BY STEP and UPGRADING TO MICROSOFT WINDOWS 95 STEP BY STEP, both from Microsoft Press.

097-000-681

The
Step by Step
Practice Files Disk

The enclosed 3.5-inch disk contains timesaving, ready-to-use practice files that complement the lessons in this book. To use the practice files, you'll need the Windows 95 operating system and Excel version 7 for Windows 95.

Each *Step by Step* lesson uses practice files from the disk. Before you begin the *Step by Step* lessons, read the "Getting Ready" section of the book for easy instructions telling how to install the files on your computer's hard disk. As you work through each lesson, be sure to follow the instructions for renaming the practice files so that you can go through a lesson more than once if you need to.

Please take a few moments to read the License Agreement on the previous page before using the enclosed disk.

Register Today!

Return this
Microsoft® Excel/Visual Basic® Step by Step
registration card for:

✔ a Microsoft Press® catalog

✔ special offers on
Microsoft Press books

U.S. and Canada addresses only. Fill in information below and mail postage-free. Please mail only the bottom half of this page.

1-55615-830-0A   *Microsoft Excel/Visual Basic Step by Step*   *Owner Registration Card*

_____
NAME

_____
INSTITUTION OR COMPANY NAME

_____
ADDRESS

_____
CITY   STATE   ZIP

Microsoft®*Press*
Quality Computer Books

**For a free catalog of
Microsoft Press® products, call**
1-800-MSPRESS

BUSINESS REPLY MAIL
FIRST-CLASS MAIL   PERMIT NO. 53   BOTHELL, WA

POSTAGE WILL BE PAID BY ADDRESSEE

MICROSOFT PRESS REGISTRATION
MICROSOFT EXCEL/VISUAL BASIC
STEP BY STEP
PO BOX 3019
BOTHELL WA   98041-9946

Register your Microsoft Press® book today, and let us know what you think.

At Microsoft Press, we listen to our customers. We update our books as new releases of software are issued, and we'd like you to tell us the kinds of additional information you'd find most useful in these updates. Your feedback will be considered when we prepare a future edition; plus, when you become a registered owner, you'll get Microsoft Press catalogs and exclusive offers on specially priced books.

Thanks!

I used this book as
○ A way to learn the software
○ A reference when I needed it
○ A way to find out about advanced features
○ Other_____

I purchased this book from
○ A bookstore
○ A software store
○ A direct mail offer
○ Other_____

I consider myself
○ A beginner or an occasional computer user
○ An intermediate-level user with a pretty good grasp of the basics
○ An advanced user who helps and provides solutions for others
○ Other_____

I will buy the next edition of the book when it's updated
○ Definitely
○ Probably
○ I will not buy the next edition

The next edition of this book should include the following additional information:

1● _____
2● _____
3● _____

The most useful things about this book are _____

This book would be more helpful if _____

My general impressions of this book are _____

May we contact you regarding your comments?   ○ Yes   ○ No
Would you like to receive a Microsoft Press catalog regularly?   ○ Yes   ○ No

Name_____
Company (if applicable) _____
Address_____
City_____ State_____ Zip_____
Daytime phone number (optional) (_____)_____

FOLD HERE

NO POSTAGE
NECESSARY
IF MAILED
IN THE
UNITED STATES

BUSINESS REPLY MAIL
FIRST-CLASS MAIL   PERMIT NO. 108   REDMOND, WA

POSTAGE WILL BE PAID BY ADDRESSEE

ATTN: MARKETING DEPT
MICROSOFT PRESS
ONE MICROSOFT WAY
REDMOND WA 98052-9953

FOLD HERE